THE GEOGRAPHY
OF
YOU AND ME

THE
GEOGRAPHY
OF
YOU AND ME

A Memoir

Amy Bickers

Grateful acknowledgement is made for permission to reprint lyrics from the following:

Better Man

Words and Music by Robert Peter Williams and Guy Chambers

Copyright (c) 2000 BMG VM Music Ltd. And Kobalt Music Publishing America, Inc.

All Rights for BMG VM Music Ltd. Administered by BMG Rights Management (US) LLC

All Rights Reserved Used by Permission

Reprinted by Permission of Hal Leonard Corporation

The Chair

Words and Music by Hank Cochran and Dean Dillon

Copyright © 1985 Sony/ATV Music Publishing LLC and Universal Music -Careers

All Rights on behalf of Sony/ATV Music Publishing LLC Administered by Sony/ATV Music Publishing

LLC, 424 Church Street, Suite 1200, Nashville, TN 37219

International Copyright Secured All Rights Reserved

Reprinted by Permission of Hal Leonard Corporation

Mr. Blue Sky

Words and Music by Jeff Lynne

Copyright (c) 1978 EMI Blackwood Music Inc.

All Rights Administered by Sony/ATV Music Publishing LLC, 424 Church Street, Suite 1200, Nashville, TN 37219

International Copyright Secured All Rights Reserved

Reprinted by Permission of Hal Leonard Corporation

Part Of Your World

from Walt Disney's THE LITTLE MERMAID

Music by Alan Menken

Lyrics by Howard Ashman

(c) 1988 Wonderland Music Company, Inc. and Walt Disney Music Company

All Rights Reserved Used by Permission

Reprinted by Permission of Hal Leonard Corporation

Publisher's Cataloging-In-Publication Data

Bickers, Amy, author.

The geography of you and me: a memoir / by Amy Bickers.

pages cm

ISBN 978-0-9965260-0-5

ISBN 978-0-9965260-1-2

ISBN 978-0-9965260-2-9

1. Bickers, Amy. 2. Divorced women--United States--Biography. 3. Abused wives--United States--Biography. 4. Divorced men--United States--Biography. 5. Suicide victims--United States--Biography. 6. Autobiographies. I. Title.

HQ834.B53 2015   306.89'30973092
                        QBI15-600145

First printing: 2015

In memory of Charles

And for our children, Kate and Jacob, with all my love and
gratitude for your presence in my life

The Geography of You and Me is nonfiction. Most names have been changed to protect the privacy of individuals or to reduce confusion.

Out beyond ideas of wrongdoing and rightdoing,
there is a field. I'll meet you there.

When the soul lies down in that grass,
the world is too full to talk about.
Ideas, language, even the phrase "each other"
doesn't make any sense.

—Jalal ad-Din Muhammad Rumi, 13th century

prologue

In the nightmare, I am crouched by the front of my car when the shotgun goes off. After the sound of the blast echoes through the garage, I don't scream. I say, "Oh my God." I say it quietly, like I've been punched in the gut and there is not enough air in my lungs to scream. I repeat it to myself as I go to the stairs and lean over your body to push the button that will open the garage. The button is on the wall next to the kitchen door, above the fourth step. I do not look down at you. I say, "Oh my God" as I go back down the stairs and cross the garage floor and see your flesh, no longer part of you.

When I see your flesh, I think that this is something most people never see. They know only in theory that bits and pieces of your body could be separated from you and become something that is no longer human. I think this as

I run past the back of the car and duck under the garage door that is still sliding open on its tracks. I run out into the driveway and across the front yard, the lawn soft and squishy beneath my bare feet.

"Oh my God. Oh my God. Oh my God."

It is not a prayer, but maybe God is here. Maybe he is carrying me and it is really his feet feeling the lush green lawn under his one set of footprints, and maybe I can write a damn inspirational poem about it and needlepoint it on a pillow. There are people who will tell me he is here simply because I am alive. I am the survivor of a scenario that most often results in two bodies. It's the type of story that is splashed across newspaper pages and evening news-casts and, if you are pretty enough or blonde enough or famous enough, on the cover of People *magazine. The po-licemen will say to me again and again, "This isn't usually how it happens."*

Maybe God is here, but all I know is that the garage is Hell on earth. If anything is in there, it is the Devil him-self, or maybe a lowly demon assigned to ride on you until you finally gave in to the pain, until you buckled under the weight of carrying that evil monkey on your back.

I will wish the next year away as if the sun will rise on August 4, 2010 and shine on a new world, a world where I am Over It. Over It *is a field bursting with crimson pop-pies, the Emerald City in the distance.* Over It *is some Technicolor version of me in red, sparkly shoes carrying a little dog. This scenario is a sorry lie I tell myself so that I can make it through each day in this afterworld.*

I will never make it up and over the hill if I am still in the garage with you, always trying to edit the scene. I change what you say, and then I change what I say. In order to do this, I have to see the original again. I have to know the truth to create a lie. I have to hear you say, "You can remember that's the last thing you said to me before I did it."

And then I have to know again the horrible thing that comes next.

A friend will arrive one evening with an enchilada casserole. It has corn in it, so our son won't eat it. Our daughter, always game for trying new things, will eat a small portion. The rest will sit in the freezer for weeks, growing a colony of ice crystals.

I will tell my friend what I said to you before you died, and she will say, "You can leave that part out of the book."

I suspect that many of us navigate life's difficulties by turning them into stories so that we can set them loose from our hearts that are heavy with sadness, and perhaps lighten the load a bit.

"You can leave that part out," she will say.

Because, obviously, that's how bad it is. It is a secret I should carry. What I want to hear is that it is not my fault, no matter what I did or said in the minutes or months or years leading up to your suicide.

Instead:

"You can leave that out."

With this, I will know it isn't something that can easily be forgiven. No amount of editing can change it. I will forgive you, but who will forgive me? You were the only other person in the garage with me, the only other person in this nightmare that never ends, but you are gone and I have no idea how to find you again.

1

Nothing ever ends without signaling the beginning of something else. When God closes a door, he pushes you out a window. I used to say this a lot. I probably thought it was funnier than it really was.

So this was the beginning, this moment on an Alabama summer evening when I ran out of my garage and into a world entirely different from the one that had existed before a gun went off.

It was a clear night, and I'm sure it was warm, because it was August in the South, but I can't recall the moisture of perspiration or the weight of humid air on my skin that might have indicated the temperature. It was after 9 p.m., and it was dark. When I had gone into the garage a few moments earlier, the sky was lighter, a soft purple that it becomes when half the world is bright and half the world has succumbed to nightfall. So now, in my memory, everything before is light. While I was in the garage, the sun disappeared for good.

I ran out of the driveway and onto the grass in my bare feet. The ground gave way slightly as it might after a good rainstorm, but the earth was dry. The blades of grass were the kind that are wide and have a seam in the middle so you can pluck them one by one and split them down the center. It is odd how it only takes a moment to register these thoughts. While you run from the most horrific thing you've ever witnessed, you can find yourself focusing on the green ground under your feet and everything else fades into the background.

I live in a suburb of Birmingham on the corner of a street that is a cut-through for people avoiding the interstate as they make their way from one side of the mountain to the other. The side street is short and only has one house facing it and seems rarely driven on by anyone other than my neighbor or me or the trash collectors. Before I made it to the side of the house, I could see that the young woman who lives there wasn't home. The driveway was empty and the lights were off.

I'd only met the neighbor two weeks before, when my house was broken into. She saw the flashing lights of the police cars and came over to see what was happening and to tell me that her house also had been robbed a few weeks earlier. She brought me a board and two metal brackets to put against my now-broken back door. She gave me her cell-phone number and offered to let me and my two children, Jacob and Kate, sleep at her house if we were afraid. She was a graduate student at an area school and lived alone. She was the sort of young woman who seem to exist in great numbers in the South, naturally lovely and kind, ready to open her house to near strangers.

"No, we're fine," I had said then. "But thank you so much." We'd exchanged cell-phone numbers. Just in case.

My ex-husband, Charles, was there that night. I'd called him immediately after I called the police to report the break-in. I'd spent the afternoon driving to Pearl, Mississippi, to meet Charles's mother at the Cracker Barrel along I-20. We often met there to exchange the kids. It was about halfway between Birmingham, Alabama, and Shreveport, Louisiana. Charles's parents would buy me a Yankee Candle in the gift shop—my favorite scent was Honeydew Melon—and treat us to lunch in the dining room.

My children had spent most of the summer in Louisiana, and while they were there I'd bought a house and moved us in, unpacking their rooms and throwing away things they would never remember having in the first place. They'd never seen the inside of the house, though I had driven Kate by the outside early in the summer and shown her the vast, fenced-in backyard with its trampoline and play fort.

When we arrived at the house, it was about 5:00 or 6:00. Instead of pulling into the garage, as I normally would have, I stopped in the driveway so we could go in through the front door. I wanted the kids to get the grand tour, beginning where these things should begin. I pushed the door open and saw immediately that the back door, directly across from the front, was open. I stepped in and leaned forward enough to see that the flat-screen television was no longer in the living room on the red-painted trunk my grandfather had built decades earlier.

I immediately stepped out and pulled the kids back with me. Kate began to cry while I called 911, the first time I'd ever had to do that.

Then I called Charles on his cell phone. He was staying at a weekly rate motel nearby and had been for at least a month. Despite our divorce, he was the person I called when such things happened. He was supposed to be the person who was there for us, who would help me take care of my children and provide a sense of security.

Charles arrived after the police and stood on the porch as I met my new neighbor and turned down the offer of a place to stay. He said he would stay with us and sleep on a mattress on my bedroom floor. That night, both kids slept in my bed with me.

That's how Charles got back in my house. Fear. The children were afraid, and I knew that having both parents there would make them feel better. I could have stayed there alone. I should have. But Charles insisted. Once he made up his mind about something, I would have to fight long and hard to change it. I didn't have it in me that night. After that, it was my sympathy for him that allowed him to stay longer than necessary. My sympathy is why he was still there two weeks later, while the children were spending one last week in Louisiana and I stayed in Alabama working.

"You have to be gone before the kids get home," I'd said. "We can't go through this again. You have to figure out what you're going to do."

When I realized my neighbor wasn't home—that I didn't have to meet her for the second time with wide, wild eyes and a horrific story—I turned back and ran through my own front door. I passed the doorway to the kitchen on my left. Across the kitchen was the open door to the garage and Charles lying right outside it. I didn't look to my left.

I ran through the living room to the kitchen's other pass-through, right next to the garage door. The phone was on the small section of wall between these two doorways.

I couldn't see Charles because the open door blocked my view, but I could see his blood. It was more black than red as it spilled out of him on the white tile floor and spread toward the refrigerator. I couldn't look away from it. Everything else faded in color and importance. There was only this maroon puddle with hundreds of tiny bubbles marking the surface. I picked up the phone and dialed 911 for the second time in two weeks, the second time in my life.

Why did it have so many tiny bubbles in it? Who would I even ask for an explanation? When you watch horror movies and you think they use gratuitous amounts of blood, I am here to tell you, it's not a gratuitous amount. It's really not even a realistic amount.

The 911 operator answered. "What's your emergency?"

"Someone has committed suicide in my house," I said.

Charles and I met through mutual friends when I was 19 and he was 21. As so often happens with these things, a good friend of his was dating a friend of mine. The friend arranged for us to go to the Natchitoches Christmas Lights Festival with the guy she was dating, Mickey, and his good friend Charles. We rode down in Charles's dad's truck and listened to an Indigo Girls album, the one with "Closer to Fine" on it. It is odd now to think of a time when I didn't know Charles, when he was only a friend of a friend.

We watched the fireworks display from a pontoon on Cane River and drank beer. Afterward, we stopped by my mom and stepdad's house. They'd gotten married and moved to Natchitoches from Shreveport the previous year. My grandmother was visiting for the weekend, to see the fireworks and the millions of sparkling lights lining the banks of the river. We all had the happy buzz of beer and holiday cheer. Mickey and Charles took turns dancing with my grandmother.

Charles made a good impression on people. He was friendly, and if you met him once, he would remember you the next time he saw you. If he saw you out in your yard, he'd pull his truck over and say hi and ask how things were going. When we were married, I would try to keep us on track to wherever we were headed, saying, "No, no, just wave. Keep going."

Over the next year and a half, I saw him out at bars in Shreveport, and he always came over to talk or buy me a drink. At the Christmas Lights Festival the next year, Charles came by my parents' house with a drunken friend who ended up walking "home" at the end of the night and landing in a bed at some random fraternity house at the local college. Like a snoring, beer-scented Goldilocks, he was found there sometime in the wee hours by the frat member in whose bed he was passed out.

Charles visited Natchitoches pretty often to see his good friend Camme. We decided the next time I went, he would come, too, and we'd all go out. So two or three times, we drove the 45 minutes south and spent the weekend hanging out at my parents' place, throwing darts with my stepdad and mom.

One weekend, my mom asked me to come down and stay with my brother, who was then in high school, while she and my stepdad, Ted, went out of town. It was the kind of "babysitting" job in which I was expected simply to make sure my brother didn't have a wild party and burn the house down. Charles came with me. If I'd had even an inkling that I might like him, I would never have invited him along. I would have been too nervous for that. By then we'd established a friendship, and I was comfortable with him.

That night we hung out on a blanket in the front yard with my brother and his friends. I smoked a cigarette, and Charles brought it up for years afterward. That was probably one of four cigarettes I'd ever smoked in my life. Charles insisted that I was trying to impress him, and I would forever deny it. "I was drunk!" I'd say. I was never worried about impressing him. I was always myself with him.

Later, when my brother was safely in bed—or, more likely, safely smoking weed in his room with his friends, the lights off and the black light on—Charles kissed me. Or I kissed him. We had an ongoing debate, as couples often do, as to who made the first move. He said I did, but I remember well him turning to me and leaning in. It wasn't expected, but it wasn't unexpected either.

I remember the room around us. It was dark, and we'd pulled out the sofa bed. We'd slept in it before, once with my former college roommate Carol Anne in between, all of us sleeping off too much beer. The sofa was plaid, and on one wall there was a poster of a dog in a tuxedo at a dinner party, an advertisement for a New Year's Day Hair of the Dog Party.

And when Charles leaned in, so did I.

If I went back in time, would I go back to that? Would I try to play the whole thing out differently? Or would I go back farther and make sure we never met?

After Charles died, my mother warned me against "what-if"ing myself all the way back to 1973.

There is no way to know where to go in the time machine, because, eventually, the only solution becomes to "what if" yourself out of existence.

"Someone," I had said. "Someone has committed suicide." Later, I decided that was weird. When I told my mother the story, she said maybe I was simply giving the information in the most concise manner possible.

In *The Year of Magical Thinking*, a memoir on the year after the death of her husband, Joan Didion is described by a social worker as "a pretty cool customer." She is the cool customer who assures him she has money for a cab ride home from the hospital. She wonders, when she arrives home, "what an uncool customer would be allowed to do. Break down? Require sedation? Scream?"

I think if there were a Cool Customer Club, I would have been in it with Joan. It would be a quiet club in which no one wails or demands sedatives or flails about. I don't even know how to be that kind of person. I don't know how anyone has the energy for all that screaming when the world is spinning out of control and you are desperately trying to hang on.

The 911 operator asked me what happened and who the victim was. She said, "Where is he? Where are you?" and I told her I was right next to where he did it. I was using the only phone in the house.

I'd been holding my cell phone when I was in the garage. I'd been on a phone call in the driveway and had walked back in through the garage. I'd dropped it when I tried to walk up the stairs and Charles came toward me with the gun. I'd heard the phone hit the ground and I thought it bounced under the car. I was crouching, trying to see under the car, when he said what he said, and then I pulled myself up, my legs still bent under me, and looked at him.

So instead of being able to use my cell phone, I had to use the only landline. I'd never installed a filter for it, so it buzzed and squealed because of the interference from the Internet connection.

I apologized to the 911 operator for the annoyance. I said, "I never bought a filter. I'm sorry." It seemed rude to be calling on this defective, squealing phone.

She told me it was OK and to stay where I was until the police got there. Stay on the line. Stay where you are. Next to the pool of blood. Next to the source of a smell so foul it was like burning flesh. Of course, it was burning flesh. I know that now, and it is only the gift of shock that allowed me to not fully know it then. It made my nostrils ache with its intensity. That smell is what Hell smells like. If Yankee Candle had a candle called Hell with an illustrated label featuring flames and a happy little devil, it would smell like that. It wouldn't sell very well. Cracker Barrel wouldn't stock it amidst its seasonal decorations and colorful striped peppermint sticks in jars.

I wonder if saying, "Stay on the line," is lesson number one in 911-operator school. You could run off in a fit of insanity. You might have been the person who committed the crime and maybe you would jump into your getaway car. You might lose what's left of your mind and wander the streets barefoot and alone, searching for your old life, the one you had before you had to call 911.

I could have ignored what she said and hung up. I could have escaped the smell and the blood and waited on the front porch, my feet feeling the cool brick tiles, my eyes focused on the pine trees near the road. What the hell could this anonymous 911 operator have done about it? But I'd always been the kind of girl who does what she's told, so I stayed on the line.

"We're going to send paramedics anyway," she said.

Anyway? I realized later it's because I said, "Someone has committed suicide." That statement didn't allow for "maybe" or "possibly." That statement meant that someone was dead.

"OK," I said, but I knew it would be a wasted trip.

Charles was gone. I knew it because he disappeared right in front of me.

I had my back against the far wall of the living room, pushing myself into the corner. I heard the sounds of police sirens and saw the flashing lights through the kitchen window.

"They're here" I told the 911 operator, but she still wouldn't let me go. "Stay on until they come inside," she said, "and then you can hang up."

I have never heard the recording of my 911 call, though I do wonder about it sometimes. I know it would be weird to hear it. On that night and many nights since, I worried about what would be deemed completely unhinged by the outside world. Which of my post-August 3 inclinations were healthy and which were signs of permanent damage? During the 911 call, I wasn't screaming or having a meltdown. I have the sense that the sound of my disembodied voice on that night, apologizing for the squealing sound of the unfiltered phone line would be disturbing, like listening to a deranged party hostess apologizing for not having the right canapés after a guest keels over from a heart attack.

When the policeman came into the living room, I hung up that phone and went straight to him. He was the first of a series of mustaches. His was black. The sight of this stranger in uniform was the emotional equivalent of being tossed a life preserver, and I clung to him. He put his arm around me and guided me out of the house and into the front yard. We walked down the hill toward the end of the driveway.

The garage door was wide open and light poured out of it. Are policemen immune to the things they see? Had they seen something like that before? Was one of them new to the job and stunned by the scene in that garage? I hope not. Then again, maybe it's worse to be unaffected by that sort of thing because you've seen it before. The paramedics declared Charles dead one minute after they arrived. There was simply nothing to be done.

While I sat in the grass, the policeman with the black mustache asked me questions and I answered them, slowly and deliberately.

"Who can we call for you? Is there someone who can come be with you?"

I wanted my friend Stacey, but I didn't have her number. Every number I had was in my cell phone, and not one of those numbers, other than my mother's house in Natchitoches, was in my memory.

"I dropped my phone. I think it's under the car. I heard it bounce," I said, and the policeman left me and went into the garage. He emerged shortly and asked again where I was when I dropped it.

"I was going up the stairs. I was trying to go up. He had the gun and he made a movement with it—" I paused. I took a deep breath. "I dropped the phone and I ran back toward the front of the car."

The policeman asked for my number and used his own phone to call it. My ring tone was a Pearl Jam song, "Better Man." When it rang, my daughter Kate thought the lyric was *"She lies and says she's in love again."* But the lyric is actually, *"She lies and says she's in love with him. Can't find a better man. She dreams in color, she dreams in red."*

Can't find a better man. I'm not going to delve too deeply into that. I liked the sound of Eddie Vedder's voice. I was familiar with the idea of lying to oneself to make it through the day. That was all.

I imagine that phone ringing after the policeman dialed my number. I imagine the cops and paramedics hearing those words as it sang out, in all its plaid, Seattle, musical angst. They found the phone underneath Charles's body. When I dropped it, it never hit the concrete floor. It hit the stairs. That made it part of the crime scene, the officer told me, and I assume it went into a plastic bag and sat in an evidence box on a shelf in the Hoover Police Department where it would remain until they discarded it.

A detective arrived and squatted down next to me. He was a young black man with kind brown eyes and a gentle manner, wearing khaki pants and a button-down shirt. He introduced himself, and I nearly made a joke. In my mind, I actually formed some comment about his name being Clint Black. I thought up some quip about the famous country singer and almost as quickly I thought, "No one makes jokes at a time like this."

My mouth was bone-dry. Everything about me stopped working normally. I'd had a cocktail after work, a vodka and cranberry juice prepared by Charles, and the last lingering flavor of it sat on my desert-dry tongue. The half-empty glass sat on the kitchen counter where I'd left it when I stepped out into the driveway to finish a phone call I'd been on the hour before Charles died. When I came back to my house more than a week later, I pulled the vodka bottle out of the freezer and poured the remaining contents into the sink. I poured out the cranberry juice as well. The thought of drinking either made my stomach turn.

Clint Black asked me the same questions as the first officer. He might have asked for more details. He's the one who typed up the police report and left it in my mailbox a week later. It had a few minor mistakes on it, but I was certain this had more to do with my malfunctioning brain than his note-taking skills. I was moving underwater. My words came out haltingly, and I struggled to form complete sentences. It was as if the policemen were speaking another language and I had to translate their words into something that made sense.

But nothing in the world made sense anymore.

Clint Black was kind. All of the officers were. I felt like a thin glass sculpture they each handled carefully before handing me over to the next person.

The officer with the black mustache continued to ask me who could come for me.

"Where do you work?" he asked. "Where do you go to church?"

"I don't go to church. I used to, but I haven't been in a long time. I work at *Southern Living*," I said. Then I told him my boss's name, but my brain hiccupped again and I gave him the name of my former editor, not my current one. I'd been moved from the homes department to the travel department several months earlier, yet my mind opened the file to 2008 and named the person I'd worked for during the six years prior.

The question of who could come get me was one of some urgency, it seemed. I wanted the officer to stop asking me. I wanted to sit still in my front yard, the world swirling around me. But clearly the police weren't going to leave me in my house alone, with a pool of blood in the kitchen and a crime scene in the garage.

"Call my mother," I said. That is what I wanted. I wanted my mom.

Officer Black Mustache dialed my mother's number, and later I couldn't remember if he told her what happened or if I did. I somehow think he did, because I don't have a single memory of telling anyone what happened other than my two children. They were the first and only people to whom I had to break the news.

I don't know what I said to her on the phone or what she said to me. I know we discussed how to get in touch with my friends Stacey and Todd. I told her to call my boss—no, my former boss—who was one of the few people I could think of who might still have a landline, a number that could be found online. Everyone else I knew had only a cell phone. Their numbers were all locked in my phone and lost to me.

I know now that my former boss, Stanford, the man who hired me to come to the magazine six years earlier, answered the phone and took the news my mother had to give. He belonged to the Mountain Brook Country Club and had a wife who decorated houses, and I imagined my ugly story as completely out of place in his tastefully decorated home in his upscale neighborhood. Even coming in only as sound waves through his landline, it seemed like something he would want to clean up, like sticky soda spilled on the polished hardwood floors, as soon as the call ended.

He called Todd. Todd and I had worked together at the magazine until two months earlier when Todd was laid off, the news delivered by Stanford and the managing editor. Todd walked into the meeting with them and, already knowing the end was near, said, "Ah, the two horsemen." So two months later, when his caller ID lit up with the name of this man, Todd's reaction was, understandably, "What the hell?"

Todd let the call go to voice mail and after he listened to the message, he called Stanford back. Then Todd called Stacey. I don't know what time it was. It might have been after 10:00 by this point.

"Stacey," he said, "get dressed. I'm on my way to get you."

"Where are we going?" Stacey said.

Todd is known for grand adventures and nights out that turn into early mornings, so maybe Stacey thought they were about to embark on something fun. When men are laid off, they often seem to grow unkempt beards, but Todd had grown an extravagant mustache instead. It was not the kind on the law-enforcement officials around me that night. It was a mustache you would find on a stately Southern gentleman, one who might wink and hand you a flask in a dry county.

Only one day before all this, Todd, Stacey, our friend Rose Darby, and I spent the day having what we called Drunk-Ass Movie Sunday. It was organized on a whim. We went to Todd's for appetizers and sparkling wine, and then we went to a movie theater to see *The Ugly Truth*. It was, we all agreed, the worst movie any of us had ever seen. Gerard Butler played a masculine, chauvinist-pig type and spoke like he had marbles in his mouth. He was unshaved and looked to be unbathed as well. He and Katherine Heigl, in the role of uptight control freak, were nothing more than unappealing stereotypes. During the film, we whispered asides to one another that were far funnier than anything in that movie.

That is the kind of day it was—so good that even a horribly bad movie didn't ruin it. It might even have made it better. We liked to imagine a world in which we were the people writing the shows and movies, and that none of our work would be as dumb as *The Ugly Truth*.

In the movie-theater parking lot, we had an impromptu photo shoot next to Todd's red BMW convertible, an older model he had purchased with a friend for just such days. It's made for whimsical afternoon adventures and silly photo shoots. Stacey posted the photos on Facebook late that night, and not one of us could look at them later without thinking that was the day *before*.

Afterward, we went to dinner at a chain restaurant near the Galleria. While we were at dinner, Kate called me from her grandparents' house in Shreveport to ask me some important thing that couldn't wait. I know I didn't hear my phone ringing the first time—the sound muffled by the white noise of the restaurant crowd—and the next day I found that I had a voice mail from her. She must have called me and then hung up to call her dad, but instead she had pushed the button in such a way that she made a three-way call. The voice mail was a recording of her talking to Charles and asking where I was.

She said, "I love you, daddy," and he said, "I love you, too."

I didn't hear it until I was at work on Monday. When I came home that afternoon, I played it for Charles. We marveled at the weirdness of that conversation ending up on my cell phone. And then after Charles heard the message, I deleted it.

I wish I hadn't done that. Later, I wanted to hear Charles's voice talking to Kate, Kate talking to him. When I got a new cell phone and they assigned it my old number, I listened to several days' worth of voice mails. Some of them from the day after were urgent and frantic, and then, over the next couple of days, the messages became sympathetic and resigned. But the voice mail with Charles and Kate was already gone.

A few days before he died, Charles recorded *High School Musical 3* on the DVR for Kate to watch when she got home; this I never deleted. More than three years later, it was still on the list. It was meaningless, and yet I couldn't erase it. It's only that there was so little that he left behind for us.

The evidence technician came out of the garage carrying a camera and walked over to where I sat in the yard.

"I need to take some pictures of you," he said. "Could you come over here in the driveway?"

He led me over and had me stand in between two police cars, in the light of the headlights from one of them. I looked down at my shirt and shorts and saw that small dots of blood covered both the shirt and shorts. The tech asked me to turn around, and he took a photo of my backside. "OK, turn around," he said.

I turned to face the camera, but I didn't look at it. I turned my head to the side and tensed up, like someone about to be splashed with cold water from a bucket.

I was wearing what I'd worn to do an hour of power yoga when I got home from work: a red sports bra and a gray tank top with white straps; gray shorts with pink stripes down each side. Charles had come in and out of the room while I moved from one pose to the next.

Sometimes he would watch me work out, and it was easier to let him do that than to argue with him about leaving the room. He grew easily bored when I was occupied with something that didn't involve him. He would wait impatiently like a child for me to be finished. He sat in an armchair by the bedroom's fireplace, and his presence threw me off balance. I'd gone several weeks over that summer without doing yoga, and the skills required for it seemed to fly away as quickly as a bird frightened from a tree. After finally making it to level three in the spring, I was back to level one of my three-level DVD; I wobbled during standing tree, and my legs ached during extended warrior poses.

The evidence technician had a mustache, too. He came to my house two weeks earlier when it was broken into. He dusted the red trunk and the broken back door for fingerprints. I'd cleaned the trunk after he left, but the filthy black dust was still all over the exterior of the back door, the outlines of unknown fingerprints still visible.

He'd said very little when he'd been at my house the first time. This time he asked me more questions.

"Did you struggle over the gun?"

"No! I never touched that thing," I said. I remembered after the break-in how Charles wanted to show me how to use his shotgun for protection. I was sitting on my bed, and he brought it over, ready to hand it to me. I'd said, "If someone wants my TV, they can have it. I'm not going to shoot someone with a shotgun."

Charles saw I was adamant, so he'd carried the gun to the other side of the bed, leaned it against the corner by the window, and slid the white draperies over it.

Now the evidence tech asked me if Charles was left-handed or right-handed.

"Left-handed," I said. As he walked back toward the garage I wanted to stop him and say, "But he played golf with his right hand. He did a lot of things with his right hand."

Did he pull the trigger with his right hand? I didn't know. I would have had to look too closely at the image of Charles on the landing to answer that question.

The evidence tech didn't spell out to me how the photos were necessary so that they could document the blood splatter to see if this lined up with my version of events.

I went to high school with a girl and her brother whose mother was in jail for murdering their stepfather. The mother was once a cheerleader at the same high school we went to. One evening, she woke up to find her husband in bed beside her holding a gun to his own head. "Stop! Don't shoot!" she yelled. Her son was 16 at the time and heard the single gunshot in the night.

The mother was portrayed as a spendthrift who killed her husband for money. She bought a new pair of hose at an expensive department store the day of the funeral. The prosecution painted an image of a woman on a shopping spree, dipping into a $1-million-plus life-insurance policy for frivolous things.

Years later, her son fought to have the case reopened, and the mother was released from jail based on the blood-splatter evidence from her nightgown. In fact, there was no blood on her nightgown, which would have been impossible had she shot her husband at point-blank range. Before he was married to her, the husband had once attempted to commit suicide by shooting himself in the chest when a former girlfriend left him.

What an asshole. That's pretty much all I could think about that dead man.

Along with my cell phone in an evidence bag, I knew there would be photos of my garage that night, taken by the handsome, quiet evidence technician. In other boxes along cheap metal shelves, there were probably photos of other people that were equally horrific.

What did this man do to keep those images from invading his dreams?

In my memory, those hours in the yard were a series of vignettes. Me sitting in the grass with ever-changing police officers who sported a series of mustaches. A black mustache. A gray mustache. A brown mustache. There is the saga over my lost phone and who would come to get me. Me standing in between two police cars in the unblinking light of the car's high beams having my photograph taken. Me sitting on the grass again with a man who might have been a paramedic. He didn't have a police uniform on. This man assured me that Charles's death wasn't my fault. He asked me if I attended church. He said to me, as most of the men I came into contact with that night did, that this was not the way it normally happened. Typically, the police found two dead bodies. I was lucky to be alive, they said.

These people came in and out of my life that night, and I had no memories of their comings or goings. I never knew their names, only that one minute a person was there, and then he was replaced with another. I said to every one of these people that I didn't understand how this had happened. "We have the greatest kids," I said more than once.

For awhile I sat in the back of a police SUV parked in the street at the end of the driveway. The back door was open, and I hung my legs out the side as I watched people go in and out of the garage. One of them was the coroner. He came down the driveway and asked more questions. He asked who should be notified. Charles's parents, I said. The coroner said I should call them. "They'll want to talk to you," he said.

I pictured the Emorys at home in bed, asleep in another world. The universe had been split in two. I could see Kate sleeping next to my mother-in-law, not knowing she was fatherless. I could see Jacob in the guest room, a night owl playing a game on his Xbox and talking to friends online through his headset.

I didn't want to tell them. I didn't want them to know. The thought of them two states away, their fate coming at them like a tornado, was what would kill me.

Two police officers stood by the SUV. At one point, another officer came over to them. They formed a small huddle and spoke in low tones.

"We're going to pull around to the side," one of them said to me. I tucked my legs in, and he shut the door.

"Are they bringing him out?" I asked the officer who climbed into the driver's seat.

"Yes," he said. He turned and looked at me. "We'll pull on the side street so you don't have to watch."

It doesn't matter that I didn't see. There it was in my head, an image set against the black of night, blue lights flashing on top of white SUVs, Charles's body in a black bag being carried down the driveway.

I was sitting in the backseat of the SUV in the driveway on the side of my house when Todd and Stacey pulled up behind us in Stacey's car. I got out and came around to hug Stacey. Todd went straight to the first officer he saw. "I'm Todd Childs," he said, putting his hand out. "What's going on here?"

One of the officers told Stacey to be careful not to get blood on her, not to contaminate the evidence, but I'd been sitting outside for more than an hour and I'm quite sure the blood was dry.

Clint Black asked me to go inside and change and bring the clothes out to an officer.

"We'll return them," he assured me.

"No, no. I don't want them," I said. Why would I want them? Sometimes during the next year when I was getting dressed to work out, I would dig through my underwear drawer for my red sports bra, and then I would remember.

Stacey walked me in through the front door. I told her and Todd not to look to the left. I feel like I said it sort of desperately. An officer stood in the doorway to the kitchen, his arms crossed over his massive frame, his legs spread in a wide stance. Stacey led me to the right, down the hall and into my bedroom.

It was nearly impossible to function in a normal manner. I managed to change into a T-shirt and pajama pants. Stacey told me later that I stood beside the bed for a minute and shook my arms uselessly, so she helped me pull my shirt over my head. I piled the workout clothes on the floor at the end of the bed. I packed a bag of random clothing. I don't know what was in that bag, but it turned out later that there was nothing of use to me.

As I packed, I glanced at the bedside table and saw a green shotgun shell, propped like a morbid accessory next to the lamp. I pretended not to see it. I kept it in my peripheral view and kept moving. Toothbrush, hairbrush, underwear.

I picked up my pillow and a stuffed dog that sat on the bed. We'd gotten the dog at a Build-a-Bear workshop one weekend several years earlier. Kate had a bunny, Jacob had a monkey, and Charles said, "Let's get your mom something, too."

I chose a plush dog with floppy ears. In his paw was a recordable device that had Jacob's voice on it saying, "Monkey. I love you." He was obsessed with monkeys that year, and we laughed because it was as if the dog was telling Jacob's stuffed monkey that he loved him.

I held that dog for the next day or so. I slept with him for weeks, pushing the plush surface of his ear back and forth with my thumb. About six months later, the recordable device stopped working. Pressing the dog's paw would release a garbled sound like pennies rolling around in a plastic bowl. Jacob's voice the way it sounded on that day when we wandered the mall and spent money on silly things and ate snacks from the food court, Jacob's voice before it changed to its current deep timbre, was gone.

When I returned to the house more than a week later, the shotgun shell was no longer on the bedside table. One of the many people who had come and gone from my home, cleaning and packing bags for me, had removed it.

On the way out of the house, I told one of the officers the clothes were on the floor. A policeman with a gray mustache said he remembered coming over two weeks ago after the break-in. He remembered meeting Charles.

"Something didn't seem right about him," he said.

I didn't respond. Maybe someone else did. What could I say? I wondered about it later, though. Should I have known that something wasn't right? I tried to see Charles on that night. Were his eyes glazed over? Was he slurring his words? Did he look like a man who wasn't going to live two weeks more?

One of the officers walked us to Stacey's car and suggested to Todd and Stacey that they take me to the emergency room because I would need a sedative. I said, emphatically, "No."

This I remember as the one thing I was absolutely unwilling to do. In all other things I had allowed these mustached strangers in uniforms to guide me gently around my yard, into police cars, into my house, back out of my house. This I would not do. I would not sit in a waiting room surrounded by people with sore throats and sprained ankles and pathetic emergencies and wait hours to tell a horror story, the price of admission to a bottle of Valium or Xanax.

The officer who suggested the ER looked at Stacey and said, "Well, you can get her something, right?"

On the drive to Stacey's, going down Lakeshore Drive past the landscaped grounds of the *Southern Living* offices, I told them how I wanted to make a joke about the detective's name, this black man with a white country star's name. Then I barked out a laugh that was harsh and metallic and not quite real. Todd and Stacey exchanged worried looks. They thought I was about to lose it.

Even months later, this caused irrational anger to well up in me. It left in me a feeling of being separate from them, separate from everyone on the planet. I was a hysterical girl orbiting the outer bounds of sanity, someone on display, someone to be watched with uncertainty.

Humor had always been the shield that would protect me from the world. I needed it, but it wasn't right. Who was I supposed to be that night? Who was I to become? I had lost myself, and I began to suspect that Charles took me with him when he left this world.

The detective had given me his card before I was driven away from the house, and I clutched it in my hand. As we turned off Lakeshore onto Highway 31, I glanced down at it and I saw that his name was actually Clint Blackmon.

I probably could have made a stupid joke about that, too.

2

Charles and I met and became a couple when we were both in college and his addiction was hidden under a smoky haze of nights out with friends who were all drinking beer and stumbling slightly by the end of the night. Charles could poke a hole in the bottom of a can of beer, pop the top, and "shotgun" that beer in less than four seconds. I could take the stem from the cherry in my cocktail and tie it in a knot with my tongue. We were stupid humans, and these were our tricks. I was 21, and Charles was 23.

We went on our first official date to a baseball game in Shreveport, Louisiana. We'd both grown up there, but we had attended different schools. The city used to have a team called the Captains that never inspired deep devotion in the city's residents. My mother once took me to a game when I was a teenager and we used it as an excuse to tan in the sun-drenched stadium seats, being sure to watch for fly balls that might knock us unconscious.

We went on a double date with one of Charles's best friends Stuart and his girlfriend, Leslie. On the Friday of the date, the news had broken that Kurt Cobain had been found dead in his home. The coroner would later state that Cobain died on April 5, three days earlier.

I remember Leslie in the backseat of the truck, me in the front. We had stopped at a convenience store, and the men were inside, buying cigarettes and Skoal.

Leslie commented on the awfulness of it, this famous man intentionally ending his life.

After Charles died, I felt for Courtney Love. She was nutty as hell, but look at what she'd been through. I thought about how, like her, I was someone who could be blamed if people chose to do so. I was someone who was still alive while a man who once loved me was gone. People would rather punish the living than the dead. The dead typically get a pass. Maybe because it's pretty unsatisfying to aim anger and resentment at someone who can never respond.

In college, my friends and I went out to bars and drank too much and said, "Yes," to too many boys who were not yet men. The next morning we would lie around, sprawled on the sofa and the floor, with hangovers that made the world hazy and slow. We would replay the evening's events and remind each other of every funny, ridiculous moment.

During the blur of too many nights out, when I quit my retail job and stupidly lived off my student loan money, I'd had a fleeting thing with a boy/man who seemed to think he was so much older than me. I was 20, and he was 24, a negligible difference now that I look down the years at it. He was handsome and had blue eyes and a scar on his forehead that shot through one eyebrow. He sighed with irritation if you asked him how he'd gotten it. So many girls asked him this question. He had six-pack abs and, years later, my best friend Tina and I would occasionally reminisce about how beautiful he was.

"He was the hottest guy any of us ever got with," Tina would say, and I would agree.

There is foolish pride in being with the hot guy when you are 20 years old and you don't know enough to know your own worth.

But the boy/man was cruel and selfish in a way that good-looking boys often can be. The morning after the first night I slept with him, he barely said good-bye to me before having his brother's friend drive me home. I continued to sleep with him over several drunken months and endured any number of instances when he offered proof that he did not care for me beyond a few brief moments in his bed or mine.

One night after a party my friends and I had, he sat outside my apartment in his car with another girl, a blonde who had been a cheerleader at my high school, an unfriendly girl who perpetually looked as if she smelled something bad. The rest of us were on the front porch, drinking, some people smoking.

Tina yelled across the yard at him, "Come inside. What are you doing? Come in." And he said no. She continued to bug him, all on my behalf, while I said nothing. Finally, he yelled, "No!" and stretched the word out, obnoxiously. "That's one word."

I got up from where I'd been perched on the top step and I said, "Fuck you. That's two." I walked back into the house and went to bed, and that was that. The end.

It was no great love affair. Hell, it wasn't even great sex. One night in his attic bedroom, when I told him it hurt, he scoffed and said, "No, it doesn't." Once he said something to me, fed me some practiced line, and then said, "How many girls do I have to say that to before I find the right one?" I heard years later that he'd been married and divorced (probably because he was a major asshole) and was still spending most nights out in bars.

It is vitally important to experience the singular torments of wanting someone despite how meanly that person treats you. You learn to recognize this type of person so in the future you can cross the street—or a crowded bar—to avoid him. You must measure how badly you will allow yourself to be treated in exchange for the pleasure of running your hands down a flat stomach and kissing a boy with a scar and a smile that never seems to reach his eyes. You should figure out how much punishment you are willing to endure in the pursuit of love or sex or attention.

One night, years later, I saw him out at a bar and I said, "Do you remember me?" and he said, "Of course I do. Why would you think I don't remember you?" and I wanted to say, "Because you never even *knew* me."

But I only shrugged and said, "See you later," and went back across the bar.

When Charles wanted to be more than friends, when he first kissed me or I kissed him, I was ready. I was tired of mean boys and unpredictable boys and unattainable boys, boys who made me feel like I wasn't enough.

Charles was nice to me. He liked me, and he showed it. He didn't work out and he didn't have a flat stomach, but he did have spectacular forearms and muscular legs. Don't underestimate the appeal of the forearm. Somewhere inside me there must be a woman from a Jane Austen novel, who wants to lay her gloved hand lightly on the firm forearm of a gentleman leading her on a stroll through a garden scented by roses or jasmine.

Charles had eyes that changed like the sea from blue to green, depending on what he was wearing. Both my children inherited their ever-changing eye color from him. He was blonde, with a hairline that was already receding at 23, and he had pale skin, legs that would never tan, and arms with a farmer's tan. Although tan isn't quite the right term. They could be described more aptly as freckled into submission. When he grew a beard, it was red, a last remnant of his childhood hair color.

Charles didn't play games in which he tried to make me jealous or insecure. He was easy. We went out with our friends and laughed. He invited me to his house and grilled steaks and made baked potatoes. He could be silly, and I could be silly with him. He wrote me goofy poems, always knowing that romantic gestures would make me uncomfortable but making me laugh would get me right into bed. So he rhymed "girl" with "squirrel" in some nonsensical poem scrawled in a matter of minutes on loose-leaf paper. He drove me home to my garage apartment, and we sat in his truck talking and kissing for an hour until finally I ran inside. The next day I saw him again. It was as simple as that. I never had to wait for him. I never had to wonder if he would call. He called *every day*. He was always there.

Two years later, we had a redheaded son we named Jacob, who was unplanned and the greatest thing to ever happen to us. In May of 1996, he came into the world at nearly 10 pounds ("Congratulations, you've given birth to a kindergartner," one of the nurses said to me) and turned us into a family. Charles and I married a month later on a sweltering hot June afternoon.

There were good times and bad times. People almost always tell about the bad times when a relationship ends. And you think to yourself, "Why the hell did you stay? Are you an idiot?" But that's only because they don't know about the times your husband told you how beautiful you were or said that you were his favorite person in the world. How, when you lost weight, he said, "I'm glad for you, but I thought you looked fantastic already. You always look good." They don't know about the times he made you laugh until your sides hurt, the times he listened while you complained about work and he never once tried to tell you how to fix the problem. He simply *listened,* and then he said, with total loyalty, "Yeah, she's a total bitch," or "He's an asshole." They don't know how he covered the distance from Louisiana to Alabama in record time because you called him crying after your car was stolen, and the next day he drove you to the Social Security office and the DMV and the rental-car office, and then he bought you take-out Chinese food and fixed you your favorite cocktail. They don't know that he was your favorite person, too.

Maybe I didn't recognize the difference between Charles and everyone else "just having a good time" in the early years, but eventually I couldn't ignore his insatiable need for pills. During my 31st birthday, when his eyes were glassy under heavy eyelids and he slurred his words, I sat far away from him around a table at Shogun, one of those restaurants where the cook prepares the meal in front of you and makes jokes about "egg rolls" while pushing an egg across the cooktop. Our friends passed around a picture frame and a Sharpie and everyone wrote birthday messages for me. Charles signed it: "To the most forgiving wife ever."

And for almost a decade, I gave him every reason to believe this was true.

I forgave him hundreds of times. I offered up second chances like some harried doctor scribbling out prescriptions. I thought my understanding and love could be the remedy. He *needed* my forgiveness.

Our divorce was final three years before he died, but he still called me every day, many times more than once a day. For the last nine months of his life, he mostly lived in my home. He had moved back to Birmingham after brief stays in Louisiana and Colorado, searching for something he could never find.

One day he called from Vail and said, "Why am I so far away from my children?" and I said, "I don't know."

He wanted to come back, and I said he could stay with us for six months. Pay down his debts, save money for a deposit on his own place, help pay the household bills. "There will be no sex," I said. "There will be no trying to get into my bed or harassing me."

I still imagined a world in which Charles would get his act together and we could be a family, but I did not tell him this. I said, "We are not getting back together. Do you understand?"

He said he did, but what he really heard was me offering him a way back in.

Would it have been better if I'd done something so big and awful that I deserved what happened? What exactly could one do to deserve the punishment of watching a man destroy himself?

You can work hard and get a good job. You can take care of your children, pay your bills, clean your house, work out, and only drink in moderation. You can be a loyal friend. You can be kind to someone even as he repeatedly betrays you. You can make sure he sees his children and that they never hear you say a bad word about their father. You can drive that man to rehab twice. You can carefully avoid triggering his anger and jealousy by not dating. You can lock up your heart and your body and toss the key into a swiftly moving river rushing toward the sea.

You can do all this and still end up trapped in a room with someone who needs you to watch him die.

Why? Because the horrible thing you did is that you offered him hope. (The secret was that you felt it, too).

And then you took it away.

3

We went to Stacey's house, and I took a shower in the guest bathroom. Standing under the hot water, surrounded by glossy blue tile, I thought for the first time that if blood was on my clothes, there must be spots of it on my arms and legs and my face. I scrubbed myself with soap and water and thought of Lady Macbeth rubbing her hands together and saying "Out, damned spot." I thought of all the Lifetime movie shower scenes in which a character cleans herself vigorously to remove the tragedy that has come upon her.

But I lathered soap on myself *normally,* and I rinsed myself under the hot water *normally,* and I did not worry again that I had his blood on me. I held onto these small moments of deliberate normalcy as proof of my sanity.

While I was in the shower, Todd left to pick up some Valium for me—a generous donation from another friend—and then delivered it before heading home. Stacey and I sat up for a little while, me on her living-room sofa with the stuffed dog in my lap. I used Stacey's phone to call Charles's parents, Roger and Frances.

While the phone rang, I tried to figure out what to say. "Someone committed suicide in my house" wasn't going to work this time. I was relieved when no one answered.

My mother called and said the coroner needed the name of Charles's dentist. Weeks later my dental hygienist would call me with words of sympathy and comfort. We have had many good conversations during my annual cleanings, despite the fact that her hands are in my mouth most of the time I'm with her. She did not know what had happened, only that Charles was dead, a death that required identification by dental records.

The coroner had also, again, urged my mother to have me call the Emorys. They would want to hear it from me, he said. Truthfully, I sort of hated the coroner. He was an older man and seemed a little abrasive. He had an awful "bedside" manner, and I wanted him to shut up about what we should or should not do. But if we didn't get in touch with the Emorys, a police officer could be contacted in Shreveport to go to their front door and ring the doorbell in the middle of the night. My mother handled this, and when she called the police department, the person who answered said, "Charles Emory? I know him. We went to high school together."

Life might be less painful if the world weren't quite so small.

He told my mother they could send someone, but she was hesitant. She said she would try once more to call Charles's parents. This time Charles's mother answered, and when my mother told her Charles had died by his own hand, my mother-in-law said, "Oh, I can't tell Roger that." Like me, Frances had been abducted and transported to a different planet, and, for a few brief moments, her husband was left behind, asleep in a better world.

I asked Stacey if I could sleep in her bed with her, and she said of course I could. She apologized because her room was messy, her clothes and purses were spread around the floor, but I didn't mind. The mess was comforting evidence of a life that involved laundry and getting dressed for work.

The condo was filled with bright, spring-inspired colors. We'd not so long ago painted the walls of the living and dining rooms a happy mint green for a special edition of the magazine. Stacey had never painted before, so I came over and taped off the molding and showed her how to cut in along the ceiling and how to use a roller to make wide Ws on the walls and fill them in. Charles came with me one day to hang the curtain rods and put up silk draperies of pink, green, and yellow plaid.

The colors felt appropriate for Stacey's new place. She'd gone through a long legal battle with her ex-husband and she was looking for a fresh start. Earlier that day, she'd at long last signed her divorce papers.

When she brought me back to her condo after Charles died, I said to her, "Now you don't have to think of this as the day you got divorced. You're welcome."

She told me this days later, laughing. I didn't remember it, but it sounded exactly like something I would have said.

Stacey turned on the television that sat on the dresser and, for much of the night, reruns of *The Nanny* were on. I didn't watch it, but I was grateful for the noise and the light.

Stacey eventually fell asleep, and I stared at the wall. The Valium calmed me down somewhat, but I'm pretty sure it would have taken a tranquilizer gun for me to sleep. I got up many times during the night to go to the bathroom. Then I stared at myself in the mirror while I washed my hands. There was no sign on my face that I'd been transformed from a person who has never seen something horrible to someone who has. Same brown eyes, same brunette hair, same nose that looks like my dad's, same mouth that looks like my mother's. I was expressionless. I was blank.

When I got back in the bed and closed my eyes, the image of Charles on the stairs was huge in front of me. It was like sitting in the front row at the movie theater where you are so close to the big screen that you can barely focus. The stairs were wide, and Charles loomed large over me. I quickly opened my eyes again and stared blankly at the beige wall. In reality, the landing was not expansive. The stairs were barely two feet across, if that. And Charles could not have been looming directly over me, 8 feet tall and 5 feet wide, because I had been at least 6 feet away.

When I told her how memory had warped my perspective, my mother said, "Monsters are big in our nightmares, aren't they?"

At sunrise, when golden light slipped in between the window blinds, I fell asleep at last and slept for two hours. This would be my pattern for many days to come. I was vigilant against the darkness. My body—my soul—could only relinquish its lookout post when the sun rose up from the edge of the world.

When I awoke, I was alone in the bed, and Stacey's condo was silent. I climbed out of bed and padded down the hall to the living room, but Stacey wasn't there. The bathrooms were empty, too. Had she gotten up and gone to work? She was a copy editor at the magazine. I thought, "If this isn't a reason to stay home from work, I don't know what is."

The thought was in my old voice, the voice of sarcastic Amy, and it sounded weird in my head.

What was I supposed to do? I was hopeless in the face of whatever now lay ahead of me. I didn't have a phone to call anyone. My mother was getting on a plane that morning to fly to Birmingham, and she wouldn't be in until mid-afternoon. I needed people to take me by the shoulders and gently move me in whatever direction I was supposed to go next. I began to panic about being alone and I stood in the center of the living room, shaking my hands uselessly like I'd done in my bedroom the night before.

Then I looked out the front windows and saw Stacey sitting in her car. She was talking on her cell phone. She'd gone out to get something and had stayed there while she talked to someone. The news was spreading quickly and inevitably, and Stacey was rallying the troops.

For most of the day, I sat on Stacey's sunshine-yellow sofa in my T-shirt and pajamas under a strawberry-red blanket. I didn't have on a bra, and this detail strikes me as yet another way I wasn't me. I've never been one to sit around braless if people are coming over. But on that day, I was like an invalid in a hospital bed. Putting a bra on seemed pointless. Hell, getting off the sofa at all seemed pointless.

My friends came, all of them from the place we worked, and gathered around me. I can see them now, one next to me on the sofa, one on the floor, the others buzzing around talking to Stacey and making lists of what they could do. Events were set into motion without any help from me. Erin would buy me a pay-as-you-go cell phone to use until I could replace mine. Jennifer would pack a bag for me to take to Shreveport the next day. They were there, and then gone on their missions, and I have no memory of what anyone said.

I had worked at *Southern Living* for six years, and the people there came together to help me in ways large and small. I am forever grateful for all of the things they did. My boss, Spencer, who I'd forgotten the night before when asked who I worked for, came by and said the company was going to rent a car for me to drive to Shreveport. My car was still in the garage. Other coworkers went to the grocery store to fill up an ice chest with water and snacks for the drive. They brought me Kleenex and an iTunes gift card and magazines.

In the days following, they pooled their money and bought all my children's school supplies. They paid for Jacob's yearbook. They called the schools and explained why Kate and Jacob wouldn't be there the first few days (school started the next week). When we came home from Shreveport, there were two baskets filled with notebooks and pencils and folders. The refrigerator was stocked with Diet Coke and Gatorade.

While Spencer was there, a man from ServPro came. The detective had given me a card for the cleaning company—they clean up after fires and floods and crimes—and Todd had called them. The person from ServPro said I'd have to meet the crew at the house to sign papers, and Todd said to him in a tone that made clear he would not be argued with, "No, she will not. You will go to her."

So the man came to Stacey's and put a clipboard full of papers in front of me, and I signed them. They would clean the garage and the kitchen. They would clean my car, too, he said. They would bill me later. Spencer leaned forward and said, "Don't bill her. Send that to me. Here's my card. Don't call her about it. Call me."

On the business card, ServPro's slogan was printed at the bottom: "Like it never even happened." This slogan is the ultimate in wishful thinking.

It can *never* be like it never even happened.

When could I have done the thing that would have stopped this train on its tracks? When was the moment that I could divert its course away from suicide in my garage to something less horrific? Where should I "What if" myself to on this fantasy journey to the past?

After I put my sweet baby girl in her crib, a silky blanket pulled up under her chin, and kissed her four-year-old brother good night, should I then have stormed into the living room and demanded that Charles leave? Should I have said, "If I find pills in this house one more time, that's it. We're done." Should I have begged him to stop so we could keep our family together, so my children wouldn't have to grow up with a single mother and a distant father like my brother and I did?

I did those things. I exhausted myself looking for answers, looking for a way that I could be responsible for it all and, thus, be powerful enough to change it.

I could not figure out where to go in time to fix this. I could not find the moment when I could make everything OK, when I could stop Charles's growing drug addiction. I couldn't see where I could go to avoid the whole thing entirely. Was it the moment when I could have told Courtney no, I didn't want to go to the Christmas Lights Festival with her boyfriend and his friend?

That little time-travel trick wouldn't allow me to still have my two children. I could tell myself that had I avoided meeting Charles I would never have known Jacob and Kate and would never have known what I was missing. But it was an impossibility for me to paint a picture of a world without them in it.

If you must know the truth, I would have witnessed a thousand deaths if it were the price I had to pay to have them in my life.

While my children lived another life on another planet, Todd picked my mother up from the Birmingham airport on that sunny Tuesday afternoon in his red BMW with the top down. Todd said it was like a ball of fire leapt off the curb and into his car. My mother said he was like a movie star pulling up to the curb. Weeks later, she drew a picture of him in the BMW and sent it to him with a thank-you note for being such a good friend to me.

When my mother walked into Stacey's condo, I was still on the couch—I'd managed a short nap aided by more Valium—and, in my memory, the seas parted as my mother came in. Whoever was there left the room, and it was only my mother on the sofa, hugging me. She'd flown to Birmingham so I wouldn't have to drive to Shreveport alone. But really, I think she mostly came so she could hold me.

Charles's parents had agreed that Kate and Jacob should hear the news of Charles's death from me. I do not know how they managed to keep it to themselves for that day and a half. Charles's brother, Randy, had driven to Shreveport from North Carolina, but he was staying at a friend's house until the children could be told. He couldn't see his parents until everyone in the house knew. He couldn't hide his emotions from the children of his older brother.

For all of Tuesday and much of Wednesday, Jacob and Kate did not know. Jacob stayed at the house playing video games. Frances took Kate shopping. I worried that someone would see them out and say something that would give it all away, spilling the awful news on an aisle at Target, surrounded by over-sized boxes of Goldfish crackers.

My mother and I left for Shreveport Wednesday morning. I drove because my mother is afraid to drive long distances on the interstate. When my brother and I were growing up, my mother drove us halfway to Indianapolis at the beginning of every summer. We met my dad in Jackson, Tennessee, at the Shoney's Big Boy, and we rode with him to Indiana. At the end of the summer, we met at Shoney's again, and my mother drove us home. Now she was fearful of the other drivers and the big rigs that sometimes crossed the center line.

This was day one of me doing what had to be done. Tuesday I had stayed on that couch in pajama pants and a T-shirt and no bra. I had gotten up only to shuffle to the bathroom. People came and went, sitting beside me to hug me and offer words of support. But nothing had been asked of me.

I slept some of Tuesday night from sheer exhaustion, in bed with my mom in Stacey's guest room. But Wednesday I awoke to a world in which my children would learn that their father was dead.

I showered and washed my hair. I put on makeup. I got dressed in khaki shorts and a peach-colored sleeveless top. Look how presentable I was. Look how normal I was. This was day one of putting on my normal-person disguise.

My mother and I both cried a few times as I drove, but in many ways it was a typical road trip. We stopped for gas. My mother looked at the magazines my friend Sara had bought for me, and we discussed celebrities and clothes in fashion magazines that were stupidly expensive and, worse than that, ugly. Then we circled back around to Charles. This was how my life was after August 3, 2009. My thoughts and conversations with certain friends and family members always circled back around.

As the mile markers passed by us on I-20, my anxiety grew. What would I say to them? I had never dreaded anything more in my life. My chest ached with the weight of this information. Numerous times over the next week, I would look at my children and think desperately that this was wrong. My children were not the children without a father. Someone had gotten this terribly mixed up.

We pulled into the Emorys' driveway around 3:00 that afternoon. As I turned the car off and took out the key, I said, "I feel like the messenger of doom." She said, not unkindly, "You are."

She stopped me before we reached the front door and held my hands and prayed. She asked God to give me the right words.

I have never felt the comfort that some people seem to get from religion, but in the first week after Charles's death, I did feel a sense of complete trust in something larger than myself. Was it a trick of the brain, a symptom of shock explained away by medical science?

There are 60 seconds in a minute and 60 minutes in an hour, but the minute I stood outside that house was not an ordinary minute. It was a passageway. It was a wormhole. It was the difference between my children's lives as they had been and my children's lives as they would be.

It was amazing to me that I was not frozen in that spot forever. In a Greek myth, I might have turned into stone, a statue of The Mother Frozen in Time, a place around which flowers would grow and upon which rain and snow would fall and birds would perch to sing mournful songs.

Kate came running when I opened the door, and she called my name with a mixture of delight and surprise. She hadn't known I was coming. As she hugged me, Jacob came out of the guest room and said "Mom? Grammy? What are you doing here?" Only curious, not with any foreboding.

I must have said, "Hi." I must have hugged them both like a normal person would. Roger came out of his bedroom, and Frances came over from the kitchen. I said to the children, "Come sit down with me," and I led them to the couch.

This will be their story to tell one day, but I wonder now what they thought in those brief moments as I led them from the entryway to the living room, from this life to the next one. Kate was listening to music on her laptop when I arrived, and the song she was listening to was by the Black Eyed Peas about how tonight was going to be a good night. When she told me this weeks later, she said, "That song was a lie!" She said it with a sense of the ironic. I took it as a good sign that she recognized the absurdity of life. We sometimes still listened to that song and to others by the Black Eyed Peas, and we sang loud in the car while Jacob made clear by his expression that he found us obnoxious. Kate did not stop listening to that song. My girl was strong. But sometimes she asked me to skip it when it came up on shuffle, and I did.

Kate sat on my lap and Jacob sat right next to me. My mother sat on my other side. My mother-in-law sat on the coffee table across from us, and my father-in-law stood next to us. In my memory, we were as close to each other as we could possibly be, and the adults created a wall around us, a fortress against the world.

I remember some of what I said. First: "Your dad has died." They both began to cry, quietly. "How?" or "What happened?" is what one of them asked, and I think now it must have been

Kate. She was the one who asked questions in those days, and Jacob only listened.

"He did it to himself. He was sick in his head. He'd taken drugs and they messed up his brain. He wasn't in his right mind or he never would have done this. Daddy had been taking pills for a long time, and he wasn't thinking right."

I said more. They didn't look at me or at any of us. They looked down. I said that we were going to be so sad and angry for a long time and that we had to be there for each other. I told them their dad loved them and he never would have left them if he hadn't been in so much pain. I told them they could ask me anything, any time they wanted. We could talk about it or not talk about it. We could do whatever they needed to do. I did not tell them I was there when it happened. I did not say specifically that he shot himself.

Other than the moment in my front yard when I wondered how long I could go without telling the Emorys or my children who were asleep in their beds on another planet, it never occurred to me to keep Charles's manner of death a secret. I didn't consider concocting a story about a heart attack or a car accident, something typical and socially acceptable to tell my children and our friends. But I sometimes pictured Charles dying of a heart attack on a lush green golf course. In that scenario, it is possible he could have been saved. In that scenario, he would still be someone who could afford golf, who wasn't unemployed and homeless and charged with DUI. He would be someone in crisp khaki pants and a collared shirt and an LSU baseball cap, a pristine and manicured lawn beneath his feet. I could see it, the green perfection spread out around him.

"He had a heart attack" would be an easier answer to the question of how he died. It's a question that would come up regularly. If you tell someone your ex-husband passed away and you are in your 30s, they assume he was, too, and they want to know what tragic event took the life of someone so young. There is no way to answer it that doesn't make someone's jaw drop, even if you say, very simply, "He took his own life." That sentence is enough. It is a horror movie in five words.

For months after he died, I sought out books to help me understand what Charles felt and what I was feeling, what my children might be feeling and how I could help them navigate a world in which they weren't simply fatherless. They also were saddled with a family history of suicide.

I would wander up and down bookstore aisles and past library bookshelves. Friends would press books into my hands. "This helped me when my husband/wife/sister/mother died. This might help you."

There would be both comfort and sadness in reading stories and knowing this sort of thing had happened to so many people besides me. I felt like an alien half the time, a stranger in my life, and there were others like me in the world walking aimlessly through supermarkets and malls and bookstores wearing their normal-person disguises in the new abnormal world.

One book I read had an entire section on the stigma of suicide and had firsthand accounts of people who kept their loved ones' suicides secret. They felt ashamed. The book was written only 12 years before Charles died in my garage, and I wondered if we as a society had changed so much over the years or if we simply knew better.

To keep this thing a secret from my children would eventually have destroyed us. I cannot bear to think of their lives upon the eventual discovery of such a huge lie. "At the length truth will out," Shakespeare wrote. To attempt to keep a secret is futile. I am often stunned that so many people make a regular habit of it.

I felt sad for Charles. He would be ashamed and embarrassed by what he had done. As our marriage fell apart and he gambled money away or hid pills from me, he would beg me not to tell anyone. He would attempt to forbid me from calling my mother or my best friend Tina and sharing with them my pain after a fight or another disappointment. His shame was to be my baggage.

But he was dead, and we were not. We could not carry that burden for him when we already had so much to bear.

This is not to say I had no secrets. This is not to say that I didn't sometimes take my secrets out of their hiding place and use them—at night when it was quiet and my children were sleeping—to cut myself.

You do not need a knife to make yourself bleed.

Maybe I said too much, someone who was afraid to stop talking.

"You went on and on, Mom," Jacob told me later. But he said it in a teasing, loving way.

When I did stop talking, Kate said, "Daddy said we were going to get a kitten."

After I'd moved us into our new house, our cat Shadow had successfully made the move, never whining to be let out so she could trek back to the old place. Our other cat, Stripes, an orange tabby, had left the new house one day and went right back to the old neighborhood.

Charles made it his mission to find Stripes and bring him to the house. He drove through the old neighborhood a couple of times a day, and he eventually found Stripes living at a house on Empire Drive with a female cat and a litter of kittens. He told the kids they should bring home a new kitten since we could never get Stripes to come home and stay home.

When I replaced my cell phone, among the voice messages in my inbox was a call from a former neighbor. He said he'd tried to call Charles and couldn't get him, but he'd seen the orange cat on the front porch of the old house. I deleted the message. I never looked for Stripes again. It was ridiculous, but I couldn't forgive that dumb cat for leaving, and he wasn't welcome back.

When Kate asked about the kitten, we all laughed through our tears. It was a relief. The children had heard the news—at last they knew what we knew—and they were absorbing it. They were crying, but Kate also was thinking about living. In her life, which would continue despite the death of her father, she was a nine-year-old girl who was supposed to get a new kitten.

Jacob said he wanted one, too, one of his own. In Jacob's life, which would continue, he was 13 years old and couldn't be expected to share with his sister without a fight. We needed two new kittens, they insisted.

My children could have asked me for a Saint Bernard with a diarrhea problem and I would have said yes.

4

Edward, the glittering vampire from *Twilight*, stared down at me from the ceiling. The poster was attached with thumbtacks right above my side of the bed. I was in Sophie's room. Sophie was the daughter of Audrey, one of my dearest friends, and she'd read the *Twilight* series numerous times. They both had. I'd mercilessly teased Audrey about it. Sophie was at her dad's house tonight, so I was sleeping with Kate in Sophie's white iron-and-brass bed. Well, Kate was asleep. I had turned on the lamp because I couldn't handle the darkness, and now I was staring at a creature of the night whose appeal is a complete mystery to me. Pale? Cold? Glitters in the sunlight? I had to wonder about a generation of grown women who found this guy attractive when there was someone like George Clooney in the world. Sophie was only 13, though, so if she wanted to stare up at a poster of Edward from her white iron bed, I guessed that was OK.

Tonight, Kate, my mother, and I were staying in Audrey's apartment. Audrey and I went to high school together and had been friends ever since. Audrey always said exactly what she was thinking no matter what situation she was in. She had no filter. On top of that, she was always the loudest person in any room. I loved both of these things about her. When I was in college in Louisiana and she was in college in North Carolina, she wrote long letters to me about her adventures. When, at 22, we were both pregnant with our first children, we had long phone conversations pondering exactly what the hell was going on with our bodies. Months later when we both breastfed those children while sitting on Audrey's parents' bed during a holiday visit, we joked that Jacob and Sophie were having their first dinner date. When I moved into my new house that summer, she drove to Alabama with my mother and helped me haul boxes of books into my new house. Audrey and my mother both agreed: I had too many books.

Jacob was at the Emorys' where he could stay in a *Twilight*-free guest room and simply be a 13-year-old boy playing his Xbox games.

By the time my mother and I arrived in Shreveport that afternoon, Tina had already been there for six hours. We'd gone to high school together also and had maintained a strong friendship through the years. We emailed almost daily, an ongoing series of rants and inside jokes and tales of our misadventures in parenting. She'd flown out of Cincinnati on the first flight she could get on Wednesday, and while I was still driving across Mississippi, she texted me: "I'm here." She came for the visitation and funeral, but mostly, like my mother, she came so she could hold me.

One of our favorite stories to tell is about the time a guy was mean to me in a bar, and Tina, half-Cuban and fully pissed off, stomped up to him and said, "You fuck with Amy B., you fuck with me."

Tina came to Audrey's apartment, and we sat around the table with my mom and drank white wine and listened to Audrey talk about her looming divorce.

After 15 years of marriage, Audrey's husband had been caught in an affair, a discovery that had then released a countless number of other misdeeds, like bouncing balls falling out of an overturned bucket. They could no longer be contained, and each bounce gave them more power as they spread across the floor. The process of separation and divorce, which had been going on since early in the year, was turning into an unwieldy war full of accusations and selfish motives and a hundred battles.

Audrey had come to visit me one spring weekend, and we'd spent Saturday shopping and lingering over lunch. At an upscale clothing shop, as she tried on jeans and tops, Audrey told the shop owner about her divorce. The information came bursting out of her uncontrollably.

If you asked her how she was, she could not say, "Fine," or "I'm good. How are you?" She could not hold the truth of her misery inside. It came spewing out, like word vomit.

That night, 48 hours after Charles's death, she drove Tina crazy with her stories. "Charles was dead. He died in front of you, and all she could talk about was her stupid divorce," Tina said the next day.

I hadn't eaten since Monday night—other than a bite or two, the minimum amount required to convince everyone I was eating and thus get them off my back—and the glass of wine slightly loosened the tension in my neck. I didn't mind talking about something other than the reason we were gathered here. Kate watched cartoons or Disney Channel sitcoms in the living room and frequently came over to sit in my lap for a minute or two, to feel me solid underneath her, and then she went back to the sofa again. When she came over, the conversation briefly turned to things inconsequential and harmless. When Kate's attention was back on the television, Audrey's rant would begin again.

The opposite of love is not hate, it is indifference, and Audrey was nowhere near indifferent yet. She wasn't even in the same country as indifferent.

In the months after Charles died, I grew to understand Audrey's need to tell everyone and anyone who would listen that her life was not what it was supposed to be. She'd been sold a bill of goods. The universe had played a foul trick on her, and someone needed to pay or, damn it, at the very least *explain* how this had happened. How could this wrong be righted if no one knew the truth? How could the world keep spinning when there had been such an egregious error in the order of things?

Sometimes that fall, I'd be at a checkout line at the grocery store or at the counter of a fast-food restaurant and I would think how odd that this person didn't know what my ex-husband had done and did not know what I'd seen. Charles's death was so huge in my mind. It seemed impossible that it hadn't manifested itself as part of my appearance. It was as much a part of me as the fact that I'm a woman, that I have brown eyes and brown hair, that I have a tiny chicken pox scar over my lip and an ever-deepening worry line between my eyes.

I was like a kindergartner who needed a note pinned to her shirt so that whoever picked me up from school could not miss the vital information that the PTA meeting was at 6:00, or that Field Day would be held next Saturday. Except that my note would say, "My ex-husband shot himself in front of me. Before I order this Happy Meal for my child, you need to know this about me so you can be nice to me. I might break if you mess up my order or treat me rudely. Handle with care."

It wasn't that I wanted people to know. I've never been a fan of telling horror stories. It was only that I was afraid I might lose control of my emotions if I were mishandled. At any moment, the world could prove to be too much for me.

But I never did vomit words onto unsuspecting strangers. I was well practiced in the art of saying, "I'm fine. How are you?"

I eventually turned away from Edward and watched Kate breathing in and out beside me. I pushed a strand of her gold hair behind one ear. Her ears are slightly pointed like mine. I once told her it was a sign of intelligence. She looked like Charles except stunningly beautiful and feminine. It's so odd how that works. Her skin was smooth, her eyelids ever so slightly tinged blue from the veins beneath the delicate skin. She looked like what women are trying to look like when they put on blue eye shadow and pink blush and foundation to conceal the years. Charles was going to miss seeing how he made this beautiful girl, seeing his face in hers as she grows into a woman. He could have seen how his nose might have turned out if he hadn't had it broken three times and permanently lodged askew by barroom stupidity.

Sleep was impossible, so I finally got up and padded out to the kitchen. I sat at Audrey's desk and logged onto Facebook on her computer. In my inbox were several messages of condolence, one from Michael. We had gone to high school together, and I hadn't seen him since college, but he wrote me on Facebook and, in July, had asked for my phone number. On the evening of August 3, around 7:30, he called me to catch up. We discussed old friends and what each of us was up to now, 20 years after high school. Two hours later, Charles was dead.

Around 4 a.m., I wrote Michael back. I thanked him for his note of sympathy. I felt like a freak. I'd joked to Tina earlier about it. "I don't think Michael will be taking me to dinner now." I felt sorry for him that he'd inadvertently become part of a tragic event.

I logged off Facebook and crept back to the bedroom. I slid into bed next to Kate and waited to see sunrise through the mini-blinds. Then I turned off the lamp and slept for a bit. If I dreamed anything at all, I didn't remember it.

On the Thursday after Charles died, when I woke up at Audrey's and started another day of doing that which must be done, I called my father and told him the visitation would be Friday evening and the funeral on Saturday. I had the schedule and was writing Charles's obituary. Frances had asked if I would, and I said yes, of course. I wrote that he was born in January of 1971 during a Southern snowstorm, but all who knew him felt his warmth and kindness. I wrote that he loved hunting and LSU football and reading thrillers. I wrote that he was at peace. My mother suggested that. She damn near insisted. "He is now at peace," she dictated. She wanted to believe it—as did we all—and having it in black and white in *The Shreveport Times* might make that easier.

I sat at a tiny desk tucked into a nook in the entry of Audrey's apartment, and my mother and Audrey and Kate sat around the corner in the living room. I could hear them talking while I dialed my father's number.

The morning after Charles died, my mother had called my father before she left for the airport. She cried, and I imagined her saying, "I'm flying to Birmingham. What are you going to do?" She probably expected that he would get in his car and drive to Birmingham. She told him I didn't have a cell phone and maybe she gave him Stacey's number.

I know I spoke to him at some point during that long day I spent on Stacey's sofa, though I do not remember anything I said to anyone that day. I suspect I simply told a story that I would relive many times more before I died. He asked me to call him once the funeral arrangements were made, and I assumed he and my stepmother and maybe my half-siblings Katie and Wesley would come down.

My father lives in Indiana and has most of my life. My parents divorced when I was four and my brother, Tim, was a baby, and my mother moved us to east Texas to live with my grandparents. There are photographs of my father with us on my grandparents' goat farm where we lived in the guesthouse. He would make the long drive to visit us, even if only for a day or two.

My memories of that time are vague, but I do remember my grandfather feeding the goats and my grandmother sewing clothes for my Mandy doll. I remember eating dinner in my grandparents' kitchen, and one evening my grandmother scolded us for stirring our vanilla ice cream into slushy milkshakes. My brother and I were stunned by her harshness, and my mother quietly nudged us out the back door and toward the guesthouse.

Tim and I joked about it over the years. *Never* stir your ice cream in front of Grandmother or in public. The message seemed clear that it was rude or unseemly.

Later, my mother told me that the day of the "ice cream–stirring incident," my grandmother had received the news that her father, my mother's "Granddaddy," had passed away in California. I would think of this story later when I would yell at my own children for no good reason. When you're miserably sad, you can be set off by something as simple as stirring vanilla ice cream into a frothy milkshake consistency and slurping it from a bowl.

Within a year or so, my mother was ready to live on her own again and moved us an hour east, to Shreveport, and this is where we grew up. Shreveport was full of a bunch of people who lost their fortunes in the oil-bust days of the early 1980s and then tried to look like they hadn't. Luckily, my mother, Tim, and I never had any money to begin with. My father only came to visit us a couple of times in Shreveport. We went to Indiana each summer, seasonal additions to the family my father had formed with my stepmother, Carolyn, and their children, Wesley and Katie.

We loved them, and they loved us, but no one should lie and say it is easy for children of divorce. When you sleep in the guest room at your father's house, you feel like a guest. When you and your brother are not in family portraits, you feel like extended family, rather than immediate. When you live in a tiny rented house with your mother, who cannot afford to take you to the movies or buy you Guess jeans, and then you spend your summers with your father and his wife, who have a swimming pool and a BMW, you cannot help but feel an imbalance in the Force. There is a crack in the foundation of your world that you must constantly straddle as the Earth shifts beneath your feet.

When I was 21 and first dating Charles, he told me his father had attended Louisiana Tech. So had mine. We found a book of alumni tucked into the built-in bookshelves in Roger and Frances's den, and I looked up my dad. It listed him as living in Indianapolis, married to my stepmother, and the father of two children, Wesley and Katie. My brother, Tim, and I were not mentioned. I cried and I told my mom, but I never mentioned it to my dad. My mother told my dad, and he brushed it off as nothing. He hadn't filled out the information. It didn't mean anything. Except that it did, even if it only served as an illustration of my and my brother's biggest insecurity—that we weren't as important as my half-brother and half-sister, that I wasn't part of my dad's *real* life. And he wasn't part of mine.

I knew my father loved me. He was a *nice* man. I couldn't tell you one time he had ever been mean or rude or hateful to me. He had been loving. Mostly, I think he was oblivious, and I was always willing to forgive that. I was willing to stuff my own hurt into some hidden place in order to keep the peace.

I turned stories of iniquities into humorous tales. Audrey will still laugh about the time I asked my dad to help me buy a dress for my senior prom, and he sent me $25. We shook our heads at the foolishness of clueless fathers. More than a decade after that prom, Audrey told me that she had gone to her mom and asked if they could help me buy a dress. In the end, I hadn't needed the help. My mother came up with the money.

I learned to be happy with what I had. I did not ask for more. I learned to laugh off the small things. I'm no saint, but I have always known that if I am strong enough, all things can be made small.

Being the good girl who lived far away for 10 months of the year meant that I could be as close to perfect as possible for an adolescent girl. My father did not know that I back-talked my mother or rolled my eyes when she asked me to unload the groceries. He did not know I snuck out of the house to meet an older boy I had been forbidden to see while my mother was lying sick with the flu in her bed. Oh, sure, he might have heard the story later from my mother—who caught me coming in the window that night—but it was a tale told second hand, and it was days or weeks old. And my mother had already handled it by yelling at me and telling me she was going to paint my bedroom door red for "whore." Then she came down off her flu-medicine high and reprimanded me in a calmer, less dramatic fashion—no red paint involved. (Though Tim and I will probably make jokes about "red-door whore" for the rest of our lives.)

And there was no fathering required.

It is a blessing and a curse to be seen as wonderful but to know that perhaps you are not truly known.

My father had disappointed my mother deeply, and she carried it with her for years. Sometimes we carried it, too. But my father showed us love when we were with him. He called us when he wasn't with us. He and my stepmother sent us huge boxes of presents at Christmas. We made it an event to cut open the boxes and take out the packages one by one, feeling the weight of them in our hands and guessing at their contents, before tucking each one under the tree.

My father's failure was simply in not being there. He lived too far away. That wasn't his fault or my mother's fault. It was how it had to be. Once you are a grown woman with children, you see how decisions must be made, and sometimes the right thing for one person changes the lives of other, smaller people. *Changes* lives, doesn't destroy them. Doesn't ruin them. Only changes them. That is all. But a large chunk of parenthood is *being there.*

I am always here for you, I would tell my children three days later as we floated in the aboveground pool behind my mother's house. Jacob said, "What if I'm in Russia and I need help?" "I will get a passport and fly there as soon as possible," I said. "What if I'm in Antarctica?" he countered.

"I'll find a way to help you," I said.

"What if I'm an astronaut and I'm in outer space?" he said.

"Then, son, first you should call NASA and tell them, 'Houston, we have a problem.' And *then* you can call your mommy."

Over the years, I wished my father were there to know my friends or my high-school boyfriend. It seemed wrong that he would never know the first boy I ever loved. He would not know when the boy broke my heart and I cried myself to sleep, and my mother let me miss four days of school.

When Charles and I had been dating several months, one of us came up with the grand scheme to drive to Indiana with my brother for Thanksgiving and surprise my father and the rest of the family. Charles had not yet met my dad or any of the Bickers family. Thanksgiving was Charles's favorite holiday, and I did not know then what a sacrifice he was making in giving up his mother's homemade feast, his favorite meal of the entire year—a smorgasbord of turkey, broccoli-and-cheese casserole, sausage rice, mashed potatoes, stuffing, and piles of hot, buttered crescent rolls.

We recruited my Aunt Carla and her partner Sue in our plan. We would drive up on the Wednesday before Thanksgiving and stay with them overnight and then show up at my grandparents' in time for the family lunch.

It was a stunning success and one we talked about every Thanksgiving after that. We would pull out the videotape that Sue had recorded. There were images of my grandma crying when she saw us at the front door, then of my granddad coming into the living room, seeing us, exclaiming in delight, and dropping his shoes, which he'd been holding in his right hand. Then he pointed at Charles and said, good-naturedly, "Who's that guy?" Group by group, our aunts and cousins arrived and screamed and laughed and cried, and my cousin Heather chased my brother through the den to hug him fiercely.

And when, at last, my dad and stepmother and Katie and Wesley came in, my dad covered his face and burst into tears. God, it was incredible.

Charles made them fall in love with him on that trip. When we all had to pile into a minivan to drive to Michigan for Wesley's hockey tournament the next day, Charles was all for it. In the morning, in the hotel room we all shared, he woke everyone up by singing a wake-up song his mother sang when he was growing up. He always sang it obnoxiously loud, and all of our friends had been treated to it on many a hungover morning.

"Get up, get up, the sun is up
The dew is on the buttercup.
Get up, get up, the sun is up,
And you should be up, too."

Even now I still believe Charles was the kind of guy you would take home to meet your parents. He endeared himself to them so much that a decade later, when my marriage was in its death throes, he was a groomsman in my sister's wedding. Even after our divorce, my stepmother would say, "He's such a nice guy. If you two could make it work, it would be wonderful."

Of course, they were far away and they weren't privy to the daily drama. As in my childhood, they heard stories weeks or months later, and everything seems smaller through the lens of time.

My dad said he thought they would wait until I was back in Birmingham to come see me. He didn't think they could make it to the funeral. It was such a long drive, and they could be more help to me once I was home.

"Is that OK?" he asked me.

And I was quiet. Those few seconds laid heavily on my chest. I thought that I could tell him I needed him, but part of me recoiled at that and said that I did not *need* him. I had lived 37 years with the firm belief that no one *needs* anyone. So I said, "I guess so." Now I had to get off the phone and tell my mother, and we could add it to the list of disappointments that defined us.

Without malice or intent, I did not speak to my father again for seven months.

Perhaps these things were my fault. I disappointed myself by not saying out loud that I might need someone. I could go this alone. Needing was not the same as wanting.

I had trained myself not to say out loud what I wanted.

5

Later that day, I drove my mother to her house in Natchitoches. She needed to go home to get clothing and arrange to pick up my stepfather, Ted.

Ted had suffered a heart attack the summer before, a tragic moment on a treadmill in a gym where no one knew how to do CPR (or bothered to do it), and the lack of oxygen caused brain damage. He went through weeks of rehab at a facility in New Orleans, and I'd gone down there to pick up my mother and drive her home (because of her fear of long interstate drives). Ted sat in a wheelchair and rolled it around the floor of Touro Infirmary Hospital and talked to himself in low tones. All the doors were locked, but he went to each one and pushed it. He wanted out. He asked my mother to pull the truck around because he was ready to leave. He had landed in the wrong place and he wanted to go back.

A year later, his long-term memory was somewhat intact, though he sometimes asked my mom where Baby was, a dog who died years ago. He said they'd been married 10 years, though it had been 17. My mother told him about Charles, but she had to repeat the news to him more than once.

"Oh yeah," he'd say each time, as though he remembered someone telling him this before and it had slipped his mind. Then he would shake his head. "I can't believe that boy did that."

We were not unalike in the inability to hold onto this information for long without having to be repeatedly reminded that it was real.

Ted had been at his parents' house, and my mom was going to pick him up and then pick up my brother. Tim was flying in from Phoenix, his home for the past five years. He'd followed a girl there, a tattoo artist. In the years he'd lived there, Tim had acquired countless more tattoos. Whenever he came to Louisiana, he showed us his new body art.

Before we drove the 45 minutes from Shreveport to Natchitoches, my mom asked if I wanted someone to ride with me. I had not been alone since Charles's death. I called Tina at her mother's house, but I decided not to ask if she wanted to ride with me. I was OK on my own. I'm not sure what we were afraid would happen if I were alone.

We took Kate to the Emorys' house, and, before we headed out, Audrey stopped by to bring me my new cell phone. She'd gone to several T-Mobile places that morning until she convinced an employee to give her a new phone on my account. To each person, she'd presented a handwritten and signed note from me explaining that the phone was lost, what my account number was, and that this was an emergency. Finally, after several employees said no, one of them took the note, nodded understandingly, and said, "Sure, I can help you."

Barely out of Shreveport, it began pouring rain. I pulled over on the side of I-49 while 18-wheelers continued to fly by, tossing up buckets of water in their wake. While we waited for the storm to pass, I checked my voice messages from Tuesday and Wednesday and listened to the sounds of worry, the expressions of sympathy. Then we got on the road again as the rain tapered off.

I didn't stay long at my mom's. I went to the restroom and splashed cold water on my face. In the living room, my mom gave me a tight hug. "We'll see you at the visitation," she said.

And I headed out, back to Shreveport, back to What Must Be Done.

By then the sun was shining. The sky was blue and dotted with white clouds. It spread out around me like the pages of a pop-up book. When I was in Birmingham, full of its hills and winding roads and towering pine trees, I sometimes felt claustrophobic and I missed the flat land of north Louisiana, the way it spread endlessly, the sky wide and open. But today the sky felt like a low ceiling.

My mother went through an awful second divorce when I was in fifth grade. (Are any divorces not awful?) For awhile, maybe a week, or maybe it was longer, she came home from work, fixed dinner for my brother and me, and then spent the rest of the evening in her room, curled up in bed. She said that during those weeks, the ceiling of her bedroom was 5 feet high. It was so low that she could not stand up.

That is how the sky on this day, so bright and blue after the swiftly moving storm had passed through, felt to me. Barely 3 miles away from my mother's exit, I began to cry. A more accurate description is that I began to wail. Three days' worth of emotions spilled out of me, my heart straining against the cage of my chest. Like the rain before, my tears clouded my vision. I could not see past August 3.

I said his name. "Oh, Charles."

It pushed its way out of me, again and again, jagged against my throat. He was gone. Not just gone. Dead. The knowledge of it rose to the surface, set free from the place my shock had hidden it. Maybe it had been in my stomach and that's why I couldn't eat. My stomach was so full of it. I imagine that knowledge stuffed behind my liver or some other internal organ. Before that, Charles's death was like a concept, an idea that was not real. It did not register. Now, denial was an unnecessary organ my body was rejecting. It could no longer live in me. And with denial gone, I couldn't not know.

This happened multiple times over the next year. Sometimes it happened on my way to work. Other times, it happened on the way home. The knowledge crawled around in my head at night and brought me to my knees in the shower the next morning.

The stages of grief were not stages but rather continually overlapping phases of varying lengths. Denial could last a minute or a month. Acceptance blew right past, something that had to be captured but was too slippery to hang onto.

"Grief changes shape, but it never ends." Keanu Reeves said that. I read it on People.com or some other celeb-focused website, and it stayed with me the way a quote from C. S. Lewis or Euripides might. In 1999, Keanu Reeves's girlfriend gave birth to a stillborn daughter. Two years later, the girlfriend died in a car accident. These are the kind of things journalists want actors to talk about while they promote their next film projects. A piece of publicity will cost you a piece of yourself. That seems to be the deal.

Grief was going to come for me again and again, in many forms. I wanted to work through the phases and be done, but it's like I was trying to learn physics. Just when I thought I had a grip on acceptance, it changed shape and slipped out of my grasp and was gone. And I did not fight against its retreat because I never cared to learn this shit in the first place.

When I got to the Emorys' about 45 minutes later, I'd managed to pull myself together. Kate was at a friend's house around the corner, playing like a little girl should, something that seemed right and normal, and Jacob was in the guest room playing a video game. There were other people there, but now I don't know who besides Roger and Frances and Randy. The kitchen counters and the dining table were lined with casseroles and snacks and sweets. Over the course of four days, I probably ate four bites total of whatever was in those containers.

I stuck my head in to say hi to Jacob, and as I turned back down the hall, Frances stopped me to ask about the details of the funeral.

"Did Charles want to be cremated?" she asked.

"He sort of cremated himself, didn't he?" I thought, proof that constant snark should probably be classified as a mental illness.

"Should we have an open casket?" Frances asked.

We were still standing in the small hallway of the Emorys' home. I could hear the sounds of low conversation in the living room. I started shaking my head, and it felt like I couldn't stop. It was like the stammer I had developed in the past three days, which came out at night or in my worst moments. Something in me got stuck, and I couldn't stop it.

I had to tell her there was too much damage to repair, but that would mean telling her what he'd done—to himself and to me. I still wanted to protect him, as I always had, keeping secret the cruel things he did in anger and desperation.

Frances said, "There's a lot they can do." Not understanding. Not knowing. But I was still shaking my head, and then she motioned, lifted her hand like a handgun to her temple, like a question.

I couldn't seem to say it, so I held my hands like I was gripping a shotgun under my chin. "Oh," like an exhale, like I'd punched her in the gut, she said, "Oh, I didn't know. I didn't know you were there."

Later, I went out to the extra refrigerator in the garage to get a cold Diet Coke, and that is when I first realized that getting out of that garage in Birmingham was going to take more than hitting a button and running out. As I took the soda out and closed the refrigerator door, the heat trapped in the garage began to wrap itself around me, and the faint odor of oil began to unlock my memory. My heart was racing, and I ran back into the house, out into the living room.

And then I could hear it, Jacob's video game. It was a first-person shooter game, and the guns were constantly going off. Frances is the one who noticed me standing there and that something was wrong with me. She jumped up off the sofa. "What should I do? What can I do?"

"Tell Jacob to turn it down. Tell him."

I was not out of that garage. It was inside me. It had come with me down the miles of I-20.

Jacob later told me that he knew I was there when his dad died because the sound of the guns on his video games bothered me. Whenever I needed to speak to him, I would stand outside the door and first say, "Turn that down, OK?" and then I would walk in and avoid looking at the screen. "I figured it out, Mom," he said. And I should have known he would.

For several months, I avoided television shows or movies that might have guns. But I realized quickly that it didn't take actual guns to send me back. I could watch a sitcom and be forced into the wormhole. I didn't have statistics, but if you asked me, the most popular joke on modern-day shows is the suicide joke. People constantly put their fingers to their head—boom—to indicate boredom with someone. "I'm going to blow my brains out. Isn't that so hilarious?"

I began to document them, these suicidal gestures on film. I made a list in my journal. An episode of *Friends*. An episode of *How I Met Your Mother*. An episode of *Cougartown*. The movie *40-Year-Old Virgin*. A character in the movie *Julie & Julia* made the gesture to illustrate how her husband died. On an episode of *Ugly Betty*, Betty's sister said, "One day [your boyfriend] is saying 'Miss you much'; the next day—pop-pop murder-suicide." On *Today*, Nancy Sneiderman discussed her response if she didn't keep her New Year's resolutions: "Well, I won't put a bullet in my head." I could have written a book titled *500 Suicide Jokes in Five Months*.

The worst crime is that the jokes are all so unoriginal.

It wasn't just on TV. In early fall, I went with friends to see a comedy show at Bottletree, a restaurant bar in Birmingham. My friend Christopher, an artist and graphic designer at the magazine, was doing the introductions for Janeane Garofalo and Al Madrigal, and we were all so proud, out in full force to support him. And during Al Madrigal's set, he made a suicide joke, something about shooting oneself. It was nothing unusual, and yet the entire room disappeared around me. I was alone with my memory. I wasn't the only one affected, of course. Christopher was backstage, and the joke stopped him in his tracks; he worried about me out in the crowd. And at the theater watching *Julie & Julia*, I swear I could feel the collective tension of my friends sitting around me on the tenth row when that woman put her finger to her temple.

One night over Thanksgiving, I went out in Shreveport with two friends from high school and we saw three couples having dinner a few tables away. They were people we had also gone to school with, clean-cut men in khaki pants, collared shirts, and blazers—the uniform of the well-behaved Southern boy. Their wives were the kind of people who would always be described as "sweet."

"If I had to be over there, I'd shoot my face off," one of my friends said.

And I knew what she meant. But I was suddenly in the garage again. Everything in me stilled for a moment.

It's like when you buy a blue Camry and suddenly you seem to notice nothing but blue Camrys on the road. When this happened, for that second while I was still, I hoped the person wouldn't realize what he or she had said. I hoped they wouldn't apologize to me. "Let's keep going. Keep the conversation moving, keep it normal. I want to feel normal," I'd think.

It didn't actually matter that Charles did not put a pistol to his head. His gesture that night was not that of the jokes on TV and movies.

Only one time have I seen the suicide gesture done the way he did it. It was on *The Daily Show* during a discussion of Ernest Hemingway. Later, I searched for information online about the famous writer and read that he had committed suicide with his favorite shotgun. It was worded that way in account after account. "His favorite." And he, unlike a million comedians, had to make a gesture like Charles did, or something close to it anyway.

Whenever I heard references to Hemingway, I felt angry. An article about his love for hunting would make me sneer. A reference to his home in Key West, kept like a shrine, made me roll my eyes. A book about his first marriage made me want to shake his first wife and yell, "Why aren't you leaving this asshole?" This long-dead, famous author was a good target, because I wasn't willing to direct those feelings at Charles.

Eventually, I would direct them at myself.

Months later, Jacob and I went to the bookstore and, while he browsed the teen section, I wandered around the personal-growth department. I picked up book after book on grief or suicide, searching the index for "posttraumatic" or "witness." Every one of them had a page number and then, when I flipped to the page, I would find only one line about it.

I needed more, some evidence that I wasn't alone. I wanted something that indicated that witnessing a suicide is not a one-sentence event and it does not have a one-sentence effect.

Every day I had to work to get out of the garage in my mind and to stay out of it, but a word or a motion from someone could send me back there.

It didn't even take a real reference to suicide. A person might speak of someone "losing his mind" or that the news of something might "make his head explode," and I was there again.

In a figurative world, I had too many literal images to reference.

I sat on the sofa with Randy, who was using his laptop to look up songs that might be played at the funeral. It was mid-afternoon. Kate was still at her friend's house, Jacob still on his Xbox. People had wandered in and out, bringing food.

"Charles always said to me they would play 'He Stopped Loving Her Today' when he died," I said.

This was part of a scene he played out with me a hundred times after we divorced.

"If I died, would you come to my funeral? If I had a heart attack, would you come to the hospital to visit me?"

I thought about how he had this idea of himself as the one with the undying love, and I was the one who got away (though I never really did, did I?). In every scenario, he was in pain, wasn't he? He was really saying, "Will my pain bring you back to me? How big does my pain have to be?"

Randy pulled the song up online, and, as a clip played of it, Frances walked by us and said, "Not that song. No." I was embarrassed that she might think I would want that song played. Even now, I cringe to think that she might have thought that.

I felt ashamed, too, because maybe the truth was that I wanted him to love me and never stop. Maybe Charles knew that. It had been in the air.

But also in the air was that I wanted him to go away because that would be the only real way for me to escape, too.

6

On Saturday, the day of the funeral, the sky was cloudless and the sun was blazing down. We would not be huddled under large black umbrellas around a muddy grave while the sky cried. We'd be sweating our asses off.

I got ready at Audrey's apartment and then drove to the Emorys' house so I could ride with them and Kate and Jacob to the funeral home. Somehow, during these days of rites and rituals, I was able to set aside how Charles died. At night, I lay awake and afraid in the darkness until I inevitably gave in to the urge to turn on the bedside lamp. I would draw close to the edge of something gaping and bottomless. But in the daylight hours, I was able to hear stories of him and laugh. I was able to see clearly that he was a man in pain, and I could separate his pain and his tragic end from my own pain and trauma. For now, the long job of reckoning was night-shift only.

The night before, we'd had the visitation, and people were lined up out the door and around the corner of the building. If you want your funeral to be standing-room-only, die young. The Emorys and I greeted mourners one by one, accepting condolences. Occasionally, I felt myself at the edge of the hole, and suddenly Jacob would be at my elbow, saving me. Kids never know that they do this, rescue their parents again and again, simply by being there at the right moment.

"Hey, Mom."

"Hey. Are you OK?"

"Sure. Do you want a Diet Coke? I can go to the snack room and get you one."

"Yes, thanks. I'd like that." Then I'd watch Jacob's red hair, as he would weave his way through the crowd toward the door.

Most of the folks at the visitation simply offered their sympathies and moved on, but some asked questions, carefully worded yet probing.

"Had he been depressed?" Some asked this of me directly. Others whispered to the bit players on the periphery of the tragedy: "What happened?"

Had he been depressed? I knew people were picturing Charles alone in his hotel room, listening to sad country songs and weeping over a suicide note. Maybe they imagined warning signs in the days leading up to it, like Charles going around giving away boxes of his stuff and saying meaningful good-byes to friends. People have ideas of suicide based largely on movies and books and their own personal fantasies of how they might pay back all the bastards who've done them wrong.

In this scenario, Charles threatened suicide one minute before he went through with it. There was no time to leave anyone a parting gift. Except for me, of course. I got a big ol' box full of fucked-up that I could carry around with me for a lifetime.

I'd only heard Charles threaten suicide once before, when we had first separated five years earlier. We were standing outside an apartment we'd moved to after selling our house in Birmingham. We couldn't afford the house or the SUV, which we'd turned in for what they call a "voluntary repossession." We lived on the second floor of a brown building that was supposed to look muted and natural tucked into a wooded lot. For a time, a drug dealer lived with his grandmother in the first-floor unit. He was a teenage boy, and he sold little baggies of weed out of his bedroom window. I called him the McDonald's of Marijuana for his drive-up window service, open all night. He was actually rather beautiful. He had smooth, milk-chocolate skin, light copper-colored eyes, and a regal nose. Charles gave him rides now and then because the boy didn't have a car. I'm sure the boy returned the favor with discounted weed.

Sometimes it would get so loud in the apartment downstairs that I would stomp on my bedroom floor and someone below would pound on the ceiling. It was a pointless ritual that left me exhausted and hating that place, which was always impossible to cool in the summer and heat in the winter.

That day Charles was distraught over the pending divorce. He couldn't bear the thought of losing his family and living on his own. I didn't realize then that he was incapable of living on his own. He'd come over to plead his case, to beg me to change my mind about letting him stay there.

"I might as well kill myself," he said.

I stopped where I was, with my hand on the driver's side door. I wanted to drive out of there and away from him.

"That's ridiculous and selfish," I said. "You would break your children's hearts. You know that, right?"

I suspected a lot of men said what Charles had, when they were faced with the end of their marriages, staring into new lives not of their choosing (but absolutely the result of their choices). This was a last desperate attempt at control.

When my mother moved my brother and me from Indiana to Texas, my father said that if she took us away, he might as well be dead. My mother told me that she said, "Well, we're moving in two weeks, so you better do it before then because we're not coming back for your funeral."

People say these things, and they don't have to be the last things that are said.

Charles didn't mean it. I believe he thought, "If I threaten the worst, I can get what I want."

What is so sad is that Charles could have had us. At so many moments, he could have taken the road that led him to what he wanted. On too many days, I held the door open to him and held my breath.

But Charles was powerless over the thing he needed more than us.

When we pulled into the lot behind the funeral home, people were already arriving. As family members, we went in the back door into a private reception area to wait for the funeral to begin.

I was wearing a new gray dress my friend Gabi bought for me the day before. We'd gone to a dress shop where Gabi picked things off of racks for me and brought them to the dressing room. She picked out faux pearl earrings to go with the gray dress.

Gabi had also picked out a black-and-white print dress for me to wear to the visitation and a casual gray knit dress for a gathering to be held the night of the funeral. When we went to pay, she pulled out her credit card and waved me away. Afterward, we went to the mall to look for something for Kate. Kate enjoyed the outing, but I was like a zombie wandering around Dillard's. We'd briefly separated while we were there, Kate and Gabi going to the juniors' section while I went upstairs to buy new undergarments to wear under my funeral dress. When I came back down the escalator and into the girls' section, I couldn't find them anywhere. I checked the dressing rooms on one end. I wandered around to the shoe department and then through the men's department and toward the doors we'd come in through earlier.

As minutes passed and I couldn't find them, I began to panic. I stood in the middle of the stacks of button-down shirts and crisp khaki pants and turned around slowly. Inside I was spinning.

"Hey, Charles." I heard someone say, and I turned toward the escalator and saw an employee carrying a cologne sample. This was Charles, a tall, skinny guy in his early 20s, ready to spray people with some musky scent while he earned minimum wage.

This is where I lose it, I thought. This is where the woman goes insane in the shopping mall.

But I didn't. I breathed slowly in and out and I made my way back to the juniors' section and found another set of dressing rooms. And here was Kate, twirling around in a rhinestone black party dress best suited for a disco while Gabi held up a sweet sundress, bright and beautiful with a tie around the waist, and persuaded Kate to try it on, too.

The simplicity of my new sleeveless shift dress made me think of *Vertigo* and Kim Novak's gray suit, the one Jimmy Stewart makes her purchase to look like his lost love. It looked like something I could have worn to a funeral 50 years ago.

People came up to me before and after the funeral and said, "Well, you look good."

And that was something, anyway.

We, the family members, walked in through a door at the front of the room. It was as if we were on display for all the other mourners, already seated in rows of wooden pews. Are they called pews if they aren't in a church, if they're in a long, nondescript room of a funeral home?

Roger, Frances, Randy, and one of Frances's elderly aunts went into the first row ahead of me and Kate and Jacob. I had a brief moment of worry that I would have to sit next to the old aunt, someone I didn't know really well.

The children didn't seem to be paying attention to where they would sit. Neither was clinging to me or holding my hand, and I began to panic, thinking neither of them would be next to me. I would be alone. My mother and brother and stepfather were on the second row, already seated. No one was trying to sit next to me, to offer me comfort or to hold my hand. That was something Charles would have done.

As we moved toward the bench, I reached for Jacob and whispered, "Sit by me."

I grabbed Kate's hand. As we got situated, Jacob was on one side of me and Kate was on the other, but Kate leaned in and said, "I want to sit by Pop."

Did Roger hear her, or did we whisper this to him urgently as everyone settled into their seats? I can't remember. Roger moved down to our end of the row to sit on the other side of Kate.

Warm bodies next to me couldn't really remedy the panic I experienced. There were endless moments during the service when I felt unmoored. I was adrift, thousands of miles from anyone, lost on a sea that no one around me even knew existed.

I felt like I needed Kate and Jacob more than they needed me. That would feel true every day that followed. It was a fact that I tried to keep from them as we went about our lives, as I was busy being the mom and they were busy being kids.

Every once in a while, I would grab a hand. I would pull one of them toward me.

"Sit here," I'd say. "Just for a minute, sit by me."

Charles's friends got up one by one and spoke of their love for Charles. They had each known Charles for 20 years or more. It is no exaggeration to say that at least three men began by saying, "Charles Emory was my best friend."

Stuart said, "Charles was good at everything he ever did. He could play golf. He could play pool. He could shoot a gun."

There's a pause in the world when these things happen, when a person says something and then immediately knows it is wrong, that it is a trigger (like this) or that it hits too close to home (there's another one). Language is a tricky thing. It can lead you down a path you didn't intend to take.

I felt it, this pause, and I thought, "Oh no, Stuart's going to feel bad about that."

And he did. Later, he said to me, "As soon as I said it I knew. Did it make you think..." and our minds filled in the blank of that sentence, me with a real image, and him with an imagined one. "Yes," I told him, "but it's OK. I'm never not thinking about it."

No one should ever feel bad about reminding me. It is not possible to remind me. It's like reminding me that I am alive, that I have two children, that I must breathe in and out. That

Charles took his life in front of me is part of me now, and I could not pinpoint a day over the next two years when I did not think of it within an hour of waking in the morning or within an hour of going to sleep at night.

Stuart told of good times watching LSU football, of going fishing and hunting. He told a story of Charles killing a deer in the dewy early morning of some hunting season years before and how they'd had to drag the animal through the woods because it was so far from the truck.

Stuart went on to tell a story about a Sunday evening nearly a decade earlier when he and Charles drove out to Boothill Speedway in Greenwood, Louisiana. Stuart is a recovering alcoholic. While the rest of his friends still drank, Stuart had started along the hard road to sobriety.

"I'd had a bad day," Stuart said. "I wanted to drink. When Charles picked me up, I said stop so I can get some beer. Charles said sure, but let's drive a little farther before we stop. He kept stalling me. Finally we got to Greenwood, and I said stop at this gas station so I can get some beer, and Charles said, 'Sorry, they don't sell beer on Sundays here.'"

Charles's lifelong friend Chris, who went to the University of Alabama and lived in a suburb outside Birmingham, spoke of their annual bet over the LSU/Alabama game. The loser had to buy the winner a steak dinner. He said, "I'm going to say something now for Charles. Go Tigers."

The crowd laughed (the laughter was such a relief during the funeral), and I thought that I could not wait to tell Charles what Chris had said.

More friends walked to the front, stood in front of the closed casket, and poured their hearts out. Kristen spoke of silly songs and stolen lighters.

"I did a little dance called 'The Humpty Dance' all the way to the Chevron, where I purchased several lighters, on the Chevron card, of course, to replace the ones that mysteriously disappeared. On my way home, I spotted a tornado and decided to see if I could catch up with it, and then I realized I didn't have my copilot. My best guess was that he could be found at Julie and Dan's or Leslie and Stuart's because, after all, it was Christmas morning, or was it 4th of July, or New Year's? Better yet, there was probably an LSU game on. You were a big part of all of our lives for these reasons and so many more. I can still hear your voice calling my name, good or bad, happy or mad, aggravated or frustrated, and even sometimes glad to see me. What a sweet sound I have ringing in my ears now and forever."

Charles's friend Julie didn't take off her dark sunglasses as she stood at the lectern. They hid half her face and, with her sunny blonde hair and black top, she looked a bit like a celebrity come to pay her respects. But, really, the sunglasses were simply hiding her eyes, red and puffy from crying. Julie was married to Dan, another of Charles's lifelong friends, and she told stories about how Charles was like a member of her family. He spent countless hours at their house when we still lived in Shreveport and whenever he visited. She spoke of how Charles spent most of Dan and Julie's wedding night with them, running around the casino hotel with Dan—Julie tucked into bed and watching television in the room—into the wee hours. When Julie found out she was pregnant, Charles knew before Dan. He was waiting outside the bathroom when she emerged with the pregnancy test.

In the midst of these lovely tributes, I suddenly felt as though I did not belong here. I felt sad for this person's friends, all sitting together on the other side of the room, walking one by one to the front to express their sorrow. I felt disconnected, like the friend of a friend who has ended up at a party without an invitation. I felt like I was not one of the main players in this drama. Sometimes it seems that the mind's coping mechanisms are really some version of insanity.

I had lived with Charles for most of the past 15 years. I knew him better than anyone on the planet. As people said, again and again, "Charles was my best friend," I wanted to stand up, too, and say, "I was Charles's best friend." But then, in the same instant, I thought that I did not really know him at all. His friends had memories of him that were fun and full of laughter.

What did I have? I had one memory that had crowded out all the others. To go up there to the front of the room would be to take this elephant and set him right on top of the casket. I could not stand in front of all these people and express my love for him.

I was not even supposed to love him anymore. This love had been off-limits for some time now. I spent endless years pushing him away when he wanted to hug me. When he insisted, I would hug him lightly and pat his back. He would say, "Don't give me the back pat." The back pat is the universal sign for "I don't really want to hug you, I'm only humoring you. Move along now."

I felt I had no claim on him. We were divorced, so my lack of claim was official, court-ordered, and part of some black-and-white document in a file somewhere. Maybe his desperate need to hold onto me was because I refused to hold onto him, because he always knew I could live without him.

We had been desperately off balance. If I was the lifeboat, he was the drowning guy trying to pull himself out of the sea. But the lifeboat can't do anything to save you unless you heave yourself over, gasping for breath, salt water dripping from your drenched clothing. The lifeboat bobs along fine whether you get in or not. It stays afloat while the desperate man drowns beside it.

I didn't belong here on the front row. I was not his best friend. I was not his wife. I was only someone who had failed him.

For a while I pressed the sharp edge of this statement against my flesh to see if I could make myself bleed. True or not, it was a weapon I kept hidden from others so I could use it against myself while everyone else slept through the night.

A priest from Roger's church spoke next. When Frances had asked me if Charles wanted to be cremated, she had said, "Roger would like a headstone to visit."

In truth, at some point during our years together, Charles probably told me he wanted to be cremated. We'd had discussions of this nature. We both wanted our organs to be donated, if possible. Neither of us wanted to be kept on life support or feeding tubes like Terry Schiavo. But I couldn't remember if he felt really strongly about cremation or not.

I'm certain he wouldn't have chosen a priest to speak at his funeral. He would have preferred someone like LSU coach Les Miles or maybe former coach Nick Saban (before he defected to Alabama).

Charles had lost whatever faith he might have once had. This world and its pain, and his inability to overcome it, seemed proof enough to him that we were merely spinning pointlessly on a globe in the middle of a vast universe.

That spring, a high-school friend of Charles's named Ryan had passed away. He'd complained of a headache and gone home to take a nap on his sofa, and this was where his wife, his high-school sweetheart and mother of his three children, found him dead from natural causes, some rare heart condition that had been like a silent secret inside him.

Charles was heartbroken over it. He told me stories, some that had been told many times but still made us laugh, like the time Ryan was at the Emorys' house and got his foot caught in one of those old-fashioned school desks. The seat had folded up around his foot like a bear trap. They'd had to call the fire department to get him unstuck.

And now this man was dead and his wife and three children were alone and why did this happen, Charles wanted to know. "He was a good man. A *good* man. If there is a God, he's an asshole anyway."

I told Frances, "Let's bury him. If that's what Roger wants, we should do that."

Charles had never expressed an adamant wish to be cremated, his ashes scattered across some golf course or a football field or into the wind blowing in off an uncaring ocean. If it comforted Roger to have a headstone, we should have one, I had said. If he wanted a priest to speak, then we would have that, too.

What I recall of the priest's words is next to nothing. I can remember no direct quotes apart from this one: "God, why hast thou forsaken me?" I do not remember how it began or how it ended. I know he clutched a crucifix in his hand. I can picture his long robe. I know he spoke of Charles's despair. He acknowledged Charles's pain. He did not pretend Charles had died of a respectable heart attack on a golf course. The actual words he spoke will not come back to me now.

All I know is that when he finished speaking, I felt a loosening in my chest that was beautifully akin to relief. When the funeral ended, Frances said she felt the same. My mother came over to us and said that she felt such comfort from the priest's words that it was like a physical sensation, that of a weight being lifted.

Maybe I could believe then, for that moment in time, that there was a god who would comfort Charles now, take him in like the lost child he was and love him enough to fill up all the empty places that Charles had tried to fill with pills.

If I believed the devil was in that garage five days earlier, did I have to believe God was somewhere in this world, too?

At the graveside services, Kate asked to put flowers on the casket. We did this at my grandma's funeral in Indiana a couple of years earlier. After the casket was lowered—the great-grandchildren had watched the mechanics of it with unveiled fascination—we all tossed in daisies. Those bright-eyed, unassuming flowers were Grandma's favorite.

Kate liked the idea and wanted to do the same for her daddy, but where he was being buried they don't lower the casket during the service. They wait until later, when all the mourners have wandered back to their cars and back to their lives beyond the cemetery gates.

I don't like this. Some people might get upset at the idea of their loved one being lowered into the earth, but I was more upset by the idea of leaving Charles aboveground, still vulnerable to the world that had broken him.

Kate passed out flowers to family members and the pallbearers and, one by one, we laid them on top of the casket. Randy laid a crucifix on top, as well, something a friend had given him only days before.

Friends paid their respects, spoke to each of us, hugged good-bye, and retreated to their air-conditioned cars. We made our way back to the funeral-home limousine, the first Kate had ridden in. Despite the circumstances, she was very excited about it. Oh, my sweet girl, that should not have been your first.

I stopped and looked back at the casket.

"Are we going to leave him here?" I wanted to ask. It felt wrong. Frankly, I didn't want to go. If my life was not 99 percent doing what others expected of me, I might have stayed there, waiting to feel like it was OK to leave him alone. Had I done that, I might still be there.

I'd spent years knowing Charles could not be left alone, and now I was expected to leave him here in this cemetery in some random section of Shreveport in an area of town so far from where we'd grown up that we might once have described it as being in East Jesus or BFE (bum-fuck Egypt).

Charles hated being alone. It's why he had so many friends, so someone would always be there. Even when he died, he was not alone. He needed me to be there.

We went back to the Emorys' house where people were going to gather for food and visiting. The kitchen counters and the dining-room table were covered with casseroles and bowls of chips and dip and platters of iced cookies. I spooned shrimp pasta salad from Monjuni's on a paper plate. It's one of my favorite dishes, and whenever I visit Shreveport, it's on my list of things I have to have (along with a frozen daiquiri from the liquor store and a "Humphrey Yogart" from Counter Culture). I sat down in one of four metal folding chairs that had been set up in the living room next to the fireplace across from the sectional sofa. I had a Diet Coke, too, and set it down next to the chair leg.

There were only a few people when we first got here, but now they were arriving steadily, two and three at a time. Jacob retreated to the guest room to play video games. I have no idea where Kate went. I search my memory, and the whereabouts of my daughter are lost to me. Did she go to a friend's house to play and pretend that a mere hour ago she hadn't been at the funeral of her father? I'm certain she did. When she is grown, will she look back on that? Will she remember playing Barbies or watching music videos, singing along to Fergie or Miley Cyrus or whoever girls were into at the time? Will she remember keeping the grown-up knowledge of her father's death at bay while she steadfastly remained a little girl?

I couldn't eat the food. I only held the plate so people might believe I would eat it. One woman, the sister of one of Charles's good friends, arrived carrying an open can of beer and said to those gathered near the door, "I didn't know if we were allowed to bring drinks, but then I thought 'I'm an adult, I can have a drink if I want one.'"

This "adult" also had been seen making out with one of the pallbearers in the funeral-home parking lot after the visitation the night before. Or so I'd been told.

Roger was a recovering alcoholic, sober for more than two decades, and Frances didn't drink. I'd never seen alcohol in their house. Neither of them said anything. I thought most people were embarrassed for this woman and her need to loudly justify her afternoon drinking. I wasn't against a little afternoon drinking—hell, if anyone should have had a drink in that room, it should have been me—but I did respect Charles's parents.

I knew suddenly and without a doubt that I couldn't remain in the room with all these people. Not one more second. I went into the kitchen and threw my uneaten food in the garbage can. On the way back through the living room, I stopped and picked up my can of Diet Coke and then went to where Roger was sitting on the sectional.

"I'm going to go in your room for awhile, if that's OK."

Roger stood up and hugged me and said, "Of course."

The master bedroom was right off the living room and had a huge flat-screen TV set up on a desk. The TV was always turned up too loud because Roger was at that age when men tend to pretend they can still hear just fine. I sat down in the recliner across from the TV.

It was already turned onto a news channel, so I flipped channels until I found the movie *Holes*. In it, Shia LaBeouf is sent to a work camp where Sigourney Weaver forces boys to dig holes, searching for buried treasure. I turned down the volume a bit and watched it. Mostly, I stared at the screen and listened to the white noise of the people in the living room and kitchen and dining room, the rise and fall of conversations. I ate some candy that was sitting on the TV tray next to the chair. The bag of Sprees might have belonged to one of the kids, or it could have been Roger's. He had a weakness for sugar that sent him searching for a fix late at night. The kids usually hid their treats because if they didn't they'd wake up in the morning to find them gone. I took off my heels and curled up in the chair and waited to feel up to going back out there.

Meanwhile, Shia LaBeouf dug holes.

I'd read stories that painted him as a bit of a douchebag in real life. He was in a car crash and charged with DUI. He'd been in some bar fights. People hate to hear celebrities complain about their fame, but I've always thought that being famous must be awful. Everyone watches you. Everyone judges you. If you get divorced, people you've never even met will pick sides and buy T-shirts that read "Team Brad" or "Team Jennifer." Someone has to be the bad guy.

This happens on a smaller scale when you are part of a tragic event. People spread the news of it and ask themselves how this could have happened. I thought they were probably picking sides, too.

The other thing about famous people is that they get to be praised if they come back from the edge. Good for you, Robert Downey Jr. And what if you could be the wife of that man and sit amongst an admiring crowd while your redeemed husband accepts an award? You could listen to speeches in which you are the reason for and the support behind his sobriety. You are the reason he is all he can be. You can be the wife who pulled him back from the darkness.

It's a nice story. You can watch it in *Walk the Line*. Joaquin Phoenix plays Johnny Cash, and Reese Witherspoon is June. Look how he got sober because he loved June and theirs was a true love. No one ever talks about Johnny Cash's first wife and how difficult it must have been to be married to this man who drank and cheated and couldn't change for her.

Who are you when you are not the wife who pulled her husband back from the brink?

You can know that there was nothing you could do. You can know that it says nothing about who you are. It does not mark you as a bad person.

But you can know something and not know it at the exact same time.

You can still hear someone who is standing outside the master-bedroom door say to people gathered around, "I didn't agree with everything she did..."

There might be a "but," something to blunt this, a statement about how you didn't deserve what happened, but that part is muffled or might have been silenced by a "shush" from someone who knows you are behind the door, sitting still and quiet in a chair.

You can sit there and obsess over things you did with which people could disagree, the mistakes you have made that can never be remedied.

I turned up the volume of the movie. Shia LaBeouf would find a way to climb out of the holes. He would get his reward at the end. I leaned my head back against the puffy leather uphol-stery. My stomach was sore and sour from not eating real food, from filling it with fizzy diet soda and sugary candy, and from swallowing all my guilt.

When Kate was six months old, I began to experience excru-ciating pain, usually in the evening. The pain would radiate through my lower back and knock the breath out of me. Late one night while Charles and Kate and Jacob slept, I filled the bathtub with steaming hot water and slid into it, desperate for relief. Eventually I fell asleep and woke up later in cold water. Another night the pain was so intense that I called an emergen-cy room and described it to a nurse. "You could come in and we'll check it out," she said, but I decided not to. I could han-dle it. It wasn't a big deal.

I have a friend who is an admitted hypochondriac. Every new bump or pain causes her to worry that she has cancer. "It's not a tumor," I say to her, doing my worst Arnold Schwarzenegger voice. I am her polar opposite. If someone shot me in my left arm, I would say, "Let's not make a huge deal of this. Calm down. I have another arm."

I ignored my episodes of pain over several weeks until one Sunday when I was at my mother and stepdad's house in

Natchitoches, picking up the kids after an overnight visit. Sitting on the sofa, I was suddenly wracked by pain that made me double over and exclaim, "This is worse than labor." My mother rummaged through her medicine cabinet and found a pain pill for me. I slept in the backseat of my car while she drove me home, and my stepdad followed us in their car with Kate and Jacob. My mom called ahead to make sure Charles would be home waiting at the house to help with the kids and take care of me.

When we got to Shreveport, my mom helped me to the sofa and tucked a blanket around me. She made me promise to go to the doctor the next day. Then she and my stepdad headed home. And Charles left.

"I'm just going to the grocery store," he said when I protested.

"But why didn't you go before, when my mom first called you? You had an hour before we were going to get home."

He didn't see why it mattered. He was *just* going to run up there. No big deal. Just was his favorite word. I just wanted to have a drink. I just wanted to spend a little money. I just wanted to go out for awhile. I just want to talk to you for a minute. Just hear me out.

If, at the end of our lives, we could calculate which words or phrases we used most often in a lifetime, Charles's would be, "I just."

Mine would be, "Have you brushed your teeth?"

Charles couldn't understand why it mattered, so I dropped it. By this time, I knew well the deal between us. Charles left for an hour, and I sat up on the sofa and took care of Kate and watched Jacob, who was four at the time, as he ran around the living room.

The next day I went to a doctor who asked me if I was always yellow, and I said, "What do you mean?" Then she pressed her warm hand against my bare stomach, and Charles said I nearly flew off the table.

An ultrasound showed I had gallstones, and one of them was caught at the entrance to my liver, blocking its function and causing jaundice, making the whites of my eyes yellow. I had surgery the next day, and during the laparoscopic procedure, the surgeon cut a vein at the base of my liver. Hours later when I was rolled out of surgery, I was as pale as a ghost, like a victim of a vampire's relentless bloodletting, and I had a long scar across the right side of my stomach.

The doctor went to talk to Charles in the hallway, and, at that moment, the priest from my mother's church arrived to check on me. He walked with the doctor toward Charles. Charles later said he was gripped by a fear so intense that his heart raced. He thought these two men, clad in the uniforms of their chosen professions, one in white and the other in black, were coming to tell him his wife was gone and he was left to raise his children on his own.

People told us we should sue the doctor for bungling something so simple, but we weren't those types of people. Shit happens, we said to each other. I'd signed a consent form that read, and I'm paraphrasing here, "This surgery might kill you." It hadn't. We were thankful for that.

The day after the surgery, Charles harassed me to ask the doctor if I could go home the next day. He couldn't stand being home alone. The doctor, of course, said no. I'd nearly bled to death the day before. My blood pressure was so low when I first came to that the nurse wouldn't give me pain medication, because it would cause the blood pressure to drop even lower, nearer to death.

"Does she typically have really low blood pressure?" I heard her ask Charles. My eyes were still closed. The answer was yes. Then the nurse insisted I open my eyes, despite the pain. In my memory, she was a rude bitch, but maybe in reality she was brisk and matter-of-fact, or coming to the end of a long shift.

Without a gall bladder, my digestive system changed and left me with horrible stomachaches if I ate the wrong thing. Translated, the "wrong thing" means anything delicious. In the years after my surgery, I compiled a list of what not to eat. When my stomach would clench up in angry defiance against mayonnaise or ice cream or irresistible coconut soup from the local Thai food place—soup that, frankly, I could pour directly into the toilet and achieve the same result in the same time—I would lie down, and Charles would smack his hands together and then rub them together like Mr. Miyagi in *The Karate Kid*. Then he would curl up next to me and put his hand flat on my bare stomach, and his warmth would spread across me.

And that would always ease the hurt.

He was good at that part.

7

The day after the funeral, the kids and I drove to my mom's house, where we spent the afternoon in her aboveground pool. It was tucked up against a deck that my stepdad built on the back of their manufactured home. Sometimes my brother and I would joke that our mother's house was a "redneck paradise." It was situated off a dirt road, and there were multiple cars in the yard. Before my stepdad's heart attack, he was the master of finding a deal on a rundown Volkswagen and then working on it until it was drivable. There was a lime-green Karmann Ghia and a blue VW Beetle convertible parked under the carport, and a baby blue Volkswagen station wagon next to the storage building.

My mom and my stepdad loved the idea of being somewhere without neighbors nearby. They strung a hammock between two trees in the backyard. On chilly Saturday mornings, my stepdad used to trek out to a deer stand on the back of the property. Of course, he couldn't do that anymore.

The week before, I'd told my mother that I couldn't wait to come pick up the kids and come to her house so I could float in the pool and drink a margarita from Maggio's, the drive-through liquor store in town. In Louisiana, you could get a frozen beverage in a Styrofoam cup topped with a plastic lid. A strip of Scotch tape secured the lid in place and covered the hole for the straw. I guess that made it a "closed container." Even after seven years in Alabama, a margarita didn't taste right to me without the scent of Scotch tape right under my nose.

Kate and Jacob splashed around and dove to the bottom of the pool to pick up nickels and pennies. I balanced on a float with my Styrofoam cup in one hand and looked up at the sky between sprawling overhanging branches. It was bright blue and clear, much like the day I'd driven from Natchitoches to Shreveport and cried out for Charles. There was something about the sky that made me wonder where he was and if he could see us. Maybe it was the feeling of being out in the open, exposed. Maybe it was a childish idea of heaven. When you're little, you are told that heaven is in the sky, and no one mentions that beyond the blue layer above you there are galaxies, punctuated by stars and full of gas and dust, that fill a vast universe that goes on forever.

I imagined Charles sitting in a tree, maybe in my stepdad's deer stand, searching the woods for signs of life. I pictured him watching us from a distance and thinking, "What the hell have I done?"

This was the brief respite between the funeral and the rest of our lives.

Two days later, we rode back to Birmingham with Randy. He was going to pick up Charles's silver Audi and drive it back to Shreveport so his parents could have it repaired. Charles had damaged the front end in a fender bender on a narrow bridge. Was he on pills? Probably. After getting it repaired, they would try to sell it.

Todd and Jennifer had cleaned out the Audi for us. They found fast-food restaurant bags filled with half-eaten burgers, the smell rank and greasy. They went through the house and gathered everything of Charles's and packed it into the back seat and trunk.

There was some back and forth about this. Frances said Randy probably wouldn't want to ride back to Louisiana surrounded by Charles's clothes. She asked if my friends would mind taking those items to the Goodwill or the Salvation Army, but I had a sudden moment of regret at the thought that everything of Charles's would be gone without me seeing it again. So Jennifer emptied the car and piled clothes and shoes in a cardboard box in the garage.

When we arrived back at the house, I found a pile of mail and a separate pile of papers that also had been in the Audi. The kids went to their rooms and dumped their bags and books. I stood in the kitchen next to the trash can and threw away junk mail. I opened condolence cards. In the other pile of papers, I found a pawn slip from a store on Highway 31, one exit away from us on the interstate. Charles had sold a portable air conditioner that had been in my basement. His parents bought it for the kids and me two years earlier so we could cool off the west-facing apartment we'd lived in at the time.

As I threw things away and grew agitated, I heard Randy in the living room say, "You don't have to do all that right now." Of course he was right, but what was I supposed to do?

What I wanted to do was throw things away and stomp around the kitchen and wander the house in despair, and I needed to be the only adult there while I did it. And I wanted to go in the garage.

I had thought I wouldn't go in there for months, that I would lock the door and pretend there was no garage off the kitchen. I would use the basement garage on the other side of the house. Until when, I didn't know. Until the magical day when it didn't bother me? When I bumped my head on a kitchen cabinet and was struck by selective amnesia?

Once home, I found that I wanted to go in there. I needed to see where this thing had happened. I didn't know at the time, but I was looking for answers. I was looking for Charles. The garage would be the first place I had to look.

Randy wanted to leave. I could tell he was uncomfortable. He'd promised to buy Jacob a video game, so he suggested we drive to Best Buy in two cars, and he would head back to Louisiana from there. At Best Buy, I went to the service counter because Charles had told me a few weeks earlier that his laptop screen had gone out. He'd taken it to Best Buy to have it sent off for repair.

I wonder now if I believed the laptop would actually be there. Did I really think this story was true? Maybe I did. The fact that I went to the service counter and asked about it must prove that I believed it at least a little. Maybe I wanted one more person to say, "No, sorry, your ex-husband was a liar, liar, pants-on-fire who was busy pawning everything he could find to pay for his pills and his sad little hotel room with the nasty kitchenette, and—tsk, tsk, tsk— you're a pathetic little fool for believing him."

The problem with being sober in the world of an addict is that you can never keep up with the many ways in which the addict will try to get what he wants. Every one of those ways will involve lying to you in some form. Not surprisingly, the

Geek Squad guy at Best Buy could find no record of Charles's laptop in the system.

A few weeks later, the police detective who was investigating my break-in called me and asked if a laptop was one of the items stolen from the house back in July. He'd found one that Charles had sold at the same pawnshop where he sold the portable AC. The detective was never able to locate the televisions or my jewelry, but that was no surprise. I hadn't written down my serial numbers, and the jewelry was little more than costume, other than a pearl, sapphire, and diamond ring that was a high-school graduation gift from my mother. I didn't have much that was valuable beyond sentiment. When the price of gold had started going up the year before, I'd gathered anything of worth, including my wedding ring, and I'd sent it all to my stepdad so he could sell it for me.

The night of the break-in, I'd gone to bed and discovered another item missing—my pillowcase. I guessed that the thief used this as a makeshift bag, like a little kid going trick-or-treating, and loaded it with the contents of my jewelry box.

Ten months later, I had lunch with Todd at one of our favorite cafés downtown, and our conversation turned to those dark days the previous summer. I said, "I can't help it. I still wonder if Charles was the one who broke into my house. What if he wasn't? I mean, my pillowcase was gone and Charles wouldn't have taken my pillowcase."

Todd looked at me and arched his brow, and we burst into laughter. A man who would take your television sets and jewelry would certainly take your pillowcase, too.

It was ridiculous that I still wondered if Charles was the thief, and that I felt guilty for thinking it might be him without more proof. But if I knew it wasn't him, then I could remember how he drove me to Lowe's and helped me buy new locks for the doors and tinted film for the windows in the garage. I would remember how he comforted me when I started crying at the end of an aisle, surrounded by home-security products. I could remember all this and not feel like I was the stupidest person on the planet.

It was absurd to think that Charles would not take a pillow-case from my bed when he was willing to steal so many other things from me.

Like the proof I wanted that Charles was the thief, I had of-ficial paperwork to show that Charles was gone, that the night of August 3 was not a nightmare in my head but a paper trail of death and phone calls. Detective Blackmon had left the po-lice report in my mailbox, and this was the first in my collec-tion of documents.

The police report read that the 911 call was placed at 9:26 p.m. on August 3. The police arrived at 9:34 p.m. Charles was pronounced dead at 9:35 p.m. When I first read the report, I didn't know what time I'd gotten off the phone call with Mi-chael, so I didn't know what time I'd walked from the driveway into the garage. I know I was only in the garage a few moments, but it seemed wrong. It felt more accurate to call it a lifetime.

I put the police report with the pawn slip for the portable air conditioner. I added the Local section of *The Shreveport Times* from August 7, folded open to Charles's obituary. I slipped all this into a large manila envelope.

I found another stack of papers that had been cleared off the kitchen counter and the side of the refrigerator during cleaning. Nellah, the editorial assistant in the travel department, had cleaned the kitchen after ServPro had finished. She washed all the spatulas and tons of other cooking utensils that were in a green, wooden container on the counter. She'd wiped down the items that were on the refrigerator, salvaging what she could. She stacked papers on the fireplace hearth next to a basket of school supplies for the kids. In the stack, there was a bat mitzvah invitation for one of Jacob's friends—the party was the next weekend—and it had brown spots all over it. I wrote down the party information on a clean sheet of paper and threw the invitation in the trash can.

Also in the stack was a receipt for Kate's school-registration fees. I'd registered both Kate and Jacob for school while they were still at their grandparents, and Charles had come with me. He'd watched while I turned in proof-of-address paperwork—power bills and gas bills and a copy of the mortgage. He'd listened while I explained to the volunteers that I had gone back to my maiden name in June, and I handed over a copy of the name-change documentation. He'd been angry when I told him about it. He'd said, "You're only doing this because your friends are."

And it was true that Audrey had changed her name on Facebook, though not legally, and Stacey was changing her name, too. We were going to make a day of it and go to lunch and then sit in the Social Security office waiting room together.

But my name change had nothing to do with my friends. When I first got divorced, I didn't think I would change my name. I liked the last name Emory, and I'd had it my entire writing career. I thought, too, that it might be simpler for the kids. But eventually, I felt the need to distance myself from Charles, and I was tired of carting around a married woman's name. That married woman didn't exist anymore.

The receipt for Kate's school-registration fees was printed on an 8.5-x-11 sheet of paper, and the fees only covered the top third. Scrawled at the bottom, in Charles's handwriting, was this note, "I'm so sorry. This is very hard."

Was this a suicide note? It was messy enough that Nellah wouldn't have really noticed what it said. I always told Charles he had a rock-star signature (much like his rock-star drug habit, I guess). The note wasn't signed. It didn't have my name on it. It didn't say "Dear Amy" or "To my family" or "Good-bye, cruel world."

I took the note from the hearth in the living room and carried it into the kitchen. I stood at the sink and looked out at the driveway. I pictured Charles standing here, watching me through the window as I stood in the driveway talking on my cell phone. I imagined him snatching up a pen and the first piece of paper he saw and scrawling this message, and then I saw him heading off to find his gun.

Maybe he thought he'd do it while I was still outside. Maybe he didn't plan for me to see.

I read something once about how all suicide notes are unsatisfying, whether they are one line or 100 pages. Charles's note is a variation on the theme of a thousand notes. I read about a famous French singer who left a note that said, *"La vie m'est insupportable...Pardonnez-moi."* ("Life has become unbearable for me... Forgive me.") A British comedian left a note that said, "Things just went wrong too many times."

While I collected actual documents, I also collected snippets like this, things that I might have tacked to a huge bulletin board in my bedroom if I were crazy and wanted everyone to know it. Instead, I tacked them to a wall in a room in my mind, jottings and notes and images, scenes torn from books and movies, words torn from the minds of the lost and alone.

I looked at Charles's hastily written note. There were no big confessions here. Charles was focused on himself and how hard things were for him. To hell with what anyone else might feel. To hell with how hard and sorry he was about to make the lives of those who loved him.

I took the police report out of the manila envelope. Detective Blackmon's card was attached with a paper clip to the top of it. I dialed the number, and when he answered, I said, "I think I found a suicide note."

Later that day, he came by with another detective. He led him into the kitchen and told him what had happened. He gestured toward the door to the garage and said, "We found him in there. We couldn't even get to him from the kitchen because of all the blood." He looked at me then. "The service did a good job cleaning."

"Yes," I said. "I guess so."

I handed him the note and I followed him and the other detective to the front door.

Detective Blackmon stopped at the door and turned to me. "I was thinking about you last week. How was everything? Was his family OK to you?"

"Oh, sure, of course," I said. "They've always been wonderful to me."

He smiled kindly, shook his head slightly, and said, "It's not always that way."

Then he held up the note. "I have to take this back to the station. I'll make a copy for you, but we'll have to keep the original. Just in case someone questions it one day."

So Charles's inadequate attempt at explaining the worst decision he would ever make would not stay in the hands of his loved ones. The note would sit in an evidence box on a cold metal shelf in a storage room somewhere. I would have a photocopied version, the warmth left by the copy-machine printing process long gone.

My friend Lollie, who I'd known since the sixth grade and who'd moved to Birmingham when we were in high school, offered to ask her friend Tess to come over and burn sage when we got back to Birmingham. The sage was supposed to drive negative or evil spirits out of the house.

"Sure. Why not?" I said. I don't know if I believed there was negative energy in the house or not, but I thought it would be interesting to see what Tess had to say.

On August 13, Tess came over with Lollie. She had long, red hair and carried a bag of sage, candles, and other items necessary for "smudging" the house. Lollie, Kate, and I decided to drive to Chick-fil-A to pick up lunch—chicken sandwiches and nuggets and waffle fries, things that seemed mind-numbingly normal in the face of the supernatural.

Jacob was still asleep in his room, so we left him there in the unbreakable sleep of the teenage boy. On our way out, Lollie stopped on the threshold and asked Tess, "Does she need to show you where...?"

Tess said, "No. I know where."

When we came back 20 minutes later with our sacks full of food, Tess was sitting on the front porch writing in a notebook. I set Kate up with her nuggets, fries, and soda in front of the television in the living room. Then I went into the bedroom with Lollie and Tess. I sat on the end of my bed, and Tess sat in an armchair in front of the fireplace across from the bed. Lollie sat at the desk to my right.

"There were three things in the house," Tess began. "He was still in the garage—"

Lollie gasped and said, "What?" and Tess gave her a stony look that silenced her. The message was clear: No drama. I was on board with this.

"The spirits of people who commit suicide tend to linger in that place longer. There also were two, what I would call, monkeys on his back. One was in here." Tess pointed at the corner of the bedroom, right next to the fireplace. "And it was lying in wait. It was short and fat, and I told it to get out."

Tess explained that she saw these things as shadows that shouldn't be there, darkness where light should be, and that the information she received came as if someone were whispering in her ear.

"The one in the garage was much larger. Charles had been carrying this one around for years, and it grew bigger and bigger until it was consuming him. It was in the corner, filling the space from the floor to the ceiling."

When Tess had walked back up the garage steps and through the kitchen door, she felt it grasping for her ankle. She slammed the door shut and was so unsettled that she immediately called her mother. When she got off the phone, she went about casting these things out. She burned sage and told each of them to leave. She went outside to sit on the front porch and to make sure the big shadow left and did not linger.

I imagined this dark thing, like a storm cloud, floating up and away through the tree limbs and over the rooftops. Maybe it went back to Hell and the devil gave it a reward. Maybe the devil gave it a new assignment, someone else cursed with carrying this monkey that would ride him to his death.

Tess looked down at the papers she'd written on while she was sitting on the porch. These were all the things that came to her while she was in the house, she said. When she left, she gave me the two loose-leaf sheets, notes jotted on them in curly cursive. Now she read it to me.

"Things started changing after the baby, the second baby, and Charles saw that the focus was becoming less on him. He was jealous of the attention toward the kids, and of your success. He was very resentful of this, and he became increasingly more and more self-centered."

I thought about that time after Kate was born. Had things gotten worse? Yes, sure. Charles gambled more. He took more pills. We moved to Birmingham when Kate was three years old and Jacob was seven. I'd been working at the newspaper in Shreveport and, burned out on the pace of a daily, I'd quit in March of that year and started freelancing. I also applied for a job at *Southern Living* as a homes editor. By the end of July, we were setting up house in Birmingham, and I was starting my new job. Charles never balked at moving, even though we'd both lived in Shreveport our entire lives. He was totally supportive. We packed up the kids and two cats and headed east.

I never once felt like he resented me or my job, but it was the type of job that inspired envy in others. Upon hearing what I did, people would say, "Must be nice." I scouted homes for photo shoots and wrote stories about beautiful bedrooms and bathrooms and kitchens, about beautiful lives. (I don't have to tell you that much of it was smoke and mirrors, do I?) Eventually, I moved to the travel department, and I went to beach music festivals and spas and surf camp. I spent countless nights under down comforters in luxury hotels in Nashville and New Orleans and many other locations where I was must-be-nice'd into exhaustion.

But in Birmingham, life was a battle against the forces of Charles's demons.

As the years passed in our new city, we would sometimes pick Birmingham as our whipping post. It was an easy target at which to aim the blame of things gone wrong. (Where "things just went wrong too many times.") Our finances suffered because Charles couldn't get enough hours at work. He would drive to Shreveport on random weekends to visit friends. He'd take Kate and Jacob with him and drop them at his parents' house. Then he'd spend hours at the riverboat casinos gambling away what little money we did have.

A few months after we moved to Birmingham, we made an offer on a house, and, almost immediately, I knew it was wrong. I was already dealing with money missing from our account. I wanted to withdraw the offer, but the realtor told me fear was from the devil. Then—oh the irony of this—he made me afraid that if we withdrew the offer we could be subject to a lawsuit. When we'd signed the offer a few weeks earlier, he had asked to hold hands with Charles and me as he prayed over it. While the realtor had his eyes closed, Charles looked at me and rolled his eyes and stuck his tongue out.

We went through with the house purchase, and our landlord sued us for moving out of the rental before the lease was up. He'd quickly rented the house out to new tenants, but he still wanted us to pay for six months' rent.

It was a long ordeal in which I looked for every possible solution. I wrote him and his wife a letter and I begged them to simply take the money for the two months when the house was empty. I begged them to allow me a payment plan or to show some mercy. It was a letter in which I laid bare the frayed edges of my marriage. I wrote that we were struggling, and I was doing all I could. Please, I wrote. Please.

The wife called me and was unsympathetic, so I found an attorney, and we went to court. Our attorney asked the judge if he and opposing counsel could meet with him in his chambers. While we waited in the courtroom, never making eye contact with the landlord or his wife, our attorney was in the judge's chambers pointing out to their attorney that in Alabama a landlord cannot collect rent on one property from two separate parties at the same time.

Our attorney came back out, nodding his head at us and smiling. We ended up writing a check for the original amount I'd offered to give them. The landlord, wearing stupid black tennis shoes and black socks, never looked at us. Neither did his wife. I hated them both. People in Birmingham were assholes, Charles and I said to each other. Now, more than five years later, I lived not more than a mile away from those people and I passed their house daily. Sometimes I would imagine shoving used cat litter in their mailbox. This was an improvement. I used to fantasize about setting their lawn on fire.

But when it comes down to it, Birmingham cannot be blamed for all that went wrong. I had foolishly hoped that moving away from Shreveport would help us, would make Charles's problem go away, as if we could pack up everything and we could accidentally leave the box labeled "Addiction" in the attic of the old house in Shreveport.

Birmingham was the setting for something that had been set in motion years before.

Here in Birmingham, my husband continued the pill taking that began in Shreveport. Here in Birmingham, he passed out on Christmas Eve while the kids and I stood on the front porch and watched Santa Claus ride by on the back of a fire truck.

Here in Birmingham, Charles went to our basement during the commercial break of some hour-long drama we were watching on television. He slammed his hand with a hammer, an "accident" he didn't even bother to explain with a good story, so that he could go to the doctor for pain pills.

Here in Birmingham, I sold our beautiful house, a Victorian-style two story with an upstairs porch, and moved us into a cramped apartment. Here in Birmingham, I told him to move out. He stayed in weekly rate motels and loaned my car to a drug dealer (who never returned it) and smoked crack (a fact I didn't learn until after he was dead).

Here in Birmingham, I continued to work and pay my bills and care for our children. I made friends and drew strength from their unwavering support. I worked hard to pay off the debt I had built with Charles. I decorated my apartment just as I had our house, and I believed that things would get better.

Here in Birmingham, I did the dance of "the addict and his wife." One step forward, two steps back. One hundred apologies, one hundred lies.

Here in Birmingham, I hoped.

It is not the fault of a place. Wherever you go, there you are. But I thought that I would be relieved if we moved. Sometimes Jacob and Kate and I would dream up places we could live. "New York?" I'd ask, and they'd say, "Yes!" "California?" I'd suggest, and they'd say "OK!" Then Jacob would say, "Let's move to Japan!" and I'd say, "No way." But I was thrilled that his dreams were without boundaries.

When we no longer lived here, it would mean that we'd moved on to the next phase of our lives and that this one was over. I wanted to believe that it could be over.

"He wanted to wreck your happy little world," Tess said. "I talked to him and—"

Lollie cut her off. "You *talked* to him?"

"Well, I had to tell him to leave," Tess said, calmly, as if this should have been obvious.

She turned back to me. "He is very sorry, but he feels that his apologies are falling on deaf ears."

It must have been true that I was deaf to the whispers of those who were dead but not gone, because I did not hear any apologies. I had gone into the garage the day Randy had said good-bye to us at Best Buy, and the children and I had gone home alone. I'd stood in the place I stood that night and I'd turned to face the stairs. My knees gave out, and I reached my left hand up to grasp the white wire shelving on the wall. I'd steadied myself and I'd thought, "So people's knees really do give out beneath them in fear."

C. S. Lewis wrote that "Part of every misery is, so to speak, the misery's shadow or reflection: the fact that you don't merely suffer but have to keep on thinking about the fact that you suffer. I not only live each endless day in grief, but live each day thinking about living each day in grief."

Since the moment Charles died, I had spent every minute mourning and grappling with trauma and also *observing* myself mourning and grappling with trauma. I was constantly two versions of myself, the one who experiences the pain and the one who watches herself. And, let's be honest, who judges herself.

"He knew you would do a better job without him," Tess said. "And he wanted to hurt you. He did this to spite you. He thought he could handle it, but he couldn't bear to see you with someone else."

He never did see me with someone else! I wanted to shout this. Despite being divorced for three years, Charles never saw me with anyone else. What he saw was me on the telephone with someone I'd known in high school, someone who was reconnecting with old friends. Nothing more. I always knew in my heart that dating anyone was unthinkable. I'd been willing to seal off the part of myself that needed love or sex for an undetermined amount of time. I was waiting Charles out. I had never imagined that simply answering the phone was wrong as well.

Tess continued to read from her notes.

"This is a blessing, not a curse. It was going to get worse—much, much worse. Kate and Jacob will remember fond memories and won't be scarred by this. You will turn tragedy into inspiration and, actually, you are relieved deep down. You feel you can breathe again.

"You do not have to look for love. Love will find you."

This part comforted me. I was, in secret, a girl who wanted to be loved and to love in return. I was a girl who wished on stars and eyelashes. I was a girl who recited the alphabet as I twisted the stem from an apple to see which letter I'd land on when the stem broke off. I was a girl who read horoscopes aloud, laughing at the silliness of them while privately hoping that September 16 or some other random date on the calendar really would be a good day for love.

Tess wrote a few more things on the paper and then told me that she'd put "a wall of fire around this house and family" so that nothing bad could get in.

"Angels are at every door and window. There is a canopy of peace over this house that passes all understanding."

The last thing she'd written on the paper was "God is with you and your babies. You have nothing to fear!" She had capitalized the last part and underlined it.

Tension drained out of me as she spoke. I didn't know how this world worked, but maybe some people did have the ability to hear and see things the rest of us couldn't or wouldn't. I wanted to be comforted. I wanted to believe that my children would be OK and that maybe I would be, too.

"Can I give you a hug?" I said as I stood up from the bed. I felt grateful to Tess for telling me what I needed to hear.

More than anything else, on that day and every day after, I wanted someone to give me answers. I looked for answers everywhere, in books and movies, and I tried to find stories of people who had seen what I'd seen.

That night, after the sun had gone down, I went to pick up Kate at a friend's house. When I pulled out of the driveway into the street, I suddenly felt that I wasn't alone. Fear made foreign a street that I drove on every day, and I felt lost.

"You stay away from me," I said out loud. "Don't ever come near me again. You aren't welcome around me no matter where I go on this earth."

Was it Charles? I don't think so. Was it one of the shadows, still waiting for me? Was it only my own fear, twisted and sour in the pit of my stomach?

I constantly wondered where Charles was. I pictured him sitting in the trees across the street from our house because he was no longer allowed to be here. I'd put a spiritual restraining order on him. Sometimes, after I said those words banishing him from my life, I felt like I'd given up my chance to ask him the question I needed to ask.

The next morning I went into the garage, opened the door, and let the sunshine and air in. The garage smelled sickly sweet, and, at first, I worried it was some weird scent of death. The room had been cleaned, and a group of my friends, including Todd and Jennifer and Rose Darby, had painted the walls bright white. But the smell was stronger than fresh paint. I discovered a red scented candle in a glass jar sitting next to one wall. The summer heat had made the wax soft and pliable and released its odor, one of those fake smells named for a fruit but that did not actually exist in nature. I threw it out. Every day for a week, I opened the garage door and left it open.

On this day, my aunt Carla and her partner Sue helped me throw things away. They live in Indiana, but they'd been on vacation in Tennessee and had driven to Birmingham for the weekend, arriving the night before with an ice chest full of food and a gift for me, an angel carved from wood with wire wings. Carla, my dad's sister, is the aunt I look the most like. She had long, shiny brown hair, olive skin, and brown eyes. She and Sue had been together nearly my entire life. I had photos of me at four years old visiting them at Ball State. It would offend none of the members of my family to say that Sue is the most awesome member of our family. They would say it, too. She was the one who played with all of us cousins and tossed us in the swimming pool. She played ping-pong with us in the basement. Sue always had a video camera on her shoulder ready to film every family gathering.

Sue is the one who found the Christmas stocking with Charles's blood on it. It was on top of a box of holiday decorations. The stocking was plush and red with a furry white trim. There were dots of dried brown blood on the white fur. I looked at it for a second at most and then tossed it in the large trash can we'd dragged up from the driveway. I did not labor over these things or cry over them. We went through a box of items that the cleaning crew and my friends had saved. Things that were heavily damaged had been discarded without my input, and that was fine. I'd asked for that. But it was disconcerting to look for things and suddenly know what had happened to them. It took two days for me to realize that the kitchen rug, with its stripes of pink, blue, yellow, and green, was gone. Another day I looked for my leather computer bag and then realized that it would have been tucked against the wall between the kitchen door and the cabinet. I always set it there when I came home from work. Now it was gone. I thought about how Charles had purchased it for me one Saturday at the mall.

"Wait here," he'd said. We were sitting in the food court. "I'll be right back."

Not even 10 minutes later, Charles came back with a large plastic bag and handed it over. "Something to celebrate your promotion."

I'd been promoted from assistant to associate editor earlier that week. I pulled the soft, camel-colored leather satchel from the plastic bag. "Thank you. This is wonderful." And I hugged him, a real hug, and I didn't pat him on the back or push him away too soon.

Now the leather bag was gone, and instead of feeling something about it, something I couldn't handle quite yet, I tucked the knowledge away.

I tossed out Jacob's tennis shoes, which had been on the landing when Charles died. I closed up the box of Charles's clothing. I wasn't ready to go through it yet. I wanted to do that alone.

I stood in the spot where I'd stood that night and again the day I came back from the funeral, and my knees did not grow weak. I stood still. I looked at the ceiling of the garage. Fragments of the white-painted drywall had been scraped away to remove blood and brain matter. Left behind was a discolored constellation, something overhead that could be charted, something to remind me that this thing really did happen. I would stand in this spot many times over the years after Charles's death to remind myself, not that a tragedy occurred, but that I could and would survive it.

After we cleared out the box, Carla and Sue went back into the house, and I walked down to the mailbox at the end of the driveway. There was a letter addressed to Charles from the Alabama unemployment office. As I walked back up the driveway, I opened it. The letter said that he did not qualify for unemployment, because employment was terminated due to a failed drug test after having been previously warned. He'd told me he'd been laid off the third week of July, but, in truth, he hadn't worked since the beginning of July. According to this letter, his last paycheck was for $48.

How was he surviving? Even as I wondered this, I knew the answer. He wasn't paying child support and hadn't for months. He was pawning everything he could get his hands on. I pictured him shaking my pillow from the white cotton pillowcase. Then he held my jewelry box over the case, its contents sliding in—earrings and bracelets and necklaces, the tray they were all housed in. Underneath the jewelry tray, I'd kept a random selection of photos and notes. There was a photo of Charles from a New Year's Eve party Audrey and I hosted in the late 1990s. In the photo, he was wearing jeans and cowboy boots and he's bare-chested, swinging his plaid, button-down shirt over his head. There was a photo of me with the first boy I ever loved, Austen, dressed for the prom and standing on Austen's front porch. We were smiling at each other rather than at the camera. The photos were gone now. Had Charles thrown them out? They were worthless at a pawnshop. Maybe he could no longer judge the value of things beyond their worth in pills.

I had tried to avoid the obvious answer to the mystery of the break-in. Stacey worked with a woman who always said "obviously" wrong. She pronounced it "obliviously." We laughed about it when she told me, but this was me. I was obviously oblivious.

I could look back now and see the obvious to which I was oblivious—that when Charles stayed in my home the last three weeks of his life that he did his best to frighten me and make my fear big and unmanageable. He called me when I was away from the house to tell me that the back gate was open when it had been closed earlier in the day. One day after I'd been in the shower, he said he'd gone in the backyard and, through the shutters, he had been able to see a sliver of light and mirror and me leaning over the sink. "You should close the shutters more tightly," he said.

Later the same day, as we pulled into the driveway after another failed attempt to find Stripes, the cat who ran away and never came back, Charles said, "Look, that side gate is open."

I'd put a lock on it, and it would have taken a great deal of force to make the metal handle give way.

The night before that, I'd told Charles that he had to leave soon. The children were in Louisiana, and he had to be gone before they came home the next week. Charles was going to move back to his parents' house, but he had to be back in Alabama for a court appearance later that month. He'd been arrested in May for driving under the influence. He was frustrated that I was making him leave.

"How will I explain why I have to be back on a Tuesday? Am I supposed to tell them I'm visiting the kids for a long weekend?"

"You could tell them the truth," I said.

But the truth was never an option. His father wouldn't help him then, he said. His father would be forced to give him more tough love. His father would make him go to 90 meetings in 90 days and Charles didn't want to listen to all those pathetic stories and talk of steps and a higher power and one day at a time. "You have two choices," Roger would tell him. "If you don't sober up, you can end up in one of two places—in jail or in the ground."

So did Charles go outside that night or the next morning and shove his weight against the chain link fence? Did he think that the price to be paid for staying in my home longer was the currency of my own fear? It was a price he was willing to pay.

I have asked myself why I allowed someone to prey on me, to lie to me so often, to tower over me while I cowered in a corner, to intimidate me, to stand in front of me and commit a horrific act of self-murder.

My answer was that I allowed a stranger to do those things to me because he was disguised as Charles.

I also had to ask myself if I was, like Tess said, relieved that he was gone. I had to answer yes. I was relieved that I could breathe. I was relieved that the stranger was gone.

But I did wish that he hadn't taken Charles with him.

Dream: Wedding

I have been afraid that I will dream about you dying, that I will find us in the garage again, where we were on August 3, where we will always be. But my first dream of you is of our wedding day.

We are at my grandmother's house, and I am wearing the cream-colored lace gown my mother bought for me. You are wearing a blue suit, and your head is shaved, and you have that scruffy red beard I like. It scratches my face when you kiss me, but I don't mind. It makes you look strong. Whenever you shave, your skin is too smooth and tender, and you look like someone who bruises easily.

You are across the room from me when my mother comes over to give me a cameo necklace that belongs to my grandmother. She stands behind me to work the clasp while I hold my long, dark hair out of the way, and she whispers to me, "He is going to die."

This does not surprise me. I say to her, "I know. He is dead already."

"But you must marry him anyway," she says.

And I know this, too.

8

Throughout August, shock wrapped itself around me like a fog. Life, on the surface, looked as though it had returned to normal. The kids started school, Kate going into fourth grade and Jacob going into eighth grade. On their first day, I made them stand on the front porch for a photo so I could send it to the grandparents.

I was still off work. Friends delivered meals three times a week. We ordered pizza once a week like we always had. I fed our cat, Shadow, and cleaned the litter box. I carted dirty clothes down to the basement and ran the washer and dryer. I folded clean clothes, warm from the dryer, and made a stack of shirts and pants for Kate and a stack for Jacob.

One weekend, I went to a 40th-birthday surprise party for my friend Laurey, a photographer at *Southern Living*. I drank beer. I posed for photos with Rose Darby and Stacey, silly pictures in which one of us would stretch her arm out to hold the camera and snap the shot. I smiled and laughed in group photos.

I was me as I was determined to be.

I sometimes felt as if I'd already forgiven Charles. This version of me could forgive him because I had seen his pain. I had seen what he needed to show me.

In private, at night, I would hate him. I would think that I could never forgive him. I would cry and feel afraid and write notes to him in my journal.

Dear Charles, I hate you today.

They were diametrically opposed thoughts running around the circle in my brain, racing toward some end that would never really be an answer, that would never even be a conclusion. It would only be a constantly moving point, like a bead on a slender necklace chain.

At night, the two versions of me would wage war against one another while I stared into the dark.

During the day, I did what I was supposed to do. On August 19, I went to the Birmingham Social Security office to file a claim for the children to receive survivor's benefits. Charles didn't have life insurance, but at least there would be something to help in the lean days ahead. I'd gone quite a few months without child support, and my salary could barely cover my expenses. I was still paying some debts that I'd taken from the marriage.

The Social Security office is on the edge of downtown in a beige building with beige walls and beige floors and plastic plants in beige plastic pots. I went twice that day, and I was probably at risk for turning beige, too.

The first time I sat near a young woman who was reading "Bill's Story," a small red pamphlet about Alcoholics Anonymous. I decided she was bored and had probably picked it up from some wire shelf by the door marked with a sign that read "Complimentary." Someone should create a series of pamphlets marked "Complimentary," filled with nice words. "You are beautiful." "You are smart." "No, you shouldn't have to be here, but you can get through this. You are strong."

When my number was called, I went to the designated window tucked into a back corner. The woman on the other side told me I needed my marriage certificate. She made a copy of my divorce agreement and told me I'd have to come back. Yes, it should have been obvious that Charles and I were once married since, otherwise, we would never have been divorced, but never underestimate a government agency's ability to remain oblivious to the obvious.

When I returned that afternoon, my number was S163. I sat, yet again, in a hard, molded-plastic chair. I looked at my marriage certificate. We'd gotten married on June 22, 1996. I'd always gotten the date mixed up and sometimes thought our anniversary was June 20. But here it was in front of me, proof of when exactly we'd officially tied our lives together.

If marriage is tying the knot, then it's never just one knot. Every day, another knot is tied on top of that knot. Another and another and another, day by day, until your lives are so knotted together that when you attempt to unravel the ropes, it seems nearly impossible.

Our divorce was final June 12, 2006, ten days short of a 10th wedding anniversary. Which year of our marriage marked the beginning of the end? Maybe the end was already in motion that day in my grandmother's living room, nervously looking at the pastor as we repeated our vows.

"You *can* look at each other, you know," he'd said, teasingly. And we'd laughed.

Had there been a way out of this? There had to be a turn we'd missed somewhere.

There was an intersection of Toledano Street in New Orleans where the right corner had a one-way sign pointing left and the left corner had a one-way sign pointing right so that the arrows pointed at each other in the most absurd way. You couldn't turn either way so you had to stay on the street you were on. You had to keep moving forward along your current path and find another way to loop back around and turn on Toledano.

I examined each memory for the signs that could have pointed me right or left, but every one is like that intersection, blocked with opposing one-way signs. So I drove a little further down the road looking for the next place to turn. Once I drove another block, I had forgotten about changing course. Charles was just a guy who needed to learn to say "no," and I was someone who thought she could handle her problems while staying on the same route.

In this beige place, the other people clutching their numbered tabs of paper were on the same road as me. They looked tired and underdressed and unshaven. They wore cheap shoes. They looked like people with difficult lives filled with money problems and family issues and a list of disappointments paid out over time.

I was one of them.

"I am here because Charles is dead," I kept thinking.

When my number was called, I carried my marriage license over to the designated window and slid it across the desktop. The clerk briefly questioned the seal. The raised gold foil seal had long ago fallen away from the document, which had been tucked into a file folder in a box in a basement. The glue couldn't hold up to the years. The woman behind Window #1 accepted it anyway. She made a copy and gave the original back to me. This time the government didn't need the original. I could take it home and put it back in a cardboard box in the damp basement.

If I was a walking cliché, a chapter in a book on grief and posttraumatic stress, Charles was a cliché of a chapter in a book on alcoholism and drug addiction. His life became increasingly unstable in the years after we divorced. I suspected it was only superficially stable before because I was there to prop him up.

In the beginning, as far as I knew, he was a guy who drank beer on the weekends and maybe a night or two during the week. So did all of his friends. So did everyone I knew in Shreveport. People wandered from Mama Mia's on one side of the street to Sports Pub on the other, binge drinking, before ending up in the Taco Bell drive-through. I often thought that whoever came up with that whole "Fourth Meal" ad campaign must have been living the same type of life in college.

Charles seemed no different from anyone else then. I look back now and wonder how you are supposed to identify the ones who are addicts from the ones who are just having fun and will later settle down. It would be helpful if they were labeled accordingly.

Charles's abuse of pills began in small amounts before Kate was born, but it really gained momentum after her birth, after my botched gall bladder surgery six months later. He dipped into my pain pills. He stole Xanax from a friend with anxiety issues.

When we moved to Birmingham, Klonopin became his drug of choice. Klonopin was a benzodiazepine and muscle relaxant, prescribed for epilepsy, panic attacks and other anxiety disorders, Tourette syndrome, and schizophrenia. When I looked it up online, I found that it was sometimes referred to by the cute little nickname "K-pin." If I ever heard someone using that term, I'd have a hard time not smacking that person. Hard. The same goes for people who talked about "eating" pills. No, it is not a meal. It is a medication. You swallow it with some water. You do not eat it.

Charles figured out that he could go to multiple physicians at doc-in-the-boxes all over town and tell each of them he had restless legs syndrome, and each of them would write him a prescription. I could launch into a rant now about the pharmaceutical industry and foolish doctors and a system that is unbelievably lax; about how people think drugs aren't deadly, because some company legally manufactures them and doctors legally prescribe them; about a culture of people who want to cure every problem with a pill; about a nation that is medicating itself to hell and back. But what's the point, really?

Two of the side effects that could be seen with Klonopin were rage and impulsivity. Drinking while taking Klonopin only intensified these effects.

Here is how it would go with us.

Step one: I would notice his eyes. They would be glassy and half-closed. If I said, "What is wrong with your eyes?" Charles would open them wide and say, "What? Nothing's wrong with me. What are you talking about?" In the beginning, I would question myself. I would have doubts about my own ability to discern whether he was on drugs or not. Later, there was no doubting it. Sometimes it wouldn't begin with the eyes. Sometimes what I noticed was that I couldn't stand him. We would go out to eat, and suddenly I would realize that I couldn't stomach another minute of this person who didn't listen, who was easily distracted and couldn't follow the thread of conversation, who snapped in irritation at the children.

Step two: I would look for the pills. They were never in the bathroom. Too obvious. They were always in the glove compartment of his work truck. I would wait for him to fall asleep (or, really, pass out) and I would take the keys to his truck and go out in the dark of night and open his glove compartment. I would jump at small sounds, afraid he would come out and catch me going through his truck. There I would find the most recent prescription bottle. If he'd gotten it filled the day before for 30 pills, there would be possibly 16 still left. He took one after another, and the next one was never enough.

Step three: I would confront him in the morning. He would cry. He would beg me not to kick him out. He would yell at me for invading his privacy. How dare I go through his truck? I had no right to look through his things. What business of it was mine? He would apologize. He would say he loved me, that he couldn't live without me.

Step four: He would promise to go to AA or NA, 90 meetings in 90 days. Two times he promised to go to rehab. Once I drove him to a facility about an hour from Birmingham. We left the kids with friends and, on the way, we stopped at a gas station so Charles could buy two cartons of cigarettes to hold him over while he was there. He put them into his duffel bag, packed with jeans and T-shirts and his Dopp kit.

It was a Sunday, and, when we arrived, there were other people in the waiting area—a husband and wife, another family with a daughter in her late teens. Charles went into a private room and spoke with an intake counselor, and then she called me back. I answered questions about Charles's pill abuse and its effect on us. Then the woman said something to us that I will never forget.

"Well, it really sounds like he just needs to learn to say 'no.'"

I was stunned into silence. "No DUH," I wanted to scream at this woman. I didn't. I rarely screamed the things I wanted to scream. What I did was nod. Maybe I hadn't told my side of the story well enough. Maybe my aversion to drama and self-pity made it all seem less serious than it was.

Did she put us off our intended course because it was a Sunday evening and the facility couldn't confirm our insurance? The woman gave Charles a number to call so he could sign up for an outpatient program. She sent us on our way, and we walked back out to the parking lot, defeated. Charles tossed his duffel bag into the backseat and we drove to Birmingham in near silence. We were like would-be vacationers full of adrenaline and good intentions who had arrived at the airport only to find that our flight had been canceled.

Charles never did go to the outpatient program. On that Sunday, he was a man who recognized that he was powerless in the face of his addiction. And by the time the sun rose on Monday, he was a guy who just needed to say "no," and how hard could that be? He could do it on his own. No big deal. We would simply remain on the road we'd been traveling all along.

Maybe all of this could be that woman's fault. I could drive out to that place and deliver this tragedy to her. I could watch her stagger under the weight of it while I tell her that she is a complete and utter failure and she should find a new line of work.

Step five: For awhile, Charles *would* "just say no." He would work hard to prove he was on the straight and narrow.

He would do whatever it took to get me back. (But only ever *just enough* to get me back.)

Then it would begin again. In the early days, this process took months. Near the end, it felt like the process took mere hours.

In 2006, the year I finally filed for divorce, I took him back for the last time on a winter Sunday. He'd been living in a studio apartment in downtown Birmingham. He'd been sober. He'd been desperately sad. He was always stopping by, asking us to dinner, pleading with me to let him hang out with us.

We had taken the kids to see a movie, *The Chronicles of Narnia: The Lion, the Witch, and the Wardrobe*. And in the dark, with him sitting to my left on the fifth row, I'd taken his hand. Even now, four years later, I can recall the intense feeling I had that I should do that, that it was right.

Afterward, I felt hopeful. He'd been sober (as far as I knew) for many months. I called my mom and told her I was going to give it another shot, and she was fully supportive. I said, "I feel really good about this. This is the right thing. I know it." And she said, "I think so, too. I'm so glad."

And by Friday night, standing in line at a Chinese buffet off Highway 31 in Hoover, Alabama, I thought, "I've made a huge mistake. I don't even *like* this person." At 8:00, when Charles was passed out on the sofa, I went out to his truck and opened the glove compartment and found the pills. He'd filled the prescription the day before. He'd already taken 14 of them.

I called my mom, standing in my bedroom—for some reason I have this clear vision of the TV on top of the dresser, of *Larry King Live* being on CNN and James Frey sitting next to his mother while he defended his memoir, of Oprah calling in and defending the emotional truth of it. I remember scoffing at that. As a writer and as a human being I was offended by the idea that one could tell a lie and defend it by saying "Well, I *felt* like it was true."

I had given a paperback copy of *A Million Little Pieces* to Charles not so many months before that. Charles always hated AA so much, and I'd read the book, this "true" story, about a man who sobered up without working the steps of a 12-step program. I thought it might help. So ridiculous. He read it and recognized something in it. But unfortunately, I know now that he recognized the lie. He wanted to believe the book's macho premise that James Frey, the protagonist/douchebag, didn't have a problem big enough for rehab or AA. He was a man. He needed to quit on his own, or, as the intake counselor had said to us that day, he just needed to "learn to say no."

After Charles's death, I reread something Stephen King wrote for *Entertainment Weekly* in 2006 on the topic of James Frey. After Frey got a verbal spanking from Oprah for making up 98 percent of his "true" story, Stephen King wrote, "The amazing thing is that anyone—including Oprah—believed any of Frey's stories once they realized he was trying to manage good sobriety without much help, because this is a trick very few druggies and alcoholics can manage. I know, because I'm both."

I wish every day that I knew then what I know now. I wish I had known that 12-step programs are almost the only way to get sober, and that even those don't work for most addicts. I wish I'd known that James Frey was full of "emotional truth" and little else. Like that book, addicts are full of lies. They will tell you the sky is green and then tower over you and scream at you for daring to suggest it's blue while you cower in a corner and wonder how you ended up on the floor, how you ended up in this life. "Are you calling me a liar? Are you?"

I forgive myself for not knowing this then. I grew up in a family without alcoholism. I didn't know what it looked like. We never had a stocked bar in our house. My mother did not have an evening cocktail. My grandmother always had one at 5:00 (not one minute before), but she had only that one. I had no close family members who were actively using or in recovery or who went to AA. I wasn't familiar with the language of the program. I wasn't familiar with Al-Anon speak—words like projecting and codependent and enabling.

I've always been a horrible liar. I am the world's crappiest actress. It's not simply that I'm bad at it. I don't like it, that feeling of knowingly telling a lie. I've never understood the purpose of it. One of my many flaws was that I constantly assumed other people thought the same way I did. Because I wasn't lying, I trusted that the other person wasn't either. Was it naïveté? More likely, it was ego. I was a liberal elitist who thought she was so damn smart. Now I know better. Now I wonder if what I'm hearing is true.

I'm not sure what would have happened had I known, though. Would I have worked harder to get Charles into rehab? Would I have become Mother Hen, constantly pecking at him to go to a meeting, driving him there, and watching him walk in so I could be sure he went? Would I have kicked him out and never looked back, knowing that he was beyond help, that he was unlikely to be on the good side of the statistics?

I wish I'd had Uncle Stevie to give me some of his hard-earned wisdom then.

I looked up the date James Frey was on Larry King—I tacked it to the bulletin board on the crazy wall in the room in my head—and it was January 12, 2006. A Wednesday. So it couldn't have been the same night I found the pills, which was most definitely a Friday.

How did I know that? Because the next day, Jacob had a basketball game and those were only ever on Saturday mornings. And I stood over the sofa and shook Charles awake. I kicked him out before I woke up the children. I told him not to show his face at the game. After the game, I took the kids to Burger King for lunch. We sat in a booth next to the window that looked out on the Blockbuster Video next door. I said, "Dad isn't going to live with us after all. I'm so sorry." And not for the first time, my son wanted to cry—his eyes filled with tears—but he refused to let the tears fall. That is how I knew it was a Friday night. This was how I knew my children were sad on a Saturday.

It must have been the same week. Now I had rolled those two nights together in my mind, so the picture in my head was of me standing by the TV and holding the phone in one hand and an orange prescription-pill bottle in the other, while on the screen a lying liar told lies.

I had realized along the way that it would not always be my job to prop Charles up. My children would eventually take on the role. There would come a time when he was out of my life (this was when I still believed he could ever move on), but he would not be out of theirs.

I imagined Kate sitting cross-legged on a twin bed in a dorm room taking a call from her drunken father. I imagined Jacob, a muscular 20-year-old, helping his dad move again, another journey to a destination that might provide the geographic cure.

I was on a trip for the magazine the first time I fully realized that my children could not remain unaffected by their father's addiction. I don't remember exactly where I was, but I was on a photo shoot with Laurey. We usually traveled together, and we knew so much about each other that at one of my birthday parties when Stacey created a "How Well Do You Know Amy" quiz, Laurey answered every question correctly.

On the second day of the trip, Charles called to tell me a story about Jacob, about how proud I should be of him. Jacob was seven at the time, a second-grader, and Kate was three.

"You're not going to believe this," he said. "Last night I fell asleep on the couch, and at bedtime Jacob took Kate upstairs and told her to put on her pull-up, and they went to sleep in his bed. I found them there this morning."

He was so impressed with Jacob's level of responsibility, the way he took charge of his sister, that not once did he consider the reason Jacob was putting his three-year-old sister to bed. He did not see that it was because Jacob's father was passed out on the sofa, too far gone to be shaken awake by a child. He did not see that his seven-year-old son was already taking on the weight of adult things.

Maybe I asked Charles why he was asleep at 7:30. Maybe he answered that he was tired, his job was hard, he was exhausted, and it wasn't on purpose, Jesus, what's the big deal? That is how those conversations always went. There was no reason this one would have been any different.

When I hung up, I told Laurey the story of my seven-year-old son putting his sister to bed because his dad was asleep on the couch. When you tell stories to other people, you see them for what they are. You see the reaction of the person who is on the outside looking in. You see the sadness in them that you could have ignored had you never told your stories out loud.

While life seemed normal in August, to say that I was OK would be a misstatement. There was plenty about me that was off.

I couldn't watch certain movies or television shows. I avoided anything that might be violent or have guns. If I was watching a movie and I thought something violent was about to happen, I would hurriedly change the channel or at least hit the mute button and close my eyes. I often was caught off guard. One night I watched a late-night talk show, and on the screen suddenly was the image of a man's head exploding. Was it supposed to be funny? I hurried from the bed to the bathroom, dropped to my knees in front of the toilet and threw up my dinner.

The problem, the shock of it, was because I hadn't been ready. I would have to keep my guard up all the time, not only during shows about crime. I would have to be prepared to hold myself steady no matter what I was watching.

Typically, I surrendered control of the television to Kate. That meant we most often watched Disney Channel and Teen Nick. You could always be quite certain there wouldn't be a gunfight on *iCarly*.

I cursed at strangers, random telephone representatives. I hung up on an Indian man working for DirecTV for some offense I couldn't remember later.

Another day, I cursed at a woman at Blue Cross Blue Shield. Each month for the past three months, I'd received a bill from the insurance company stating that they'd overpaid the claim on Jacob's braces. I'd deposited the $600 check (sent to me one year after the first treatment) into my checking account and promptly spent the money so that now I most definitely did not have it. I leaned against the kitchen counter and called the number provided on the bill, and, when finally connected with a real person, I asked if I could get a letter explaining exactly what the mistake was and why they didn't owe more on the claim. I also asked if I could set up a payment plan.

"No." That was all. No options for working with me on resolving the issue. No suggestions. Just no. She was uninterested and unfeeling.

"I don't have the money all at once. I'm sorry. If we could set up a monthly payment, I could pay it off pretty quickly."

"We don't do that, ma'am."

"You all are the ones who made the mistake, but I'm the one being punished for it." I was getting agitated. I needed to show her the note pinned to my chest, the one that said "My ex-husband shot himself in front of me. Please be kind."

She put me on hold, and when she came back on, she said, "We can send you a letter, but we can't put you on a payment plan."

"Fuck your letter!" I said, and it was really too bad I was on my cell phone instead of a good, old-fashioned landline. You can't slam down a cell phone without having the back pop off and go flying across the room, your battery falling out and bouncing off the countertop.

For months, Blue Cross Blue Shield sent me bills, and I continued to ignore them because I did not have the full amount. The company threatened to withhold all future claims payments until I paid, but I didn't care. By then my employer had switched us to a new insurance carrier. Early the next year, I got a tax refund and finally paid the bill. Even then I had not recovered from my desire to tell off strangers. It took all my restraint not to write, "Fuck you!" on the memo line of the check.

Of the nearly $5,000 cost of Jacob's braces, I paid all but $600—despite the fact that insurance should have covered the bulk of it. By the time Jacob had his braces removed the next June, the year had been too much. It was all too overwhelming to fight and try to figure out why I didn't get the money the insurance companies owed. I didn't have the energy to track down phone numbers and fill out forms and talk to more unfeeling assholes during more pointless phone calls.

This is how these companies make their money. They wear you down. They wait for life to beat you down a little or a lot so that you will give up, throw your hands up, and say, "Oh, forget it," and you'll put a check in the mail so they'll leave you alone.

That's how the bastards win.

I tried to get back into my former workout routine, but I couldn't still my mind enough to do yoga. I could never forget that I'd been doing yoga on August 3, and Charles had come in and out of the room. In the past, I could mentally swat away distracting thoughts like annoying gnats, but Charles's death was a never-ending buzz from an insect that wouldn't fly away.

The weeks of eating as little as possible left me feeling fragile. Aerobics seemed like too much bouncing around. I'd lost nearly 10 pounds and I frequently joked that I really wanted to hang onto my funeral weight loss. It seemed like the least the universe could do for me. But even if my skinny jeans fit, I was weak. I wanted to be strong again.

I decided to walk on the trail near our house so I could listen to my iPod and get out of my head. Kate, however, was not on board with me going anywhere and leaving her alone with Jacob for an hour. Kate also didn't want to go in her bedroom by herself. She wanted me to leave my bathroom door open when I was in there and she was in my bedroom, curled up on the bed reading or watching television.

Kate had been sleeping in my bed since the divorce, and I'd told her she had to stop before she started fourth grade, but now there was no way I could kick her out of my room. So I couldn't cry in bed at night unless I did it silently after Kate fell asleep. I couldn't take a walk to clear my head because Kate didn't want to be home without me. Jacob, always sequestered in his room playing Xbox games, wasn't enough. Her neediness was understandable, but it was also familiar. It reminded me of how Charles always needed so much of my attention.

Panic would rise up in me at the idea that she was like him. I would pray desperately, "Please, please, God, don't let her be like him, codependent and sad and filling an empty pit with pill after pill." Then I would remind myself that Kate was a nine-year-old girl. Her neediness in the aftermath of her father's death, a death that took place in her home, was natural. It was not some inherited character flaw.

But we were both needy. I needed to get out of the house. I needed to be free of the weight of it all for an hour of walking, of nodding at strangers who would not give me sympathetic looks as they ran past, of listening to songs that were not sad. Because I couldn't escape, I grew angry and frustrated. I lost my patience and paced the hall and yelled at Kate when she whined.

One evening when I told her to finish her homework and she argued and talked back, I spanked her. She began to cry and she said, "I want my—" and I caught my breath and I waited for her to say "daddy." For one horrible, long second, I thought, "She will say 'daddy' now to hurt me or because she really does want him. Because she misses him and now she has only me, this impatient person who yells too much."

I did that to my mother sometimes after my parents were divorced. She would yell at me, and I would go to my room and cry for my daddy who was not there. It is the magical thinking of the child of divorce that the absent parent would never be as unfair and mean as the one with whom you live.

After I spanked her, Kate said, "I want my mommy." After I lost my patience and forgot her pain and wallowed in the selfishness of mine, after I yelled and smacked her bottom and called her a brat. "I want my mommy," she cried.

And maybe hearing that hurt even more than the other would have.

On a Saturday afternoon that August, I loaded Kate's purple bicycle into the trunk of my car, and we drove to the tree-lined trail along Lakeshore Drive. I walked while Kate rode ahead of me. She turned around and pedaled back to where I was before turning and speeding ahead again. We did this for 4 miles. Back at the car, Kate sat in the front seat, panting like a dog and sweating, her cheeks bright red, while I hefted the bike back into the trunk.

"This was child abuse!" she declared when I got in the driver's seat.

But she was happy, and so was I.

9

I chose to go back to work on Friday, August 21. That way I'd only have one day in the office before a weekend. I knew holding myself upright, smiling at appropriate times, and talking to coworkers might easily exhaust me. I also thought there might be fewer people in the office on a summer Friday and, thus, fewer visitors to my windowless office in the travel department. It seemed wise to ease back into things.

On my desk, there were numerous sympathy cards in a pile. Gene, the garden editor, left a leafy green houseplant for me. A yellow sticky note on the copper container read, "Doesn't need light. Easy care." Sara, the healthy-living editor and my work "mom," brought me a 12-pack of Diet Coke. Buffy, one of the photo stylists, made me a card using letters and images cut out of magazines, ransom-note style, and left me a bar of soap that had the word HOPE carved into it.

In the corner behind the door there stood a life-size cutout of Elvis. Some of my friends had moved him in from another office and covered the King's face with a photo of George Clooney. My love for George was well known around *Southern Living.* I'd managed to mention him in at least three stories having nothing whatsoever to do with George Clooney. There are very few people who know me who don't think of me when they see news of the movie star. I often joke that this is my master plan. Eventually everyone in the world will think of me when they see news of George, and one day George himself will wake up and look in the mirror and think, "Amy Bickers." Then he will find me and we can take trips and spend a lot of time laughing, and I will never have to worry about him wanting to marry me or hang onto me so tightly that I can't breathe. This plan is very slow working and might have to involve some elderly dementia on poor George's part. George, wearing his Elvis outfit and looming large in the corner, was good for a laugh, but he also tended to frighten people who weren't expecting to see him there.

I went through emails and voice messages—catch-up work— but really I had very little to do. I'd moved into my office in the travel department only a few weeks before Charles died. Up until the move, I'd been in a cubicle in the homes department, where I used to be associate homes editor. Todd, who was assistant homes editor, had been in the cubicle next to me, and we'd popped out a panel in between to create a window. Through the window we would read each other bits of our stories of which we were particularly proud. Or one of us would comment about the latest ridiculous celebrity news and we would launch into conversations peppered with the pop-culture nuggets of our generation, references to *The Facts of Life* theme song or dialogue from *Grease* or a very special episode of *Diff'rent Strokes.*

(You know, the one when poor Dudley gets molested at the bike shop.)

I was named associate travel editor early in 2010, but I'd stayed in the homes department for months, first wrapping up a special edition on before-and-after projects, then simply staying put because no one seemed anxious for me to move.

The magazine was in the midst of a massive and poorly executed transition following the fall 2008 retirement of John Floyd, who'd been editor of the magazine for nearly two decades. John had been the patriarch of our little magazine family. It was the most wonderful place I'd ever worked. The atmosphere was not cutthroat. If you were at work past 6:00 on a weekday, you were likely there with very few other people. Staffers were encouraged to have a life outside the office. "Don't tell me this job is your life," John said in his Southern drawl. "This isn't my life. My life is Pam and the boys."

Three times a week we had "fruit of the day," and baskets around the office would be filled with bananas (on Mondays so they wouldn't rot over the weekend) or granola bars (Fridays). I went on photo shoots of beautiful homes. I did makeover projects in my own house. We were allowed to take vacation time at Thanksgiving and Christmas (something that was never allowed at the newspaper I'd worked at before coming to *Southern Living*). I never had to worry about working holidays. I never had to work an election night and sit at some cold polling place in Bossier City, Louisiana, waiting for election results at 11 p.m. I picked up my children after school. Sometimes I took my children on trips with me. Both kids had been models on a few photo shoots.

If you'd asked me during the first four years I worked there, "How's the job?" I'd have answered without hesitation, "It's the best job ever." When people said to me, "Must be nice," I would agree that, yes, it really was.

The offices in Birmingham were in huge glass buildings amidst towering pine trees, and there were waterfalls and creeks around the building and in the atrium. Sometimes geese would wander the property, and we liked to imitate John's accent, his high-pitched Alabama cadence, when he said, "What are we going to do about the goose poop problem?" We would draw out the words "goose" and "poop" for comedic effect.

Often, a group of us would gather in the atrium next to the waterfall to eat lunch. One day, Rose Darby, who was our department intern at the time, and I launched into the song "Part of Your World" from *The Little Mermaid*. Christopher had never seen the movie, so we started singing, off-key and punctuated by laughter, the lyrics about a girl who has collected many wonderful things and seems to have it all.

"Look at this stuff
Isn't it neat
Wouldn't you think my collection's complete
Wouldn't you think I'm the girl, the girl who has everything?"

Certainly, the job wasn't perfect since nothing is. It wasn't easy. We all worked hard. We complained about minor things like photo reshoots and story edits. But these silly moments involving goose poop and Disney movies show a lightness of spirit that faded after multiple rounds of layoffs.

Days after John's retirement was announced the previous fall, a number of people had been laid off from various departments. It was a time of despair and depression and outright absurdity. We heard that a magazine upstairs laid off people in alphabetical order, a strategy that became apparent around the letter C. Rumors ran amok. Morale plummeted. I voiced the theory that some prankster had published a book called *How to Destroy Morale and Mismanage People* and put a fake cover on it that read "Magazine Management for Dummies." Clearly, our parent company had purchased copies of this book in bulk and passed them out.

What was happening in the offices of *Southern Living* and the other magazines in our Birmingham headquarters was happening everywhere at that time. The economy was in a tailspin. Magazines were folding every day. Our parent company eliminated hundreds of jobs. News stories, written by journalists equally fearful of losing their jobs, likened the layoffs to "storms" and "a beast" making its way from New York to Alabama. Reports of the layoffs read like stories of mass murders with an ever-growing tally of victims. Hyperbole was rampant.

While longtime staffers grappled with the loss of jobs, the new editor-in-chief brought in a selection of staffers from her previous magazine (one of the numerous publications shuttered that year). One day the office manager came around and put sticky notes on two empty cubicles near Todd's and mine. On each note was the name of a new editor who would be in the homes department. This was done without a word to the staff about new hires. Around 3 p.m., the two new editors came in pushing their new office chairs piled with boxes. In other cubicles around the building, the laid-off employees were still packing their boxes to leave.

Later that day or the next, the editor-in-chief held a staff meeting in which she compared the magazine to a family. Families grow and contract, she said. It was an apt description because everyone knows when you get a new stepmother the first thing she does is bring in her better, brighter, shinier children to take your place.

In another meeting, our executive editor said to us, "OK isn't good enough anymore." This was the new world order and all those who had been with the magazine under the previous regime (days of great success, mind you) were put on notice that our work was subpar. We were now expected to take it the "next level." There is no better way to get good work out of people than to tell them how much they suck. (I think that's in chapter three of *How to Destroy Morale and Mismanage People.*)

In the midst of the change, I heard a rumor about myself, and eventually the editor-in-chief confirmed it. I would be moving to the travel department. It was a lateral move with no pay raise or title upgrade, but it was an opportunity for me to write more first-person stories and features. I'd written several over the years. In between stories about kitchens and bathrooms and curb-appeal makeovers, I would sneak in features about travel or essays about Southern life for the back-page column.

When the new editor arrived, I'd recently had a piece published about spending a week at a wellness retreat in Dallas. The lineup for our summer issues included another piece I'd written about a surf camp Jacob and I attended in North Carolina the previous summer. The stories caught her eye, and she thought I could do more in the travel department. I would have to travel more, and as a single mom living in a city with no relatives, that was going to be a serious challenge. But Charles had recently moved back to Birmingham and he would help with the parenting duties, right?

I was excited to have the new challenge, and I also was relieved that the new editor liked my writing.

"She had to move someone to make room for her new people in homes," a coworker in the travel department said to me after my position change was announced. And that was probably true, too.

This was the kind of time it was. People were worried about getting laid off. They were insecure about their roles at the magazine. Good news for one person was threatening to others. People who had once been confident about their work now felt they were only OK, and OK wasn't good enough anymore. Everyone was on edge waiting for the next round of layoffs. People scurried about trying to please the new powers-that-be and find ways to attract the younger readers that advertisers craved. A series of folks from Canada and the Midwest via New York— and one British woman—came to tell us what Southern readers wanted. This seemed to involve a lot of sweet tea and grits and gingham napkins and references to Mama.

Todd was laid off the following June on a Friday. On Monday, I went to the managing editor and said, "Isn't it time I moved into the travel department?" The thought of sitting in that cubicle looking through the "window" into my dear friend's empty cubicle was too much. Actually, what I said, in overly dramatic fashion, was this: "Clearly, no one here cares about my happiness." Then the managing editor (who would resign only a few months later) and I laughed. What else can you do when your friends are picked off, one by one, and you have to watch them pack their boxes while you wonder if you might be next? Sarcasm is the best way to express what you're feeling so you don't have to fully feel what you're expressing.

On that Friday when I returned to work after Charles's death, coworkers came by and hugged me and welcomed me back. When I needed a break, I shut my office door so I could sit at my desk and stare into space. I didn't do any actual work that first day. I drank Diet Coke and responded to emails. One of them was from Michael and had been sent on the morning of August 4, before he'd heard the news about Charles. "It was good to talk to you. Sorry about keeping you on the phone so long. I hope it didn't cause any trouble."

He wrote this because when I'd gotten off the phone with him, I'd said, "I have to go. My ex-husband is here and he's throwing a fit."

Yep. Those words exactly. "A fit." As if Charles was a willful child lying on the floor kicking his legs and wailing inconsolably.

Michael and I had spoken on the phone a few times in the weeks between the funeral and my return to work. We'd emailed a little and he told me about his old dog and his new boat, about how he rarely went out and liked to grill steaks at home and sit on the front porch. His life seemed quiet and calm and appealing. We were thrown into an instant friendship because I felt the need to explain things about Charles and myself to him, and I think he felt the need to comfort me and get to know me. The week of the funeral he deposited $500 in an account set up to benefit Kate and Jacob. When Charles's mother got the list of donations, she remarked on how nice it was of him, and I agreed, but I didn't say I was on the phone with him the night Charles died.

Our emails were mostly filled with banter and G-rated flirtation. It was a nice distraction from what awaited me at night in the dark. We hadn't seen each other since college. There had been a few weeks when I was 20 that he was interested in me and chatted me up at bars. We made out once, something he forgot, and he said, "Not all of us keep journals, Miss Bickers." It's true I'd found a passage I'd written about those weeks in a journal I kept in 1993, but I would have remembered it even if I hadn't written it down.

I told him that if he ever got to make out with me again he better remember it.

This statement was the closest I'd gotten to flirting in 15 years. That sounds like a joke or an exaggeration, but it's not. It was a milestone for me. I'd spent a decade and a half not flirting, first because I was married and then because I could not allow myself to flirt. I could not be interested in anyone until it was safe, until Charles would not punish me for moving forward. I was waiting for it to be safe again.

For a little while that fall, I gave myself permission to be interested in a man. Or at least to be interested in the possibility of being interested. Michael was nice and, even better, living in Louisiana. We had no expectations of one another other than to send funny emails back and forth and occasionally talk on the phone. When I felt I'd revealed too much or that he didn't share enough in return, I said that I was going to put my guard back up. I felt too vulnerable without it. Michael said, "Don't do that. We're learning each other."

So I tried to be a person who was open to that sort of thing rather than someone who was afraid of being punished for leaving the tower she'd willingly stayed locked in. I tried not to feel guilty for answering the phone when he had called on August 3 or for staying in touch with him afterward. I tried to be someone who, deep down, didn't think that hope was often the prelude to disappointment.

I said that I did very little work that first day back, but I did very little work for months. I could sit at my desk staring into space for 20 minutes and realize later that an hour had passed. My distraction was not that of a child, hopping from one subject to another, completely unrelated to the first. My distraction was that of someone unable to look away from a gold stopwatch. I was hypnotized by one lone fact swinging back and forth in front of me.

Luckily or unluckily, my lack of motivation to travel or attend meetings or write three-paragraph stories about Southern destinations coincided perfectly with the magazine's long, seemingly never-ending transition from one plan of action to the next. Also, I think my executive editor was allowing me time to recover, so I had very few assignments in those days. This was both kind and dangerous. I was left with plenty of time to think.

Sometimes I sat at my desk and fell down the rabbit hole that is the Internet. I googled "posttraumatic stress disorder" and then followed it through a series of clicks to read the symptoms and treatments. I googled "suicide" and then clicked on something about Ernest Hemingway; I found a story on his shotguns and then clicked on an image of the shotgun he used to kill himself. (Remember, it was his "favorite.") I looked up "witness to suicide" and found numerous stories on suicide bombers in the Middle East and very little on people like me.

One day, after a sleepless night when I had admitted defeat and went out to the living room to watch television, I googled *Star 80*. It had been on one of the movie channels at 4 a.m. and I'd watched in horror and fascination as Eric Roberts played an obsessed husband who shot his Playboy Playmate wife, Dorothy Stratten, and then himself. Why did I watch it? I couldn't answer that except to say that I was always looking for something that might help me understand. I was looking into a fun-house mirror for some version of Charles and myself. Of course, I was alive and Dorothy Stratten wasn't.

Sometimes I think I was doing my own version of immersion therapy. Maybe I was training myself not to react to the horrible images. If I could steel myself against the images on the screen, then maybe I could steel myself against the images in my head.

So I typed *Star 80* into Google and read the sad, true stories of Dorothy Stratten's rise to fame and her death in August 1980. I concluded that August is a shitty month. I clicked on a link about the much-older movie director she was dating when she died. This man had written a memoir about her, so I went to Amazon.com and read the not-glowing reviews. I found another link that took me to People.com. I read that after Dorothy's murder, this director became devoted to Dorothy's 12-year-old sister. When she turned 20, he married her. I read that they divorced in 2001.

I visited the website for my cell-phone service. I looked up my last bill and scrolled down the list of phone calls placed and received. I found August 3. I received a call at 7:38 p.m. The call lasted 103 minutes, so that means I hung up at 9:21 p.m. That means I walked into the garage within the next 30 seconds or so and shut the door. When I went home after work, I pulled out the police report, which stated that my call to 911 was made at 9:26 PM. I made notes of these facts in my journal, as if they were clues to some mystery that could be solved if I organized all the information.

Another day I began again.

This was a typical search: Google "Klonopin." Find out that Klonopin is one of the names for a drug called clonazepam. Click on stories about prescription-drug abuse. Find no statistics on Klonopin abuse. Go back. Click on symptoms of Klonopin abuse or overdose. Find words like "impulsive" and "aggression." Find terms like "mental confusion."

Look for answers. Click. Click. Click. Fall farther into a dark hole.

If at work I sat still and got lost in thought, at home I was on the move. In September, I spent an entire Saturday painting Kate's bedroom a rich chocolate-brown while watching a marathon of *Law & Order: Special Victims Unit* on her pink Disney TV that had purple mouse ears for speakers. (More immersion therapy.) I spent another weekend painting my bedroom a color called Meander Blue. Before, the room had been dull beige. Now it was a soothing yet happy shade, a lighter version of Tiffany–box blue. While I painted, I cried a few times. As wall after wall changed from khaki to blue, I had the sensation of moving forward in time. I remembered that Charles put up my curtain rods for me in July, when the walls had been a neutral hue. Now he was gone, and so was the old wall color. The room was different. I was different. Life was different.

When I was finished, I stood at the kitchen sink and cleaned the brushes thoroughly, running the water through the bristles until the water ran clean. I thought about nothing but getting the brushes clean, nothing but squeezing all the color out of the roller.

When we first moved to Birmingham in late July of 2003, Jacob was unimpressed with our new city's weather. "Does it rain every day here?" he asked in exasperation, driven inside once again by afternoon showers. It felt like the answer was yes. The days were hot and wet and overcast. After Charles died, it felt once again like storm clouds rolled in at least once a day. I doubt, in either instance, that the rainfall was more than the average, but perception is reality.

Rainy days and Mondays were the hardest. Because Charles died on a Monday, the first workday of the week felt like a morbid anniversary. I would mark it in my journal: *It has been exactly three weeks. It has been exactly four weeks.* I think I quit counting after 12 weeks. As for rainy days, they just suck, in general. You will never find me moving to a place like Seattle willingly.

One Wednesday in early September, when we had afternoon thunderstorms, I gave in to my urge to put pajamas on the instant I got home. This was actually more rare than you would think. Each day I had tried to follow the pattern of my old life, my *normal* life. But I'd been on the verge of tears all day. The energy it had taken to hold in my weeping left me exhausted. I spent most of the day with my office door closed. I picked up Kate from school, and when we got home I put ready-made cookie dough in the oven. Then I went straight to the bedroom, changed into my pajamas, and crawled into bed. Kate sat in the living room watching Teen Nick or Disney Channel or Nickelodeon.

I put on my Sorry for Myself playlist and indulged my urge to cry. This wasn't something I did very often, before or after Charles died. If I started crying, I might never stop. If I crawled into bed at 3:00 in the afternoon, I might never get out. But I found that I always had a reason to get up, whether it was to keep on living or to take the cookies out of the oven.

So my crying jag lasted roughly 9 to 11 minutes at 350 degrees, and then the oven timer went off and I had to pull myself together and be the mom pouring the milk, sliding the spatula under the cookies on the cookie sheet, and placing them one by one on Kate's plate.

At night when I laid down in bed—Kate asleep next to me— surrounded by my soothing blue walls, my heart would race and my mind would race along with it. I knew that reclaiming my regular sleep pattern was the best thing I could do for myself. I wanted to do this without the help of pills. I had not gone to the doctor for prescriptions of Valium or Xanax, things people had pressed into my hands during the week of the funeral. I swore if one more person suggested Lunesta to me, I would scream. I have an aversion to pills that I could blame on Charles and his drug abuse, but, really, I've always had it. It has nothing to do with fear that I, too, would abuse prescription pills. It has to do partially with the fact that I have pitiful pill-swallowing skills. It has more to do with the idea that I should handle things. Get over it. Move on. Be strong. That and don't spend money on prescriptions because you're a single mother with a looming property-tax bill due in October.

So I would climb in bed and try to focus on whatever book I was reading. I tried to read *The Girl with the Dragon Tattoo* three times. I would get to page 38 or so and give up. The Swedish names would swim around in my head. I never did finish that book, and for months I was annoyed that I was left out of the rabid devotion to the series by this dead Swedish author. When magazine articles pondered which actress would play the lead character in the American movie adaptation, I had no opinion, and this bothered me. I really enjoy having opinions.

Night after night, I would put the paperback book away and pick up my journal and fill the pages with my confusion and pain and the name Charles.

I would listen to the Sorry for Myself playlist on my iPod. Number one was "Sideways" by Citizen Cope. Number two was "Both Sides Now" by Joni Mitchell. Sometimes I would fall asleep before Joni was done. Sometimes I would cry my way through "Just Breathe" by Pearl Jam and "Everybody's Gotta Learn Sometime" by Beck. Then "Let It Be Me" by Ray LaMontagne, "Breathe Me" by Sia, and "Beautiful" by Steve

Conn. (If you can hear that song and not cry, you are dead inside). Then "Half-Life" by Duncan Sheik. "All I Need" by Mat Kearney. If I made it to the last song, "Here With Me" by Dido, I knew I was in trouble.

Sometimes the dark was too much for me. It had weight and substance, and it pressed itself against my chest. I felt its hot breath against my ear. I turned on the bedside lamp. I pulled the covers up to my ears, hiding myself from the far end of the room by the fireplace. I was afraid of the thing that had been "lying in wait" in the corner. Even though Tess had told me she'd gotten rid of these dark things, I felt a retroactive fear, fear I should have felt in the months and years leading up to Charles's death. Fear was here now, having its way with me. I turned on my side and stared at the patch of wall—painted fresh, soothing blue—between the dresser and the window. I breathed in and out, deeply and slowly.

I prayed for dreamless sleep and started my iPod again. I prayed to be asleep before Citizen Cope was finished. If this was a movie, I'd have gotten through most of the stages of grief in one lovely, melancholy montage set to this one song. It wouldn't even last the entire song, only a portion of it. Imagine that movie montage. Now imagine that grief is played out over the montage, except the montage is that one five-minute song played on repeat. And it plays at least 100,000 times.

Sometime that fall, Charles's brother, Randy, posted a request on Facebook for song suggestions. He was making the 17-hour drive from his home in North Carolina to Louisiana and he wanted songs that matched his "mellow mood."

"The winner of the best song suggestion will get a $25 iTunes gift card," he wrote.

I suggested "Sideways." (That and Miley Cyrus's "Party in the USA" because, even depressed, I'm perpetually sassy.)

Three days later, Randy posted this status update: "The winner is Amy Bickers. Congratulations. You shouldn't have been allowed to enter."

I had honed my mellow Sorry for Myself collection to perfection over the past few weeks, so going into the contest, I really did have an advantage. Or, more accurately, a disadvantage.

I think that sometimes my body resisted sleep because on the other side of sleep was another day. The alarm would go off at 6 a.m., and I'd wake the kids up for school. I'd fix breakfast and then remind them to brush their teeth. I'd get dressed. I'd wish Jacob a good day as he left for the bus stop. I'd drive Kate to school and say, "I love you. I'll see you later." I'd go into work and sit at my desk and stare into space and wonder what the hell I was supposed to be doing. I'd fall down the rabbit hole. Then I'd do it all again the next day.

Rinse, lather, repeat.

Eventually, I took George's photograph off the cardboard Elvis cutout and returned the cutout to the office from which it had come. As handsome as George is, it was unnerving to always have him watching me from the corner.

10

One of the travel editors pitched a story on the South's best pies, so everyone in the department made lists of places to sample a slice of chocolate or apple or pecan or peanut-butter-banana-diabetes-on-a-plate. This was the new way of things. The pitches that went well in meetings were the ones with the word "best" in the title, or those that indicated a certain number of things. The 10 Best Burgers in the South. The 5 Best BBQ Joints. 25 Ways to Find the Most Meaningless Number of Southern Clichés. Numbers work well on magazine covers. We were really coming up with the regional magazine equivalent of *Cosmopolitan*'s 25 Ways to Have an Orgasm. We substituted food for sex. (Note: Food is a sorry substitute for sex.)

Each editor signed up for places we could visit over the next couple of months that fall; I chose spots in Monroe and Shreveport so the kids and I could make a weekend trip to Louisiana, stopping for pie along the way. We all wanted to see the Emorys, and I also wanted to see Michael.

When we'd first started emailing, in those days right after Charles died, he told me he had come to the funeral and stood in the back. "Maybe we could talk in person one of these days," I wrote back, "and we can hug each other and tell each other it's going to be OK."

Most of our emails were fun and flirty, the sort of banter in which I told him I'd had a dream about him, and he said, "Ohhh, really?" Having a crush on Michael allowed me to fill some of the space in my mind with something other than Charles during the daylight hours.

Michael: Morning. I hope you enjoy your first Monday. How did you sleep? Any good dreams?

Me: No dreams that I can remember. I couldn't go to sleep or stay asleep. I think the over-the-counter stuff isn't cutting it anymore. Time for an Rx, I guess.

Michael: Go for the Lunesta over the Ambien. With Lunesta you will go to sleep and stay asleep. With Ambien, you will go to sleep, get up, bake brownies, try on clothes, make a mess and not remember any of it.

What are you going to write about today?

Me: It sounds like Ambien would help me get so much more done, though! I'm not really writing anything today. I wish I was. I'm planning trips and getting stories on the lineup. I'm trying to get my editor to let me take the kids to D.C. for the National Book Festival. He's worried about the photography since, apparently, nerds aren't attractive. Whatever! I read all the time and I'm awesome.

I'll probably get laid off at some point, but I figure I'm safe for the next round, what with the sympathy vote.

What are you doing? And when are you going to start having dreams about me?

Michael: They can't lay you off. You're Ms. Bickers, the greatest surf-camp writer ever. As for nerdy book lovers, there are very few of us out there who read and are so good-looking. It's a burden to bear, but I suffer through it. I can't dream about you 'cause I take Lunesta, so I have to daydream about you. Which I do.

Sometimes I would cut and paste these portions of our emails (the funny or flirty sections) and type "The Daily   Michael" into the subject line and send them to Stacey. This seemed like something I might have done in a normal world where I met someone new or reconnected with someone on   Facebook and was allowed to date and feel like a teenage girl for a bit. Rose Darby asked for his last name, "So I can put your name with his and see how it sounds."

"A lady's imagination is very rapid. It jumps from admiration to love, from love to matrimony in a moment," Mr. Darcy said in *Pride and Prejudice.*

Women do this for their friends, I think. They let their imaginations run wild, hoping that someone will swoop in and be the hero. We are raised on fairy tales and we become hardwired to believe that love will save the day. I was alone a long time, busy saving myself, and I would never change my name again, but I still appreciated friends who would playfully pair my first name with the last name of someone who is nothing more than a possibility, a flickering projection on a movie screen.

On a sunny Friday in early September, I took Kate and Jacob out of school, and we made the seven-hour drive to Shreveport. Along the way, we stopped at a tiny café tucked into a strip mall in Monroe, Louisiana, and ate pie. We were full of sugar and good spirits when we arrived in Shreveport. I dropped the kids off with the Emorys, and then I went to Audrey's, where I would stay for the weekend.

Michael and I went to dinner that evening. We'd joked back and forth via email about him taking me to Taco Bell, but he took me to Ernest's, an old-school Shreveport steak house that was considered a special-occasion restaurant by many. The steak was medium-rare and perfectly prepared. The conversation was mostly lighthearted and effortless. A magician wandered from table to table performing silly tricks, making coins disappear and playing cards appear.

I told Michael I hadn't been on a date in several years, and he said, "Whoa, that's too much pressure. Please tell me this isn't a date."

"No," I assured him. "This is not a date." I laughed.

I smoothed down the skirt of the new dress I'd bought a few days ago. I'd found it at Anthropologie, and when I took it home and hung it in the closet, I thought maybe I should return it. I'd probably spent too much on it in anticipation of a date that wasn't a date. I felt foolish, and I hate feeling foolish. I decided to keep the dress. I could wear it to work and people would compliment me, and I could say "Thank you" and feel good about myself for a minute. I could look pretty and put together, all the while keeping everyone at arm's length so they couldn't see the mess behind the facade.

By 9:00, Michael was yawning. "Sorry about that," he said. "It's Friday night. It's been a long week."

When he dropped me off at Audrey's, we stood at the front door for a minute, and I thanked him for dinner. He leaned in and gave me a hug. "Everything is going to be OK," he said.

Hadn't I promised we'd tell each other that? Maybe I responded by saying, "Yes," or "I know," or "Sure it is." But whatever I said, standing under the porch light, was a lie.

The next morning I called the Emorys. Frances answered and asked me about my evening out.

"I was home by 9:30," I told her. She laughed and said, "Roger is going to be very disappointed. He already had you married and moving back to Shreveport."

So it is not only the women in Jane Austen novels who make the leap.

Frances and Kate were going to lunch with a friend and then shopping, so I asked to speak to Roger. I invited him and Jacob to meet me for lunch and to help me sample chocolate pie at Biscotti's, a café tucked into a popular gift shop where every bride in town registered for wedding gifts.

At the café, I snapped a few scouting shots, and then we sat at a small round table in the center of the black-and-white tiled floor. We talked about what they had planned for the day. Roger was going to take Jacob to Barnes & Noble after lunch. Jacob wanted a copy of one of his favorite books, *The Lottery Rose* by Irene Hunt. He'd read it in fifth grade and wanted to reread it. Later, Roger would turn on the LSU football game.

Roger asked me about my date, and after I'd filled him in, he said, "It's not every woman who can talk to her father-in-law about her dates."

Being with Charles's father was comforting. When I worried about my children needing a good male role model, I knew that they already had one in Roger, who was kind and hardworking. I had heard tales of his exploits in college and early adulthood, when his temper got the best of him and he got in fights, but my children and I had never known that person.

On the way out of the café, we ran into the parents of my high-school boyfriend Austen. His mother is tall and blonde, his father a bit shorter than her, with a thick mustache. I remembered when we were in high school, he often wore bow ties to work. I always thought of them as people who were exactly where they were supposed to be when they were supposed to be, that they were the type of parents one could count on. When I dated Austen, they had a lamp on a timer in their living room. It sat on a table near the front window and it clicked on every evening around 5:30, flooding the corner of the room with golden light and shining onto the bloom-filled window box beyond the glass. I imagined the lamp still coming on every evening, all these years later.

They hugged me and expressed their condolences to all of us. I introduced them to Jacob, who had come to stand near me.

"I'm so sorry about your father," Austen's mother said to Jacob. Jacob nodded. He never knew how to respond to this. Or maybe he did know. Maybe the way to accept sympathy was simply with silence.

"You went surfing with your mom. We saw the story. Did you enjoy it?" Austen's father said.

Jacob said yes. It was fun.

Look how one conversation can include the worst thing that's ever happened to you and one of the greatest things you've ever done. For a week, in the early-morning hours of that summer that felt so long ago, Jacob and I had thrown our bodies onto long boards, paddled our way past the breakers. We'd floated far from shore and watched the fishing boats in the hazy distance while we waited for the good waves. We had an instructor, a gorgeous 23-year-old named Doug, who would tell us exactly when to turn and paddle toward shore. Then he would yell, "Stand up!" He would tell us exactly when to make the leap so we could stand tall and glide toward shore. I needed guidance the whole week, but eventually Jacob set out on his own and chose his own waves.

I introduced Austen's parents to Roger. I could have said this: I've said "I love you" to two men in my life, and one of them was mostly still a boy. This is the father of the man I loved, and these are the parents of the boy.

The boy told me he loved me when he was 15 and I was 16. I was driving home from Taco Bell, an "after-school snack" in the greasy bags on Austen's lap. He'd gone through the bag, and we discovered my order was wrong. I was complaining in that loud, funny way I use to diffuse my own disappointments, a rant about incompetence. Austen was laughing and he said, "I love you," like it was part of the laughing, like you would say about a movie or a book or a TV show: "I love this! It's hilarious!"

Later that afternoon, he repeated it in a serious way, and I said, "I love you, too."

"I said it earlier in the car, but you didn't say anything," he said.

I had continued on my rant about sour cream and tomatoes and drive-through wrongdoings.

It's only that I hadn't known, in the moment, that it was real, that he meant it. I know where we were exactly, driving on Kings Highway almost to the intersection of Gladstone, almost to the corner where a huge stucco house stood behind tall stucco walls, home to a family with seven children all of whose names began with the letter J.

I searched my memory a hundred times, but I couldn't find the first time Charles told me he loved me. Maybe it happened when we were drunk, and it was hidden under loud music and smoke and the weight of yeasty beer from a tap.

All I could pull up were the times later, the desperate times. "I love you. I'll always love you. I'm sorry. When I die, they can play 'He Stopped Loving Her Today.' If I died, would you come to the funeral? If I had a heart attack, would you come? I'll never love anyone as much as I love you."

On one of the days when I was searching my memory, I searched my bedroom and found Charles's last letter to me. Not the suicide note, which can only really be classified as a last jotting and not much more. This was a letter he'd written me in the spring. It wasn't dated. It had my name at the top, "Amy," like the title of poem.

You are such an amazing person. Someone I will always remember. You have a way of making a person feel special. No matter how bad things ever got, they never felt as bad when I got around you. You've always been able to make people feel good. You are so nice, funny, smart, and of course one of the sexiest people I've ever known. I know it's hard to believe but it really does feel like you suck all the bad feeling out of me with a hug, or just touching your foot or hand. Or breast. (JK) I promise you I will get over you but I also promise I will never forget you. You will always be the person I compare future girlfriends to. And while no one will ever be nearly as good as you, I will take half of you.

I did remember the last time I said, "I love you." We were lying in my bed in the three-bedroom apartment before the two-bedroom apartment before the rental house before the house where Charles died. I had lived in seven places in seven years in Birmingham. Linen drapes hung around the head of the bed, creating a canopy effect, and the walls behind the bed were painted chocolate-brown—all for a makeover project for the magazine.

"I love you," I said, and I was so glad that he was sober and I was so certain I was making the right decision. I envisioned a day not too far in the future when we might take a trip, a weekend getaway, and it would be only the two of us. We would laugh and lounge around in bed and celebrate that we'd made it through something difficult and come out together on the other side.

Five days later, I found a half-empty pill bottle in the glove compartment of his truck.

I remembered this.

I hugged Austen's parents good-bye, and then I walked with Roger and Jacob to the car. I gave each of them a hug, and they set off toward the bookstore down the street. I headed the other direction toward Audrey's house.

The next day, when I came to the Emory house, Roger said to me, "Yesterday, you introduced me as your *ex*-father-in-law. But I'm still your father-in-law. We're your family."

In the weeks after Charles died, I read many books about suicide, about people who are often blamed for someone else's last act. My in-laws never said those things to me. I would say they forgave me, but they didn't even act like there was anything to forgive.

Dream: Café

We are sitting at a table in a café and we are the only people here. The floors are tile squares of black and white laid on the diagonal. One wall of the café is entirely windows. Outside there is a courtyard, but it is filled with nothing but white light.

"The doctors saved me," you say to me.

I can see that you are here in front of me, but I also see your flesh on the floor of the garage.

"But how?" I ask.

"They were wrong in the garage. I was still alive," you say. "They fixed me. They put my face back together. It took all this time, but they did it."

I put my hand up to touch you, but I stop myself. I am frozen in my ambivalence. I am better off with you gone, and yet here you are. You are alive, but I will still not be able to love you because I must stay strong and guard myself against all the things that can go wrong.

I look closely at your face, your eyes that are sometimes blue and sometimes green. They are glossy and bright, so I ask the question I have asked so many times before.

"Are you taking something?"

"Of course I am," you say. "The doctors gave me pain-killers. I have to take them."

And I know that we are at the beginning again. What happened will happen again. It will never stop.

11

"I'm going to use the magic-eight-ball method of answering questions," Jacob said as we drove downtown for his and Kate's first counseling sessions. "Yes, no, and ask again later."

It was mid-September, and I'd checked both of them out of school so we could make it to the late-afternoon appointment on time. I picked up Jacob first; when we got to Kate's school, people were already pulling into the car-pool line. In the office, the secretary began to lecture me about checkout times and how they prefer the children not be checked out after 2 p.m. I was flustered and defensive. I wanted to point to the imaginary sign pinned to my shirt. "Here, can't you read my sign, the one that will tell you what has happened to us?"

Instead, I said, "I had to drive all the way out to get my son at Spain Park High School and the appointment is at 3:00. We don't have time to sit in the car-pool line. Should I have had her miss half the day instead of 15 minutes?" Maybe my voice rose here. Maybe I sounded like a bitch.

The principal stepped out of her office and gestured to me. "Come in my office for a minute."

Jacob stayed in the waiting area, and I went in, ready to be scolded in the principal's office.

"I'm so sorry for your loss," she said.

"Oh," I said. I wasn't getting in trouble for being a bad mom. "Thank you."

"I wanted you to know that Kate is doing really well. You must be very strong, because she's come back to school with no problems. You all must be handling this like rock stars."

Drinking, popping pills, and having sex with anonymous fans?

No, I didn't say that. I knew what she meant. She meant we were handling it like champs. We were rocking everyone's socks off, thank you very much. Hell yes, we were.

"I want you to know we'll keep an eye on Kate and let you know if she has any problems, but I think she's going to be fine."

"Thank you," I said. "That's good to hear."

This was actually our second trip to counseling. We'd visited The Amelia Center at the beginning of the month so the kids could meet their counselors and tour the building. The Amelia Center offered free counseling to children who had lost their parents and to parents who had lost children. There was a craft room and another room with toys and a punching bag. There was a tiny, windowless room with a plush sofa and a box of tissues on the side table. In another windowless room, about the size of a walk-in closet, the walls were painted black. When the lights were turned off, you could see hundreds of messages glowing in the dark, messages children had written to their lost loved ones.

Unlike Jacob, Kate loved the idea of counseling. Her therapist was young and pretty, and she helped Kate put together an album full of photos of her dad and strips of paper that said things like "I miss the way my dad _____" and "I remember when my Dad and I _____" so Kate could fill in the blanks and slip the paper into the plastic pockets. She took Kate into the craft room and talked to her while Kate painted stripes on a round box with a lid, a box to hold mementos. She called it her Daddy Box.

A male counselor took Jacob to another area of the building where they had a TV and a video-game console. The counselor told me later that it is sometimes easier for teenagers to talk if they can focus on the TV screen and they don't have to look at the near-stranger asking them personal questions.

I sat in the waiting room and ate Jolly Ranchers that the cheerful receptionist had in a bowl on her desk. I read a booklet that Kate's counselor had given me. It said, "Don't make any major life changes for a year."

Was it then that I decided to remain as still as possible? Maybe I already knew, instinctually, that I needed to stay quiet, to hide from the universe. I could freeze like the squirrels in my backyard did when they spotted the cat watching them from the patio. Here's what those squirrels were thinking, "Please, please, don't see me. Please, please let me live. Please, please, I promise not to move until things seem safe again."

Maybe those were only my thoughts. Maybe the squirrels were simply thinking: "Nuts, nuts, nuts, nuts."

Afterward, I didn't ask Jacob to tell me what he said to his counselor, but I would try to broach the subject of how he was feeling. I didn't need him to talk to me. I only needed him to know that he *could* if or when he wanted to. After Jacob's regular orthodontist appointments, we would stop at McDonald's on the way to his school. Jacob would have two bacon-and-egg biscuits (no cheese) and a Coke (no ice) and I would have a vanilla latte, and we would make up stories about the old men who regularly met for coffee at the McDonald's on Valleydale Road. We decided they were secret ninjas and they met here each day to discuss their secret-ninja missions.

During one of our McDonald's breakfasts, Jacob told me his class was reading *The Story of My Life* by Helen Keller and they'd watched a movie about her.

"Helen Keller freaks me out," I said. "I mean, not the person but the situation. I've never understood how she learned anything. She was trapped in silence and darkness. How did she break free? I don't get it."

It became a running joke between us, my inability to comprehend how Helen Keller could find her way out of that darkness and into the world. Jacob, because he was a teenager and liked to tease me, would ask me "Why?" questions about the vastness of the universe that I couldn't answer. When I would say, "It really is so hard to comprehend, isn't it?" he would laugh and say, "Yes, and what about that Helen Keller?"

But he never asked me any questions about his dad.

Kate was unafraid to say what she was thinking.

"Where was Daddy when he died?" she asked the day I told her he was dead. "Who will walk me down the aisle?" she wondered, only days into being fatherless. "I'm forgetting what Daddy's voice sounded like," she said months later.

One afternoon, when she climbed into the car after school and we pulled out of the car-pool line, Kate said, "Nicholas told me Daddy is in Hell."

She did not ask a question that time, but she looked to me for an answer.

"Nicholas is wrong. Maybe his family believes that sort of thing, but *they* are wrong. We do not believe that."

I glanced away from the road and over at her. She nodded.

"Do you understand? Daddy was sick and what happened doesn't mean he's in Hell. You're always going to find people who say those kinds of things because of their religion, but it doesn't mean they're right. They might be perfectly nice people, but you don't have to listen to that bullshit." My anger got the better of me for a second there. And look how well I'd done so far not calling Nicholas a little shit. Oh well.

"Kate, you have to remember that you know better."

She looked at me and said, "OK. That's what I thought."

One September afternoon, she and her friend Mary marched through the living room toward the kitchen. They were full of high spirits and gumption, and Kate said, "We're going to see if Dad's ghost is in the garage."

"No, sweetie, Dad isn't in the garage," I said.

"Well, where is he?" she asked.

"In Heaven."

Maybe I said it in such a way that the sentence tilted up at the end, like a question. But I hoped Kate wouldn't notice. I hoped Kate wouldn't ask me yet if I truly believed in such things.

Near the end of September, I made an appointment for counseling, too. I'd promised everyone I would. I had a reputation for not going to the doctor very often, but I knew I needed to address the growth in my brain. My brain was a garage. I'd parked the most frightening image in the world in it.

On the 21st, we'd gotten a day off work because the power in the office was out. It was definitely a treat for everyone. Unfortunately, I cried most of the day. I'd come home from the dark office around 9 a.m. and curled up on the sofa. I decided to watch the four episodes of *Mad Men* I had saved on the DVR.

During one episode, a secretary drove a John Deere lawnmower through the office during a drunken party. She ran over a man's foot, and blood sprayed everywhere. The scene showed three people in shock as blood splattered across their clothes and faces.

The scene was probably funny for a lot of viewers. I bet they burst into laughter at the absurdity of it, but I burst into tears. This wasn't a slow build-up to crying. This was an immediate and intense reaction. Burst is the right word. That expression is totally accurate.

It wasn't only guns that would set me off. It was blood, too. It was splatter.

In a flash, I was back in the garage. It wasn't hard to end up in there. The door to it was never closed.

The next day I called a counselor, and two days later I went to my first appointment. Joan was able to see me quickly because she'd had a cancellation. For many, many Wednesdays to come, I would have a midday appointment.

Joan's office was one small room in a building about five minutes from work. It was furnished with a love seat, a leather armchair, a desk, and a set of shelves filled with books and a couple of angel figurines. As it was at The Amelia Center, this office had a box of tissues on the table next to the love seat. I sat on the love seat, and Joan sat in the armchair.

"I've been joking to my friends at work that I'm going to tell you why I'm here, and then I'm going to end up complaining about the place I work instead."

(Yes, this is how I always begin things, with a joke. This is often how I end things, too.)

She laughed. "OK, so why are you here?"

Do you know what it's like to tell a story like the one I have to tell? A story that momentarily stuns people, no matter how you word it? A person could start to enjoy that, the power to shock with one sentence, the power to change what a person assumes about you with a few choice words.

I told her about the phone call and the garage. I told her about what Charles said. I told her that Charles took pills, that he'd gotten a DUI, that he'd lost his job, that he had nowhere to live.

"He made you think this was all because of one phone call when he had a hundred reasons to kill himself," she said.

I told her about my friends who took me away from the scene—on August 3, my house was not a home, it was "the scene of the crime"—and my friends who painted the garage and cleaned the house and brought me gifts and dropped off casseroles.

"You have a good support system and friends to talk to, and that's helpful. You might leave today and think you don't need to come back. You might think, 'I told my story, what else is there to say?' But you're going to need to talk about this over and over again to get through it," she said.

I looked at her and laughed.

"Oh, don't worry. I'll be back. We haven't even gotten to my father yet."

12

Eight weeks after Charles died, I found myself wishing I could go back to that night and the first day after. I didn't want to go to the event itself. I didn't want to relive that. I wanted to go back to the hours afterward so that I could be in that state of exhaustion and shock, numbed to the point of paralysis. Then I could sit in my pajamas clutching a stuffed dog.

No one expected anything of me during those hours. The world stopped, and I wasn't useless. I was simply adrift on the Sea of Disbelief. I could see myself there, curled up on a raft, bobbing along under a night sky, barely registering that the dark waters were raging around me.

Now I was adrift *and* useless. I wasn't accomplishing anything at work other than honing my innate talent for procrastination.

On the Tuesday morning after the eighth Monday since Charles had died, I took both Kate and Jacob to the dentist for their annual check-ups. The appointment was at 9:30, so we slept in and took our time getting ready for the day.

I sat in the waiting room while the kids went back for their exams. I read *The Lottery Rose*. Jacob had passed it on to me after he finished reading it. Maybe it was on this morning in the dentists' waiting office that I began to realize how much I liked waiting rooms. This one was new—the dentist had recently moved into the building—and full of brightly colored furnishings and several television sets. One was tuned to cartoons— *Dora the Explorer*; the other was on Fox News. If you asked me, *Dora the Explorer* was the more intellectual of those two choices.

In waiting rooms, I could relax. I could sit still and stare at the pages of a magazine or book without having to actually do anything. I could take a break from the world with its endless expectations. I could do absolutely nothing, and not be judged for it, because I was engaged in the very important and socially acceptable task of waiting. This was better than the far preferable but more harshly judged act of staying in my pajamas all day, watching daytime TV, and telling myself I couldn't get off the sofa because it would disturb the sleeping kitten in my lap.

Eventually, I had to stop waiting and return to the real world. The hygienist called me back, and we discussed my children's teeth. Jacob was not brushing as well as he should. This was an ongoing problem. I had no idea how to deal with it other than watch him brush his teeth or treat him like a dog or a baby and brush his teeth for him. I opted for constantly asking, "Have you brushed your teeth?"

The dentist said to Jacob, "Your mom has spent a lot of money to straighten those teeth. You wouldn't want them falling out, would you?"

Afterward, I took the kids to the McDonald's near Jacob's school. This is where the elderly men/secret ninjas met for coffee, and they were all there, sitting around a table near the beverage dispenser. We ate bacon-egg-and-cheese biscuits and McGriddles while we sat in the play area. I read the last two chapters of *The Lottery Rose*.

I remembered that the first time Jacob read it when he was 10 or 11, he came into my bedroom and his eyes glistened with unshed tears. "This book was so good, Mom. So good."

Moments like that let me know my son was going to grow up to be a good man.

Now, I had to dry my own tears with a brown McDonald's paper napkin while Kate ran up and down the play equipment in her sock feet.

"Jacob," I said, in a mock-scolding tone. "How could you let me read this?"

I suddenly had the feeling that we were on a road trip, the three of us, stopped somewhere between where we'd been and where we were going. I felt a sense of ease that comes from being en route to someplace, in the few hours when the only thing you have to do is drive safely, sing along to songs on the radio, and stop for a fast-food meal here and there.

It was a sunny day, and the promise of fall was in the air, a perfect day for driving. Where could we go if we got on the road? Which direction could we travel?

I took Jacob to school first, and he complained in that way teenage boys do, as if it is simply for their own entertainment and not because they are truly disgruntled. I humored him and explained that it made more sense to take him first since his school was on this side of town, five minutes from the McDonald's.

"Mom, Mom," he said, shaking his head. "We don't always have to make sense. We can make our sandwiches with the meat on the outside and the bread on the inside."

I dropped off Kate next, and she cried as I was leaving. I understood why. The morning had felt so good, the three of us together, and I didn't want to return to real life either. I went home and called the office. I was going to take off the rest of the day.

I had stories due soon, but I didn't want to write them. I berated myself for not getting them done. I was beginning to feel sick from carrying the weight of them, unwritten, undone.

Instead of writing, I pulled out the can of leftover paint from my bedroom. I changed into shorts and a T-shirt, already splattered with blue and brown. I turned on my iPod and listened to music while I painted the kitchen ceiling sky-blue. I worked my way from the breakfast area on one end to the area near the door that leads to the garage. I took extra care on the section where Charles's blood had been cleaned away. I looked for spots the cleaning crew might have missed, but I found none. I pushed the roller back and forth over my head and tiny dots of blue paint fell on my arms.

It wasn't as difficult as I thought it would be. It only took a few hours, and it felt good to move without thought. It felt good to slide the paint roller back and forth, covering a long space with a fresh and cheerful color. It felt good to get rid of the white ceiling that was witness to that night, to actively change the things I could change.

That afternoon, I emailed my boss, Spencer, and met with him two days later. I sat in one of the chairs across from his desk.

"I wanted to give you an update on how I'm doing," I said. "I'm not doing well. At all."

I'd begun to have mild panic attacks at work. Emails about policy changes and new procedures sent me reeling. My heart would race, and I'd feel nauseated. The last round of layoffs left the offices quiet, and many of my friends, including Stacey, were no longer right down the hall.

My counselor suggested I take time off work, but I was afraid to stop moving. I pictured myself crawling into bed and never getting out again. As a compromise, I'd decided to ask Spencer if I could work from home for a while.

I felt unsure about this, but it seemed better than taking some sort of leave. I worried that my absence from the office might put me on the next list of layoffs. I worried that I no longer knew how to write. I worried that if I relaxed for even a minute I would fall behind in the grieving process. Grieving was my responsibility, and I wanted to work through the damn stages and be done with it.

"You don't give yourself a break," my counselor said during our previous session.

"If I have to swim through a pool of crap," I said, "then I want to jump in and get that shit over with."

Words were failing me. Only cursing came without effort.

Spencer nodded. "Of course, you can do that. I'm never going to come down to that end of the hall looking for you, so don't worry about being in the office a set number of hours. Take the time you need."

What if I was never good at my job again? I missed myself the way I used to be, pre-August 3. I was such a fool in those first few weeks when I thought I could get over this and move on with no repercussions. I had never not been able to do my job. During the divorce, during the awful times leading up to

174

the divorce, the awful times after, I could always do my job. I could meet my deadlines. With little effort, I could come up with witty leads to begin stories about bathrooms or bedrooms or Southern destinations.

Now, I couldn't write because I was too busy falling, Alice in Wonderland–style, down the hole to the place where I drank weird potions, grew very small, and asked this: Why did he do this to me? Why did he hate me so much that he had to punish me?

If I was Alice, I was her in chapter two, "The Pool of Tears." I was so small I might drown in a salty sea I'd created myself. During one of our many road trips, Kate had started reading *Alice in Wonderland*. She read aloud from chapter two, "Alice says, 'Let me see: four times five is twelve, and four times six is thirteen, and four times seven is–oh dear! I shall never get to twenty at that rate!' But that's not right, Mom!"

"I know," I said.

"But she's wrong! I don't understand why she says that if she's wrong."

"Well," I said, "I guess she doesn't *know* that she's wrong, does she?"

In my journal that night, I let my pen worry across the pages.

Why can't I write these stupid stories? All I want is to complete one and not have it hanging over my head every day. Please please help me help me help me please. I'm so sad. I'm so lost. I don't want to be this person anymore. I want my old self back. Charles is going to win. He didn't shoot me first because this is worse. He didn't have to kill me to destroy me.

My first Monday working from home I planned a trip to Nashville for a photo shoot that Thursday. *You don't give yourself a break, do you?* I was writing a story about a scouting trip I'd taken in the spring during which I'd gone out for dinner and drinks with Austen, the high-school boyfriend (HSBF). He'd moved to Nashville about 10 years before and was working as an attorney. I thought the HSBF element would make a fun angle for a travel story. Who doesn't wonder what their old flame is up to? (Which, by the way, is the phrase that ended up as the title of the final story: A Night Out with My Old Flame. When I first saw it on the page, I was mortified. If that doesn't sound like the title of a country song, I don't know what does.)

We needed photographs to go with the article, so Austen and I were going to re-create our pre-dinner drinks from the spring at a restaurant/bar called Cabana. I felt ambivalent about the whole thing, which is how I knew I was officially depressed. Normally, seeing Austen would be something I'd feel excited about. He was my first love, and there would probably always be a part of me, my inner 16-year-old, which felt a rush of butterflies at the sight of him. But now I felt tired. I bought a new shirt. I was grateful I still had the effects of my funeral-week weight loss to help me fit in my skinny jeans. I hoped my face would look good in the photos and not 100 years old and exhausted like I felt on the inside.

I drove up that afternoon so I could get into town and go straight to the early-evening photo shoot. I listened to my iPod and enjoyed the sunny day as I drove north, and I didn't cry once on the way up there.

Austen looked good. We sat at the bar and ordered drinks. The bartender brought out an appetizer, some sort of gooey, baked mac-and-cheese dish that I would write about in the story. It was for looks, not for eating, and it slowly grew cold in its white dish. Austen had heard the news about Charles and, sometime in August, had sent me an email of condolence.

"How are you?" he asked.

"I'm OK," I said. I always said this. I always followed it with a joke or a sassy comment. Now would be no different.

"I used to think I wasn't screwed up enough to be a good writer, but—yea—now I am. I'm like Ernest Hemingway. So that's awesome."

I don't think he asked me for details, but I told him the worst one anyway.

I might have forgotten the look on his face at that moment if Art, the photographer from *Southern Living* who was snapping pictures from the other end of the bar, hadn't captured us at exactly that moment. A week later, I pulled up the digital images and saw the horrified look on Austen's face.

"Hey, you guys are supposed to be laughing and smiling," Art called to us, not without understanding, not without kindness.

"Sorry, Art," I said. "We'll stop talking about heavy stuff now."

And we did, for the most part.

After the shoot and a couple of drinks, we went out to dinner with Austen's girlfriend, Abbey. I was always curious about what Austen's life was like after high school, and I liked meeting someone who was part of his life now, someone he would eventually marry.

It was also a relief to be around a person who did not know Charles or me and didn't know what had happened (or, even if she did, didn't know me well enough to ask me about it). We talked about silly things like what we were like in high school and what high school must be like now with texting and, God help us, sexting. Abbey seemed like a nice person. She had au-

burn hair like Jacob's and glasses that made her look like a hipster librarian.

When they dropped me off at the hotel, I went up to my
room and collapsed. Putting up the appearance of someone who
is OK was hard work. I kicked off my shoes and shed my skinny
jeans and put on my pajamas. I turned on *The Tonight Show*
for the soothing noise. I crawled under the down comforter and
crisp white sheets of the hotel bed, and I cried.

Austen and Abbey seemed like a good couple. I felt envious
of her, not because of him, but because of appearances. She *appeared* to be living a life that was going along a normal path.
She was not yet 30, she had a job with a record label, she had a
cute boyfriend who had a good job, too. I wanted these things. I
wanted to not have a huge, tragic event that overshadowed everything else.

I rubbed my hand over the spot between my eyes where I
had a permanently creased worry line. I ran my finger up and
down, imagining that I could feel the spot, this wrinkle in time.
Here is the line I got when I was 36, I could say when I was an
elderly woman marked by one hundred other wrinkles. But this
one, this would be the one whose cause I could identify.

The worst part was that I could no longer see how any of
that, a normal life with a boyfriend, even happened. How did
people find someone to like, to allow into their homes, into their
lives? I couldn't see how it was possible. I could not see above
the walls of my self-made prison.

I drove home the next day and spent the weekend avoiding
people. Todd called. Christopher called. Michael called. Audrey
called. I never answered the phone. I wore pajamas and did
laundry. While I was in the basement filling up a basket with
warm, dry clothes, I suddenly heard Charles's voice saying to
me, "You can remember that's the last thing you said before I

did it." I heard it repeatedly. I dropped to my knees on the cold, concrete floor and put my hands over my ears.

I was trapped in my head, but I could also see myself from outside. "Look at me losing it down here."

I'd said to Austen that now I was definitely messed up enough to be a great writer, but I wondered how people wrote about anything other than the big fucked-up thing in their head.

It would be 10 weeks the next day. I was sick of August 3 and the endless loop it ran on in my head. I was sick of myself. This could have been when I started thinking about how to escape myself. Is this what Charles felt? Trapped by his own sick thoughts, his body like a prison around him until he had to do something drastic to break loose from it?

It turned out I wasn't the only one suffering from a lack of focus and a lackluster work ethic. On Monday, I went to a parent/teacher conference at Jacob's school and met with his team of teachers. They laid out the facts for me: Jacob's grades were awful. Why were they so awful? Because he wasn't turning in make-up assignments from missed days, and he wasn't doing his homework. I knew what this meant: The problem was at home.

I needed to be more tuned in to what was going on with his schoolwork. I needed to enforce limits on his video-game time. I needed to check his grades online. I had to be on top of things rather than drowning underneath them.

The school counselor had informed all the teachers about Jacob's dad, and they were all very understanding. We discussed a plan to get Jacob back on track. (They did not have a plan to get me back on track, however.) They said encouraging things

about how smart Jacob was, how enthusiastic, how he partici-
pated in class. They said his mental health seemed good.

During this meeting, I was *on*. I am a genius at being on
when necessary. Jacob came in for the last half of the meeting.
Afterward he said, "My teachers must like you. You kept making them laugh."

People are so easily fooled. One of the teachers seemed to
dismiss the effect his dad's death might have on the unfinished
assignments. She said, "I see him laughing in the hall with his
friends, so he's obviously doing fine."

In the future, I would say this teacher's name like Seinfeld
said "Newman." I decided she was a bitch.

I had had people say similar things to me. A friend sent me
an email that said, "I looked on Facebook and it seems like
you're doing pretty well." Because I was smiling in photos that
were posted of me? Because I'd written something funny about
Britney Spears's new perfume called Circus? ("Has Britney been
to a circus? It smells like elephant poo. Go ahead. Dab a little
Circus behind your ears.")

Thinking of Mrs. "Hello, Newman" as a bitch was uncharita-
ble. I knew that. I'm sure that teacher was uninformed. She
didn't know that most of grieving is the exhausting act of *seem-
ing* fine. Because if you seem fine long enough, maybe you really
will be.

13

If Charles's actions on August 3 gave me posttraumatic stress disorder, my own thoughts in December may have done the same. For years afterward, I would fear the arrival of winter. Winter meant darkness. Winter meant cold. Winter meant isolation. Winter meant bemoaning the state of my flabby midsection.

After Thanksgiving, I felt the urge to avoid other people, to hide away in my bedroom. The holiday had been difficult to bear.

More than the Thanksgiving Day meal, Charles truly loved the leftovers. Every plastic storage container we ever had was probably filched from Frances's kitchen to store our share of the spread. We never returned any of them.

Frances didn't cook this year. She prepared a ham a couple of days before Thanksgiving, and the kids and I ate with her and Roger. We'd driven to Shreveport over the weekend. Tuesday night, I headed out to visit Audrey so we could drink wine and catch up. I wanted to tell her about Michael, how I'd heard from a friend that he was talking about marriage with someone he'd recently started dating. In all his emails, he hadn't even mentioned this woman to me, and I realized I didn't know anything about him. I was spilling out all sorts of information about myself to someone I didn't really know. I felt like a fool.

I was turning onto the highway when my phone lit up with a text message from Audrey.

"I need to cancel tonight. I'm not feeling well."

I turned right into a gas station and parked so I could text her back. "No problem. I'll see you another time."

I always say no problem. I always pretend I'm fine.

I called Mom to let her know we'd be driving to her house the next day, sometime in the afternoon. As soon as she answered, I could tell she was irritated with me, irritated with the amount of time we were spending in Shreveport versus Natchitoches. I could feel the weight of it on me, the weight of every damn thing.

"Please don't give me a hard time about this," I said.

And here's the thing: I never asked anyone to let up on me. I took it, like a good girl. But now I was asking, and no one was listening.

"Why don't you try seeing this from someone's point of view other than yours?" she said.

Did I hang up? Did she? I have no memory of the end of the phone call. I know only that I cried as I pulled out of the gas station and drove down 70th Street, past the car dealerships and the Walmart Supercenter. I turned right on Youree Drive and followed it past the subdivisions and the Circle K and the driving range. I followed it until there weren't any more streetlights, only the dark sky above and the headlights of an occasional car driving north toward me. I passed wide, open fields and then, on the left, I saw a brightly lit building that looked like a small casino. Maybe it was a truck stop. Whatever it was, it hadn't been there when we still lived in Shreveport.

I had no idea where I was anymore.

I turned around in the parking lot and headed north again.

People will tell you to take care of yourself. Give yourself time. Be kind to yourself. People are full of crap. When exactly should a person do all this tender loving care of oneself? After work? After I prepared meals for my children? After I made sure they did their homework? After I did the laundry or attacked with bug spray the ants invading the kitchen? After I drove seven hours to Louisiana for a Thanksgiving holiday I would rather ignore? After I did what everyone else expected of me?

We drove to Natchitoches the next day and ate Thanksgiving dinner with my mom and stepdad and my brother and some people from my mother's church. It was a beautiful, chilly day, and we took silly photos of the kids outside. Everything went well. Everyone was fine. Everyone pretended to be fine.

One holiday down. Two holidays to go.

Why did people love this season? I only wished it away.

At work, I marked the days off my calendar, counting down to the two weeks I would have off at the end of the month. I was making a list of all the things I needed to get done before then, writing down one or two things I'd already done so I could have the pleasure of crossing them off, when Jacob's school counselor called. She told me that Jacob was failing three classes.

I might have cursed out loud. I probably did.

"I have no idea what I'm supposed to do about this," I said. "I really don't."

Within the hour, Jacob's algebra teacher called as well.

This time, I cried.

It was just me on my own, and I was so messed up. I worked at a place where 14 people had been laid off. I was exhausted from the effort of pretending my way through each workday. I didn't want to look over Jacob's homework every night. I didn't want to check the school website every day. I barely had it in me to crawl out of bed each morning. I wanted to trust that he was doing what he was supposed to be doing.

I cried and I said, "I'm so mad at him."

Mrs. Uswatte, Jacob's kind algebra teacher, said, "I know."

I'm sure she thought I was talking about Jacob.

I took Kate to her last counseling session before Christmas. Jacob didn't want to go again, and I didn't make him. I said, "I need you to know that there is always a place you can go if you need to talk to someone, or you can talk to me."

After their last appointment, I'd spoken with Hannah, Kate's counselor, privately. She told me how articulate both children were, that they were doing well.

"These are great kids," she said. "These are kids who will grow up and make a difference in this world. You are a wonderful mother, and these kids adore you. You are doing a great job."

My eyes filled with tears. I reached for the ever-present box of tissues on the table next to the sofa in this windowless, peach-colored room.

"This isn't the path anyone would choose to take, but these kids will be better for having walked it. They have wisdom they wouldn't have had otherwise. Does this make you feel better?"

It did.

So I let Jacob stay home and play video games while Kate and I went in for her appointment.

While Kate was in her session with Hannah, I sat in the waiting room and wrote in my journal. *My life feels like a waiting room. I am waiting to feel better. I am waiting to feel useful.*

I'm not getting better.

I was unable to stop the thoughts that told me this was my fault. I could have done something to stop this if I hadn't been in denial about how bad things were, or if I'd let that stupid phone ring until voice mail picked up. No one wanted to know these thoughts, so I kept them inside where they became twisted. If I kept them hidden, the thoughts could morph into something sick and untrue. In the dark, I could no longer recognize their falsehood.

If I didn't have Kate and Jacob, I could have gone in the garage and finished this like Charles did.

The thought scared me, but at night I let it loose. I read somewhere that Monday was the most common day for suicides. I read that gunshots account for more than half of all suicides. I read that people called it "The Hemingway Solution."

I read this in another book: "Happiness in intelligent people is the rarest thing I know." Ernest Hemingway wrote that.

So maybe I'd do it on a Monday as Charles had done. I would do it in the garage. I imagined it the way a person thinks up the ending of a really sad short story or a depressing independent film. Where else would my character die? The garage was where this should end.

One day I'd driven down Shades Crest Road, which winds and curves along the top of Shades Mountain, and I passed a lot where a house had been torn down. All that was left was the brick fireplace at the center of a concrete foundation. I always loved seeing fireplaces standing tall and alone in the middle of fields or tucked into a cluster of trees. In the national forest in Tennessee, there are a lot of them. People used to have houses on the land until the government bought up the property. The people moved away, and the government tore down the houses, but some of the fireplaces remained.

I would imagine arranging a room around one of these fireplaces. A sofa here facing the hearth. A rug laid across the grass and weeds and wildflowers. A ceiling that is a sky full of stars.

In the bleakest part of the night, I would picture myself setting my house on fire so this lot could be empty, too. My sick mind would do the quick work of putting the children somewhere safe. They would be at their grandparents' house. I'd be alone.

My mind put my affairs in order. Unlike Charles, I had life insurance.

I could set fire to my bedroom first, to Kate's bedroom, to Jacob's bedroom. Methodically, I could work my way through the house, setting fire to everything that represented our lives here. In the hallway, the living room, into the kitchen. Then I'd go into the garage.

There I saw myself crouched down at the front of the car where I was when Charles died. That was where I would do it. Then the house could burn around me, the curtains and beds going up in flames, the bookshelves toppling over, and the pages of all my novels and memoirs and my grandmother's first-edition copy of *A Farewell to Arms* turning to ash.

In the end, what would be left standing? Nothing but a lone fireplace and a sky full of stars.

I loved my children. I woke up every day for them. But I hated this person I'd become. I missed myself the way I was before, and I was mourning her the way I mourned Charles. The person I used to be must have done something to deserve this. My thoughts of late said that I was a bad person. I was selfish, and I was being punished for a reason. I'd done and said the wrong things. Every night, I swallowed this poison and let it run through me.

When the alarm went off in the morning, I would sit up and dangle my feet over the edge of the bed and take a deep breath. I'd lean over and turn the alarm off. I would move off the bed and head to the bathroom and brush my teeth and try again to be someone who didn't want to give up. Some days I was overwhelmed by the mere task of living. Even if I could muster the energy to pick up the bug spray and kill the lines of ants marching into the kitchen, I couldn't be bothered to clean up their tiny corpses.

After her session ended, Kate walked out to the waiting room with Hannah. Kate was carrying the memory stone she'd made for Charles. It was shaped like a butterfly. Into the soft clay, Kate had pressed colorful mementos like Coca-Cola bottle caps and glass beads and marbles she'd gathered from around the house. I'd taken her to the craft store, where she'd picked out tiny plastic playing cards and coins that said "Dad," "Son," and "Husband." She'd pressed those coins around the edges of one wing. From Charles's tool bag, she'd taken a copper pipe fitting and pressed it deep into the top edge of the right wing.

The clay of the butterfly had hardened since her last visit, so she could bring it home now.

"Will you hold it for me, Mom?"

As I grasped the edges of it to take it from her, I felt the top of the right wing, where the copper fitting was, break off in my left hand.

I felt a hot surge of tears behind my eyes and in my throat.

"Kate, I'm so sorry," I said.

Hannah took the butterfly from my hands. "This will be easy to fix. I think the copper fitting was a little too big."

Maybe there was something in Charles's tool bag that could fix it, some sort of adhesive that holds things together after they've been broken.

Hannah said, "Kate, will you wait out here for a few minutes while I go talk to your mom? Here, we'll set the butterfly in the chair next to you."

Kate had a book with her, but she was more interested in the Jolly Ranchers at the receptionist's desk. She got a handful first and then sat down to read and wait for me.

As soon as Hannah shut the door to the peach-colored windowless room, where the cushy, denim sofa was flanked by tables with boxes of tissues, I started crying.

"You're not doing well."

This wasn't a question.

I answered anyway. "No, I'm not. I'm so tired."

"You've been traumatized. It's going to take a really long time to get over that." Hannah watched me, maybe looking for confirmation that I knew this.

People often said things like this to me and then waited. Todd had called recently and said, "You must know you had nothing to do with this." And that was more like a question than a statement.

"Of course, you're tired," Hannah said. "You are constantly battling yourself. The part of you that wants to feel normal and do everything like you used to has to battle with the part of you who wants to give up, who wants to cry. That takes a lot of work. Emotional work is physically hard."

It would be nice if emotional work also burned calories.

"Even though this has stolen your joy right now, it won't always be that way. The balance is off. This trauma and grief is weighing the scales. It's huger than everything else, but eventually things will right themselves. Life will feel balanced again, but, for now, you're on autopilot.

"You're resilient," she said. "That is part of your character. So you will make it through."

I wanted to believe this. Some days I did. Some days I recognized myself as the person I used to be, who worked out and cleaned the house and stayed on the move. On Saturday, I'd gotten a visit from that person. I spent most of the day cleaning my bedroom. I'd dragged a shaggy, cream-colored rug from Kate's room into my room. All day, I'd pushed myself to keep going. I hung white garland and Christmas lights over the windows and over the gray bookshelves by my desk. I dusted and vacuumed. Once I was moving, it was easier to keep on moving.

On Kate's rug, I'd found a fortune from a fortune cookie. It read, "It is not your character to give up."

It was probably silly to look for meaning or signs, but I was grasping at anything for some comfort. I wanted to be resilient. I wanted to believe a slip of paper that said it is not my character to give up. That my daily numbers are 7 3 1. That I could win the Lotto with these six numbers: 23 30 15 21 24 46.

Hannah said, "When you do notice moments of joy, hold onto those. They can help you through this time and, eventually, you'll feel balance again."

Moment of joy:

I took Kate to her guitar lesson after counseling. The owner asked Kate if she'd like to be in a TV commercial, and Kate said, "I would *love* to be in a TV commercial!" She was wearing a sassy, black-and-white knit cap and her peace sign hoodie, and she played "Jingle Bells." It cheered me up to see her so happy.

Moment of joy:

For dinner, I scrambled eggs and baked biscuits and fried bacon. Kate helped me fix hot chocolate. We poured it into large mugs and sprayed whipped topping on top, and then we squirted some straight from the can into our mouths. We carried our plates to the table and sat with Jacob and slathered cream cheese on our biscuits.

"You know, I like your cooking, Mom," Jacob said.

I laughed and said, "It's not really what you can call cooking."

"Your meals are made with love, Mom," he said in the ironic, teasing manner of the modern-day teenager. "Maybe if restaurants served love with their meals, they'd have more customers. I'd like a Happy Meal with extra happy, please."

14

People warn you about the difficulty of the first Christmas after the death of a loved one. These people don't lie. The difficulty is due, in large part, to the simple thing that marks every "first" during the year after a death—your memories that begin with the words: Last year at this time...

Last year at this time, Charles had moved back to Birmingham from Colorado. He'd moved to Vail in September and was staying with his friend Jack, and Jack's wife and daughter. Charles called to tell me how the job search was going. Then he called to tell me he found a job. He called to tell me how the job was. To complain about living with Jack and his wife. That Jack asked him to pick up the newspaper and turn off the lights when he left. That Jack didn't do these things, so what the hell was he complaining about? What was the big deal? To tell me how he wasn't making enough money to afford his own place. To ask me why he was living so far away from his children.

By November, Charles was ready to move back to Birmingham. Charles was a big fan of the geographical cure. He asked if he could stay with the children and me for a bit while he saved money. I said yes. Was this the place where I could have saved us from tragedy? Should I drive my DeLorean through the mall parking lot and past the terrorists with machine guns to this exact minute in 2008, to this phone call?

I laid down the ground rules. As far as I knew, Charles had been sober for nearly a year. (He hadn't been. As far as I knew, I didn't know shit.) I said there would be no pills. The first sign of pills and you're out. (Did I ignore the signs?) I said you can have Kate's room, and Kate will sleep with me. There will be no sex. Do not even try. (Of course he tried.) I said you can stay here six months and help me with the bills and save money for your own place. (He saved no money.) You have to leave at the end of May, no exceptions. (I made exceptions.)

(I made mistakes.)

We spent that Thanksgiving 2008 with our friends Chris and Heather in Birmingham. Chris fixed Old Fashioneds, an homage to Don Draper and *Mad Men*. He set up a tray with the ingredients: whiskey, bitters, sugar, and oranges. Kate ate her weight in sugar cubes and oranges.

Charles didn't drink anything, but later that evening, when were back at the house, he said to me, "You know, I can drink. Drinking's not my problem. Pills are my problem. I can have a drink now and then."

"But you prefer pills. You prefer that high. So if you start drinking, all you're going to think is 'I wish I had pills instead.' Aren't you?"

"No. Not at all. It's not like that."

Did I reiterate the ground rules? Did I say, "Get the hell out for even suggesting you should be able to drink?"

I have no idea. I think I tried to reason with him.

I think trying to reason with an addict is pure folly.

Charles didn't drink in front of me until sometime that February. I had an UnValentine's party, and Charles carried around a red plastic cup. I knew it had alcohol in it. And I ignored it.

Sometimes it was fun to have him around again. He helped cook dinner and did the grocery shopping.

One afternoon, Charles and I were in the kitchen and, through the window over the sink, we saw the crotchety, elderly woman next door throwing leaves and sticks over the chain-link fence into my backyard. When it grew dark and the woman had retreated into her house, Charles and I ran out into the chilly evening and tossed huge armloads of dry and crackling leaves into her yard. Then we ran into the house and, once the back door was closed, we laughed loudly, me clutching my stomach, Charles gasping for breath.

That was a good day.

Now I thought about those months when he'd first come back, how it shifted the balance of our household. If I sat on the sofa, he wanted to sit down right next to me. If I put my feet on the ottoman, he wanted to have his feet touching mine. "What's the big deal?" he would say. I started to believe again that I was a person who made big deals out of nothing.

I was a person who made nothing out of big deals.

I knew almost as soon as he moved back that there would be no more chances for us. I'd said it aloud already to him, but to myself I'd left the door open a bit. It was open enough for a "maybe" to slide in. Maybe if he was sober. Maybe if he stayed that way. Maybe we could be together as a family. Maybe I would be allowed to love him again.

Maybe is a cruel thing. It's a word packed full of hope and possibility, but it's full of doubt, too. It's a teeter-totter. It's impossible to find your balance on the word "maybe." One of you will land on your ass.

One of you will get so high that you can't come down.

One cold evening in December, Kate and I went to the Boy Scout Christmas-tree lot near the post office in Vestavia Hills. We picked out a tree, and, after I lowered the backseats in my Passat, two scouts slid it into the trunk (leaving the trunk open). Back at the house, I somehow managed to get the tree out and carry it in by myself. I stood it up in the tree stand and yelled for the kids to come look at it while I lay beneath it.

"Does it look balanced? Is it leaning too far one way?"

"It's leaning a little to the right," Jacob said.

"Now it's leaning left," Kate said.

Finally, I got it right, twisted the screws to hold it in place, stood up, and plucked the green needles out of my hair.

Four days before Christmas, Mom, Ted, and Tim drove in from Louisiana, bringing with them a gallon of frozen margaritas and a gallon of frozen eggnog daiquiri from Maggio's in Natchitoches. They'd packed them into an ice chest with bags of ice to keep them cold on the eight-hour drive. I snapped a picture of the alcoholic beverages in milk jugs in my freezer and posted it to Facebook, proof of my mother's excellence as a houseguest. I didn't post a photo of the package of 12 rolls of toilet paper she brought, but that was pretty great, too.

I gave Mom and Ted my room. Kate and I slept in her room. Tim got the sofa in the living room. Jacob got to stay put because no one other than a teenage boy should be subjected to sleeping in a teenage boy's bedroom.

My friend Christopher came over one night for dinner, and my mom made taco soup, this fantastic concoction of hamburger meat and about 10 cans of various ingredients, including corn, beans, diced tomatoes, chicken broth, Rotel, and packets of ranch seasoning and taco seasoning. This is from whom I learned to cook, with as little effort as possible but a lot of love. "I'd like a Happy Meal with extra happy."

Christopher fit right in with my family. My brother had a man crush on him. Kate and Jacob adored him. When he came over we would call it "Art on Demand" because the kids would demand he draw pictures of whatever they came up with, and he'd do it.

Jacob: "A flying brick!" "A ninja potato!"

Kate: "Every girl from the cast of *Glee*!"

You might be thinking this is leading to a romantic subplot, a chick-lit ending in which the dear friend becomes more than a friend and everyone lives happily ever after. Get a grip. I'm telling you a story about real life and, in this real life, romantic subplots only involve George Clooney and an active imagination.

On Christmas Eve, Mom and Tim went shopping, and Ted stayed at the house with the kids and me. I never knew what to say to him when we were alone, and I guess being silent was OK. He couldn't really have a conversation, but my mom was so good at including him in what was going on. If Ted could be who he was before his heart attack, he'd have been going around my house fixing things. He would have made sure I got a new back door. I still hadn't replaced it. It still had a board keeping it closed. He would have changed the locks and fixed the running toilet. Now he watched TV.

For a while, I sat in my bedroom on the floor in front of the TV and wrapped Christmas gifts. My tradition for the past decade had been to watch *Die Hard* while I tied bows and filled out gift tags. I liked to say that *Die Hard* was my favorite Christmas movie. Don't tell me it's not a Christmas movie. It takes place during the holiday. That's more than you can say for *It's a Wonderful Life*. Most of that movie does not take place during the holiday.

What if Clarence the angel had shown Charles the world without him? Maybe I could be a lonely librarian. Would Charles have seen us better off? It made me sick and sad to think of it that way. "He knew you'd do a better job without him," the psychic said.

I couldn't watch *Die Hard* this year. The violent images would be too much. I silently cursed Charles for ruining this for me. Was it really my favorite Christmas movie? Who knows? Maybe I liked to smother sincerity with my snark and crush sentimentality under the boot heel of my sarcasm.

I pulled out the gift tags I'd saved from last Christmas. I'd had some left over, but I'd also saved tags I'd used. They were cutout illustrations of birds highlighted with glitter and too pretty to toss in the trash. I turned one of the tags over and saw that it read To: Kate, From: Mom and Dad. Another one said To: Jacob, Love, Mom and Dad. There were several of them. Love, Mom and Dad.

Whenever I was going along fine, these small things would leap up and sink their teeth into my ankles, damn it. Kate had performed with her school choir at a tree-lighting ceremony a couple of weeks before, and, as I stood there in the cold watching her stand on the risers, Christmas songs played over the loudspeakers. Couples, moms and dads, surrounded me. Charles's favorite, *The Little Drummer Boy*, came on, and I thought, "This is what torture is. Right here. Keep your waterboarding. Pipe in Christmas music." I had to shake these tiny biters off and keep moving.

I hoped the children would be happy in the morning. Jacob was hard to shop for, only asking for money or video games. It was difficult to surprise him. I usually shoved the money under a pile of new socks. This year I slid small bills between the pages of a book.

It was a blessing—of the painful, why-me variety—that I had so little money. I would have spent too much trying to make up for things for which there is no making up. I would be grateful later that I hadn't received the $8,000 first-time home-buyer tax credit, that the IRS was auditing my return and dragging out the process and keeping me from stimulating the economy with misguided gift buying.

After I wrapped all the gifts, I heated up the leftover taco soup. My phone rang, and I didn't recognize the number. When I answered, it was Mom, and she was crying. She and Tim had argued while driving back from shopping—something about he turned left and she thought he should turn right. He'd pulled into a parking lot and gotten out of the truck, slamming the driver's side door behind him. She waited for a while, and he didn't come back. Now she was in a Mexican restaurant called Sol Azteca, and I could hear the bouncy sounds of Latin music in the background.

"I'll come up there," I said. "I'll help you look for him. I'll be there in a minute."

I told Jacob I was going out for a bit, and I left Ted watching TV. Mom was back in the truck when I got there.

"I drove around a little bit, but I didn't see him walking. I didn't know which way to go. So I came back here, and they let me use the phone." Mom was crying. She didn't have a cell phone, and neither did Tim. I couldn't call him and tell him to get his ass back here and, for God's sake, calm the fuck down. It's fucking Christmas, for fuck's sake! Or something similarly soothing and sisterly.

Mom got into my car, and we drove up Highway 31. I asked how long he'd been walking and tried to gauge how far he could have gotten. It was dark and drizzling and cold. The windshield wipers thwacked back and forth, too fast for the rain when I set them on high, too slow on the low setting.

"How would he know which way to go back to my house?" I asked. I tried to follow a direct route, but I ignored the interstate because no one would be nuts enough to walk along the speeding lanes of traffic.

We turned around and went back the other direction. Finally, I pulled back into the restaurant parking lot. We sat for a few minutes in silence.

"You go back to the house and see if he's there, and I guess I'll keep driving around here," Mom said.

I gave her my cell phone and told her I'd call her from the landline at home if he showed up.

Eventually, he came in, wet and tired and full of self-righteous anger. He'd walked back on the side of the interstate, and I can only imagine the abject misery of that long journey. Tim went straight to the basement, and I could smell the faint scent of cigarette smoke. I called Mom and told her he was back.

"Thank God!" she said.

When she got back to the house, she didn't go down to the basement. She let him sit down there stewing and smoking. He didn't come up until all of us had gone to bed and he could have the living room to himself.

All I'd wanted to do on Christmas afternoon was go to the movies. *Up in the Air* was showing, and I wanted to sit in the dark and watch George Clooney and lose myself for a couple of hours. It was really all I'd asked for. That and to pick up Chinese food for dinner.

Instead I was holding a library book open on my chest, and the light that reflected off the plastic protective cover bounced onto Kate's bedroom ceiling and created a constellation of white stars. I could hear Mom and Tim in the basement arguing. Her voice was only a murmur, a muffled rise and fall. His was loud and clear.

Kate had gone to her friend Norah's house to play with some of her Christmas gifts. Jacob was holed up in his room with his new video game. Ted was in the living room.

I'd been in the shower when the fight started. We'd had a nice morning opening gifts. We'd fixed cinnamon rolls and hot chocolate and coffee for Mom. I'd given Tim a DVD of *500 Days of Summer* (he loved Zooey Deschanel), and we'd watched it after lunch. After the movie and during my shower, Tim and Mom must have untied the bonds of their unspoken truce. I could hear them in my bedroom going at each other.

I tried to ignore them. I stayed under the hot water for as long as possible, even shaving my legs, and God knows I rarely made that effort lately. I could feel the now-familiar bubble of panic build up inside me.

Most intense emotional confrontations don't erupt in violence.

It's not a catchy saying, but I repeated it to myself.

A whisper replied, "But some do."

It was this knowledge that created the panic even when the panic was unnecessary. When Stacey and I had gone to Nashville to see Kings of Leon in October, we'd gone to a bar where a fight broke out. Men, grabbing each other by the collars and shoving and yelling, had spun together in a violent dance and rolled out the door. The panic had come then, too, and, even though I sat still and silent, Stacey could see it. "Did that freak you out?" she asked me later. "I could tell."

I heard Tim yell that he hated his life and he might as well be dead.

The water was cold, so I finally turned it off and wrapped a towel around my head and put on my robe. When I finally opened the door, I saw that Tim was gone and Mom was sitting on the bed, crying.

"What's the problem here?" I said.

"He's an asshole. What do you want me to say?" She shook her head. "He's miserable. This is about him. But I guess I owe you an apology for being such an awful mother. I'm horrible. Everything is my fault."

She didn't mean this, of course. She meant, "I am the easy target of his anger and sadness about moving from Arizona back to Louisiana. I am the easy target of his feeling that his life is going nowhere. I am the victim here."

And she was. This was true.

"He told me he might as well kill himself."

I nodded. I'd heard that. I did not want my children to hear that sort of talk in this house, where someone had once said it and meant it. In the shower, I'd been thinking, "No. Not here. Not those words. Not in my house. Not today. Not ever. No."

"I don't think I should have to listen to that in my house," I said.

She turned on me then.

"You're right," she stood up and slammed down the pillow she'd been holding on her lap. "You're the only person who's ever had anything bad happen to them!"

She stormed over to the armchair.

"We'll leave. How's that? We'll get out of your house!"

I felt calm, but I think my brain had gotten really good at slowing things down for me in moments of shock, of turning off the hot water and running only cold.

"You're ridiculous. You're being ridiculous," I said.

I meant ridiculous to think they should pack up and leave this minute. Why couldn't everyone be calm and pretend to be happy until the damn day was over? Shove that shit down. It's not that hard, people. I'd been doing it for months. They could put it on hold for a day or two.

She left the room, and I heard the basement door open and close. Tim was down there again and now she was going down there, too.

I didn't read my book. I held it while I listened to Tim attack my mother's god. There is no god, he told her. Tim had no job, no girlfriend, and no home of his own. Kate and Jacob had no dad, but sure, go ahead and make their Christmas even more dysfunctional.

I pictured myself in the movie theater. I pictured the big screen. I would have taken Jacob and gone to the movie while they waged war downstairs, but the truck was parked behind my car in the driveway. I really did want them to leave.

Last night, when she'd called and said Tim had stormed off, I'd been calm. I'd tried to be helpful and rational and understanding. When Tim came in two hours after storming off, I'd said nothing accusatory to him. I figured walking two hours in the cold beside cars going 70-plus miles an hour was probably punishment enough.

They were arguing about religion now.

I was the selfish one here, right? "Why don't you try seeing this from someone's point of view other than yours?" Mom had said to me at Thanksgiving. "You're the only person who's had something bad happen to them!" she'd said to me an hour ago.

"You'll need to talk about this, and your friends will get tired of it, but you can always call me," she'd said in August.

I better get over what happened here four months and 22 days ago, and I better do it fast. I didn't want to be one of those characters in a book who is whiny and self-involved and railing against everyone around her and thinking what happened to her is worse than anything that's ever happened to anyone else in the history of the world and none of you fuckers could ever possibly understand.

Is that who I was?

I didn't think so. I wanted a Diet Coke and a pack of Sour Patch Kids and a two-hour date with the pretend love of my life. I wanted to sit anonymously among Christmas Day moviegoers. Instead I was lying here watching the prisms of light on the ceiling and constructing more walls around myself. I was helpless to stop it.

My cell phone beeped. I had a text from my friend Erin.

"Hope you had a good day with the fam and got to see your George."

No, I texted back. Not yet.

First, I had to get through this day. Mom and Ted and Tim would leave in the morning. None of us really spoke when they came upstairs later. We watched *Up*. We ate Chinese food. We avoided eye contact.

In the morning, everyone got up before I did, and Mom came in Kate's room and leaned down by the side of the bed and kissed my check.

"I love you. We're leaving."

I pretended to be barely awake. I listened as they packed up the truck and pulled out of the driveway.

I will say now that I was self-involved. I was still looking at the thing I'd seen in the garage. I couldn't look away. It was almost an entire year later, on Thanksgiving of 2010, when I had a sudden moment of clarity. Maybe my mother had not understood that I meant I didn't want to listen to threats of suicide. She did not understand that I was afraid. Maybe she had thought I was saying I shouldn't have to listen to her tell me about the fight with Tim. Maybe she'd thought I was unwilling to listen to her, that I was unwilling to comfort her. We always listened to one another, and I was reneging on our assigned roles in this family.

Until that moment, I had been unable to figure out what I might have done to become a target. I'd thought I was being such a good little griever. Look at me, buying a tree and putting out decorations and buying gifts and hosting guests and being all cool and strong and badass.

Now look at my mom. Buying gifts and driving eight hours and bringing frozen drinks I love and buying me toilet paper and slipping a check into my hand so I could buy presents for the kids. Look at my mom leading my stepdad to the dinner table and making sure he eats. Look at my mom putting an arm around his shoulder and hustling him to the bedroom so he could change his pants when he stood up from his chair in the living room and wet his pants and looked at her in confusion. Look at her mourning the loss of her husband as he once was while still loving the husband who was left behind. Look how tired she is. Look at her making taco soup and opening can after can and stirring in some extra happy.

Look at my brother. Moving halfway across the country so he could help my mom with my stepdad. Look at him changing his entire life and moving back to a tiny town he hated, where he felt judged for his tattoos and isolated by his intelligence. Look at him struggling with a big decision and trying to make peace with it. Look at him sleeping on the sofa at my house and waking up with excruciating back pain. Look at him as I hand him one of the pills from the brown paper bag someone had given me in August.

Look at the bag full of sleeping pills and anxiety medication. Look at the little yellow pill that I had never taken because it was the thing to which Charles had been addicted. Look at the Klonopin in my brother's palm, as I say that I know it's prescribed for restless legs syndrome so maybe it will help ease your back pain. Look at me acting like the world's dumbest doctor writing the world's most moronic prescription. Look at my brother acting like Charles, screaming about dying, saying there is no God.

I was sick of this year. I was ready to shove 2009 into a box and toss it out with the Christmas tree. But first I was going to lie here on Kate's white iron bed for a little while.

15

You can only lie still for so long. As the new year began, I was sick of how small I'd made myself, burrowing into my little hole of regret and fear and waiting. I did not care if it was understandable, if I needed time, if it was amazing that I was moving at all, if it was miraculous that I hadn't run away with a long-haired hippie wanderer (where would I meet one of these?) and thrown myself into a life of pot smoking and drinking and self-destruction and driving to San Francisco in a VW van. (For some reason, my self-destruction fantasies resembled the '60s.)

I mostly thought: I am fat, I am lazy, and I am useless. I tried not to say these things out loud to anyone else. "I'm fine," I said.

On the first day of the year, I got up and moved. I cleaned the bathrooms and the kitchen. I vacuumed the rugs in my bedroom. I dusted the tables in the living room. I put clean sheets on the beds.

The day before, I had dragged the Christmas tree out to the curb. It was dry, ready to burst into flames at even the idea of a spark, and the needles fell off and created a trail behind me from the front porch to the end of the driveway. The living room looked clean and spacious without the Christmas decorations. I felt like I could breathe easier now. Sorry, Christ, but your birthday is really quite taxing.

Kate helped me pack up the ornaments and carry the boxes to the shelves in the garage. We heated up the last of the leftover taco soup (yes, that recipe was like the Everlasting Gobstopper of soups) and sat down at the dining table to eat. The TV was tuned to one of the satellite radio stations, and "God Blessed the Broken Road" came on.

"Didn't Daddy like this song?" Kate said.

It is a fact that Rascal Flatts, or country music in general, will kill you—take your heart and squeeze it until you beg for mercy and put in a Ludacris CD. I told Kate that yes, he'd liked it.

I couldn't help what happened next. My eyes filled with tears, and I turned to her and smiled ruefully and shrugged my shoulders slightly. It hurt, but it felt like a relief, too. I wished I could cry out all the tears I had and be done on this day and start the next day a brand-new person.

The kids and I stayed home that night. I had barely left the house during the month of December, turning down lunch invitations and RSVP'ing my regrets to parties, and I wasn't going to change my ass-on-sofa policy on the last day of the year. I turned on the gas fireplace in the living room, and we roasted marshmallows over the flames and pressed the lightly browned, gooey sweetness between graham crackers and chocolate bars. The kids drank hot chocolate, but I discovered that s'mores and red wine are a combination made in heaven.

"Your sister makes me bonkers," I said after the sugar kicked in and Kate ran around the house, looking for ways to release her energy. It was only 9 p.m. I figured the sugar crash would take her down long before midnight.

Jacob said, "Bonkers? Is that an '80s word for 'crazy?'"

"Ha! Yes, you ass, it is."

"What was that, Mom? What did you call me?"

"An ass. Go ahead, say it."

Kate said, "I want to say ass!"

"OK, you can both say it. How's this? Five times before midnight, you can use the word ass."

They both liked this idea. Was there a better way to usher out this awful year than to indulge in the power of curse words? (What we were really indulging was the power of laughter.)

"2009 was a kick in the ass," Kate said.

"Kate, I want to kick you in your ass. I still have four left," Jacob said.

By 11:00, Kate was asleep, curled up on one end of the sofa underneath a fuzzy holiday-themed blanket, penguins in scarves ice skating on a blue background.

It was supposed to be a full moon that night, so I unlocked the back door and went out in the yard. I pulled my sweater tighter around me and looked up through the bare limbs of the pine trees, but I couldn't find the moon. It was quiet. For a minute, I stood there shivering and wishing for peace and redemption and a lot of other things I couldn't put into words. People pray in huge cathedrals and massive churches, surrounded by wood and glass and concrete, but I have always felt better in the presence of trees.

Back inside, I poured another glass of wine and turned on one of the New Year's Eve specials, waiting for the meaningless countdown. It was already 2010 in other parts of the world. In those places, was I better? Was I healing?

At 11:59, Jacob came out of his room, where he'd been playing some shoot-'em-up game on his Xbox, and said, "Ass, ass, ass, ass. There, I'm done."

In the new year, I didn't make an official list of resolutions. I never do. But I created a mental list of expectations of myself and carried it around in my head.

I resolved to keep moving.

A week into the year, I got a letter from the IRS that said they were disallowing my claim. I broke down crying and carried the business-size envelope to my bed, where I laid down and sobbed into my pillow.

It would only take a phone call or sending all of the documents again to straighten this out, but the thought of more work of any kind, of more waiting, wore me out.

Kate came in my room, and I sat up and wiped my eyes on the sleeve of my sweater. She hugged me, and I said, "It's OK. It really is. I just have to take care of some paperwork about the house."

While I sat on the bed and tried to stop myself from falling into the big self-pity pool, Kate went to the bathroom.

"Mom!" she yelled, after she flushed the toilet. "Mommy!"

I ran in and saw the toilet water spilling over the sides of the seat, splashing onto the tile floor and spreading over the threshold onto the wood floor of the bedroom.

Kate and I started yanking bath towels off the racks and throwing them down. I got the plunger and pumped it up and down until the blockage in the pipes finally gave way.

For a minute, I wanted to cry and bemoan the constant stream of shit—literal and figurative—in my life, but I decided that, "Hell, no!" I was not going to do that.

The toilet overflowing got me off the bed and moving. It made me leap into action. A body in motion tends to stay in motion. Motion is what would save me. So I kept moving. I cleaned up the water and tossed the towels down the laundry chute. I sprayed bathroom cleaner and wiped down the toilet and the tile floor. I washed my hands and changed my clothes and told Kate to change hers.

Jacob was at a friend's house for the night, so I told Kate we were going to see a girl movie. She brought her pink, leopard-print fleece blanket, and, in the movie theater, we spread it over our legs and watched *The Princess and the Frog* and shared a bucket of popcorn and a package of Sour Patch Kids.

On Monday, I sent the paperwork to the IRS. I called to make sure they received it and spoke with a woman who said it would take up to 45 days for them to complete their investigation and release the funds. Government agencies do not care that you are sick of waiting.

I resolved to be less passive-aggressive.

My last passive-aggressive act had occurred a few days after Christmas when I'd unfriended Michael on Facebook. On his birthday, no less. Confession: This made me laugh in a mean way. But to my way of thinking, he'd unfriended me first. I hadn't heard a word from him since before Thanksgiving. He'd come into my life on the worst day in my personal history and had stayed there, emailing and calling and texting for months. Then he got a girlfriend and disappeared.

If he believed his small role in that night mattered in the so-called grand scheme of things, I was sorry for that. If he had felt guilty and obligated to be friends with me and had now worked through that, good for him.

Let's all just move on, I thought.

So I clicked the "Remove from friends" button on his page. When he sent me an email sometime in mid-January, I deleted it.

Maybe it was cruel. Maybe I was unreasonable. Maybe I was envious that he'd found a girlfriend. I was envious in that way a person is when she wishes she could find love, too, but she knows that isn't possible for her and so she dismisses the people capable of finding it. Probably the way a person with a handicap might envy someone who can walk or see or hear. I heard this tale of speedy romance and instant engagement, and it was like hearing someone speak in Mandarin, with me envying them their ability to speak in a strange, incomprehensible language, yet all the while thinking, "Bullshit, bullshit, bullshit."

Maybe I could have emailed him and said, directly, "I haven't heard from you at all during these holidays and that hurt my feelings."

But it was way easier doing it this way.

I resolved to write my father a letter.

During a counseling session after the holidays, Joan asked if I'd heard from my father; I told her I hadn't.

"The first holidays after Charles's death and he didn't think to call? Did he think about how hard these would be on you?"

She was stunned, but I wasn't. I would have bet that my father did think about calling but decided against it. In the same way he'd always thought we didn't need him as long as we had our mother, he thought I wouldn't need or want a phone call from him.

He had sent me a letter in early December. *Please know that I think of you, Jacob, and Kate every single day. I pray for all of us every day*, he wrote.

Joan suggested I write him back, and I did, but I never sent it.

He'd written this: *I really don't want to continue to dwell on what happened. I know I screwed up really bad. Unfortunately, none of us can go back in time and change or fix the mistakes we've made.*

When I'd pulled it from the mailbox and saw that it was his handwriting on the envelope, I thought that I would read it and cry. I brought it inside and sat on my bed before I opened it. I didn't cry, though. Maybe it was because I got stuck against the word "dwell," like a cold and jagged boulder I had to push out of my path. I slammed my shoulder against it, but it wouldn't budge.

"Dwell" felt like a judgment. I had spent my life not dwelling on the things that hurt so that I could keep going. I was the "queen of getting over shit," I liked to tell Charles. Now I was dwelling.

What I had actually done was set my dad aside. I did not have space for his guilt or his apology that felt to me like "I'm sorry, but..." He didn't want to torment himself over his mistake. He did not want to dwell on it.

So don't, I thought. I'm not tormenting you. I'm not thinking about your (latest) mistake. (I never told you what I wanted from you anyway.) Hell, I even understand it, to a degree. I cannot imagine not going to my children in this situation, but I can imagine *you* not going to *yours*. (We had our mother.) I can imagine the reasons and the justifications. I can know that you can love someone and still hurt him or her. I can imagine making the wrong choice and having to live with it. Here, let me give you an image of a man making a choice, a man in true torment. Do you see him blowing himself into pieces? Here's a woman making a choice, too. Do you see the blood on her clothing? Here she is living with it every night when she closes her eyes. Here she is simply trying to survive. How about you dwell on that?

But I also had a storehouse of other images. Me waiting impatiently for my dad to arrive at the Shoney's Big Boy in Jackson, Tennessee, waiting to hug him after nine months. Me hanging from my dad's flexed bicep, bending my knees and dangling over the kitchen floor. I could see us on my grandparents' pontoon, with its bright-orange cushions and Neil Diamond playing on the cassette player, riding across Geist Lake. I could see us all screaming and getting wet on the log ride at Kings Island in Ohio. I could see my dad hugging me when I cried after watching *Somewhere in Time*—when I lied and said I was crying because my stomach hurt. I could see him holding me when I cried at the end of the summer, when our time was up and we stood on the front porch waving to my grandparents and my aunts and cousins as they all headed down the driveway to their cars after a going-away party.

I could see his mustache that made him look like one of those sturdy and trustworthy policemen who came to my door on August 3. His dark-olive skin as I held up my arm next to his to see if, after a day lying by the pool, I was as tan as him yet. His brown eyes. My brown eyes.

You can see why I never sent my letter, can't you?

I was 7 years old. I was 12. I was 15. I was 18. I was 23. I was 27. I was 36. I was the person I had always been and would always be. I could write a hundred letters, and I would toss a hundred letters in the trash.

My letter was too mean, and I didn't want to hurt my dad's feelings.

But, at least, I wrote it.

I resolved to cry in the shower more (and in the car less).

I needed to allow myself time to cry. I knew this because of therapy and books. It was the only way to release the constant pressure on my chest. But I was tired of crying in the car and arriving places red-eyed and unsettled. The shower was better.

Unlike a thousand female characters in books and movies, I didn't understand the crying in the bathtub thing. (I didn't understand the eating ice cream thing either.) I'd never found comfort in that. Sure, a hot bath feels good for a little while, but then the water cools and you have to get out and you're shivering and wet. Plus, it's unpleasant to cry in a bath. The sound of sobbing echoes off the water and the ceramic tile. Anyone standing outside the bathroom door can hear you. There is no running water to camouflage the sound. A shower is much better for crying. You can take one in the morning and get all that damn crying out of the way while you let the conditioner soak into your hair. Then you can rinse it out, rinse it off, and move on with the day.

I resolved to focus on work (words).

I attempted to find my way back to the Must-Be-Nice-ness of working for the country's most beloved regional magazine.

Mid-month, I took a scouting trip to Orange Beach, and Kate and Jacob came with me. We stayed in a condo in a community that was like a ghost town, only the occasional elderly snowbird wandering the grounds. The swimming-pool temperature hovered around 55 degrees, but the kids didn't care. Kate and Jacob changed into their suits the second day we were there and jumped into the chilly waters. They grabbed rafts and floated down the lazy river that wrapped itself around the property. After they'd made the loop, they ran inside to the indoor pool where the wet heat rose up and coated the windows, and Kate ran her finger through the steam to spell out her name, to draw a heart and a smiley face.

I came back from Orange Beach with several story ideas and a good interview I'd done with Lucy Buffett, who owns a restaurant called Lulu's at Homeport Marina in Gulf Shores. Lucy is Jimmy Buffett's sister, and her restaurant is like the physical manifestation of all his songs—bright colors and sand and water and frozen drinks.

A couple of weeks later, I took a weekend trip to Nashville to speak at a networking luncheon and scout out more stories. Paige and Desiree, two women from the company that booked me for the luncheon, took me to dinner and out for drinks at one of those bars decorated to look like a speakeasy, where the bartenders are "mixologists" and the cocktails are $11.

When I traveled and met new people, I realized how quickly the conversation could get to a place I didn't want to be. A person would ask if I had children, or I might mention the kids in conversation. Then the new person would ask who watched my children when I was out of town. What about their dad, they'd ask. He passed away, I would say. I had to learn later to simply say no, a friend watches them, and leave it at that. But I would make the mistake of saying he passed away. It was a fact I didn't yet know how to ignore. Couldn't they see the note pinned to my chest?

And then we would be at the precipice of it.

They would ask how he died, because they could see I was young and they would assume he was young, too.

I wished I were better at shutting it down, stopping it before it got to the edge of the hole, before they were peering into its darkness trying to see what happened.

Sometimes, after a couple of $11 cocktails, I would answer the question. I would shine a light into the hole. See that? At the bottom? There it is. And I would wish immediately that I hadn't told. It would change how someone saw me. It felt like taking a weight out of my suitcase and carrying it on my chest instead, and I had to carry it until I could get back to my hotel room and set it down and put on my pajamas.

Desiree told me about an ex-boyfriend who had called her all the time and wouldn't stop, who'd threatened awful things, until he called one day to say he'd "accidentally" shot himself in the foot. Would she come to the hospital, please?

No matter how hard I tried, I couldn't regain my balance at work. I was simply no longer any good at it. What would I do instead now that my brain was broken? I would wait to get laid off, I thought. I didn't know what the editors wanted other than short summaries and roundups, and maps with pithy little captions about shops and cafés and hipster bars that bragged of making specially shaped ice in perfect spheres from a mold made in Japan. Do you know how difficult it is to give a damn about huge balls of ice and manufactured exclusivity and bars hidden behind velvet curtains?

It was an unfamiliar feeling to be incompetent, to not understand what was required and immediately do it before deadline. I had been the deadline queen. I had been a star employee who didn't disappoint.

I disappointed myself daily.

But there was a day in December when I had ignored work completely (admittedly, I did this on too many days to count).

On this day, I had written what I wanted to write. I wrote about grief. I wrote about pain. It flowed out of me.

The stages of grief do not pass in an orderly fashion or a timely manner. They do not come one after the other. Sometimes they sit on one another and fight for attention like sibling rivals. "Look at me," anger says. "No, no, look at me," denial cries. Depression takes a backseat and only watches the fight because depression always has the upper hand. Depression is along for the ride while you bargain and cry and yell the 'F' word as loud as possible while driving down a quiet street. Depression knows it will be there after the others are put in a corner for time-out.

Thank goodness, I thought, I can still write something.

If I had a say, I'd still be in the shock and denial stage. That stage was excellent. While you know the facts, your brain is like a kindly grandmother who says, "Now, now, wait a minute, let's not do anything crazy yet. Let's pack that information in this pretty box over here. See this one in the corner? You can open it later. For now, put a smile on your face. Here, let's make this easier. Let's put a nice, white haze over everything and put this soft sweater on you so you won't feel any of the big, mean world's hard edges. There you go. Now run along and have a good time with your friends."

I stopped briefly to shut the door to my windowless office, and then I sat back down and typed more. I wrote without pausing until I was finished.

I read a story online about a woman whose insurance company cut her disability benefits for depression because someone found photos of her on Facebook having a "good time." I read the story aloud and commented on the unfairness of it, although it shouldn't be surprising that an insurance company wouldn't actually understand an illness. Kate said, "That's stupid. You look like you're having a good time and you're depressed. My MeMe looks like she's having a good time and she's depressed. I look like I'm having a good time and I'm depressed."

Kate, at nine years old, knows something those idiots at the insurance company must not: Putting a smile on your face is like hanging a Christmas wreath on your front door. It might look like you're celebrating the holidays when really you're only doing what your neighbors expect of you. Inside you might be wishing the damn holiday, with its unreasonable expectations and depressing songs, would pass already.

You might be waiting for things to be normal again.

You put your new knowledge—that normal no longer exists—in a pretty box in the corner where it fits right in under the Christmas tree.

When I was finished, I saved it in my documents folder. I copied it into a note on Facebook and posted it. There were photos of me on Facebook smiling. There weren't photos of me in my pajamas, crying. But look at this. Look at me. Here I am. Here is what I need to say.

It started to feel like this was the only thing I could write. Charles's death was like an illness that had destroyed the parts of me that had been capable and efficient.

One day, in an email, Tina told me that her boss's wife had breast cancer. "See, things could be worse," she wrote.

But didn't she know that, given the choice, I would have chosen cancer? If life worked that way and a higher power said, "You can watch the father of your children shoot himself or you can get breast cancer," I would have taken the hit. I guess I wanted to be the hero, but I had lost my chance to save Charles.

He was dead, and I felt sick.

Maybe writing was the way to get it out of me, to cut it out like a cancer that had invaded my brain.

I resolved to fight fear.

The door from the kitchen to the garage wouldn't stay closed. Jacob pointed it out to me—how the latch wouldn't click into place. I hadn't noticed. As often as I went in and out of that door, I still did it quickly. The knowledge was always there, like a whisper or something in my peripheral vision, that this was where Charles died.

I could know this without allowing it to change my daily routine. I could refuse to let it have power over me. Maybe I was pretending, faking it 'til I made it. It was a door and nothing more, I told myself.

It was a door that refused to stay closed.

There was a story I heard about some of the relatives on my mother's side of the family. They had a child who was struck by a car on the road in front of their house. The house sat on a corner, like mine does, and, after the child died, they had the pier-and-beam house moved to face the side street. They turned the whole damn thing 90 degrees. That way they would no longer have to face the scene of their worst heartbreak. Whether the story was true or simply family legend, a tragic story twisted by multiple retellings, I couldn't tell you.

Was it a good idea for me to park in the garage, to go in and out of the door and walk up and down those steps? If I could, I might have lopped off the garage entirely, knocked it down and replaced it with a butterfly garden.

The truth was, I had replaced some fears (the irrational fear that I might die, too, on August 3 even though August 3 was already past) with new fears. I worried that Charles could watch me. If this were a movie, isn't this where he would be? (Hell, if he was alive, this was where he would be.) Watching over us; coming back to wreck any new romance before ultimately giving his blessing; coming back as a snowman to enchant the children and then, cruelly, subjecting them to saying good-bye again before he melted; coming back via Whoopi Goldberg's psychic power to slide pennies under my door and save me from a sleazy banker?

I imagined him seeing me do all the things I do, good and bad, public and private. Now he knew everything about me, things he didn't know before. Now he'd know I wasn't as great as he thought I was.

After I indulged these thoughts, I scolded myself because they were really all about me. How he might not still think I'm wonderful. Didn't I always need him to think I was wonderful? Wasn't my worst act never allowing him to hate me so that he could move on and away from me? I wanted him to leave me and yet still love me.

No, that was not my worst act.

I resolved to stay behind my lovely castle walls (despite professional advice to do otherwise).

In mid-February, President's Day, Erin and I went to the spa at Ross Bridge Resort. It was like a mini-vacation. I had a hot stone massage, a facial, a shampoo and style, a manicure, and a pedicure. (The check from the IRS had finally come, eight months after I'd filed my amended return, and I'd paid off loans from my mother, my aunt, and those rat bastards at CitiFinancial.)

"What was your favorite part?" Erin asked at the end of the day.

"The massage, hands down." My favorite part of all the treatments was the same thing. During the manicure, they rub your hands. During the pedicure, they rub your feet. During the facial, they rub your shoulders and chest. Clearly, I wanted to be rubbed.

Being touched made me realize how long it had been. Every inch of my skin was soft and touchable, and there was sadness in knowing there was no one to appreciate it. Sometimes my loneliness was heavier than at other times.

While Erin was having one of her treatments, I sat in the dimly lit women's lounge, reading a book. Women in soft robes came and went from one treatment to the next. The place was busy with women using Valentine's Day gift certificates given to them by husbands and boyfriends. The spa was windowless with no clocks. "It's like a casino," Erin said.

You could spend days in there and not know how much time had passed. I could stay in there until this year was over, wandering from one dark treatment room to the next, all of them smelling clean and fresh with a hint of eucalyptus. I could take a break from the real world. In the real world, I felt like I was waiting for something, maybe to be touched again.

It is impossible to be touched when you have built a wall around yourself, one that is quality-made of lovely old stones and covered in ivy, like something outside a French castle. This sort of wall makes your self-made prison look rather inviting and enchanting, but it's all a facade.

In my chick-lit fantasies, I met a sensitive yet manly fire-fighter who understood my trauma. I met an independent-bookshop owner who looked like George Clooney.

In reality, I was closed for business.

"It's fear," Joan, my counselor, said. "You're afraid of commitment, of getting involved."

Maybe, I said.

Maybe I'm afraid someone will shoot himself in front of me, I didn't say.

"Did you meet anyone in Nashville?"

I shook my head no. This concept was foreign to me. Where would I have met someone?

"Did you even notice anyone?"

I thought back to the trip, the dinner at a restaurant in Franklin, the bar in Nashville.

"No. But when we left the bar, one of the girls I was with said, 'Wow, there were some good-looking guys in there.' I hadn't even noticed."

Apparently, my wall was high enough to block the view.

Even as I had wished for Charles to move on, I had remained in the prison I built for myself. I honestly had no idea how to get out of it. I liked it in here. George Clooney was here, and he wasn't going to hurt me, because he was not real.

There were people who thought I would love to meet George, but why would I want to meet the real man—one who dates women far younger than me and would not fall in love with me at first sight? Pretend George was a wonderful screen onto which I could project whatever qualities I wanted.

I told Joan that Spencer had set up Stacey with a friend of his.

"No one ever offers to fix me up with anyone," I said.

"And they won't. And now they'll worry that you're in mourning and they won't want to offend you."

I always thought I was a good wife. I thought I could be really good at loving someone again, given the chance. If I was allowed to openly love the person, if I didn't have to constantly protect myself from the dangers of loving an addict. For now, taking care of myself meant staying where I was, behind my walls. Eventually, I would start making jokes about how I hadn't gotten laid since the Bush administration. "Talk about a recession," I would say. At least I found myself hilarious.

On *30 Rock*, I heard Alec Baldwin's character say to Tina Fey's Liz Lemon, "You are truly the Picasso of Loneliness."

I loved it so much that I wrote it down in my journal.

"Or I am that painting elephant of being awesome," Liz responded.

Dream: White Curtains

You and I are in my bedroom. The windows are open, and a gentle breeze rustles the white linen curtains.

It's not my bedroom in the new house. It's the one in the old house, the small bedroom that I painted pale gray. The bedding, too, is gray and white and covered with butterflies. It is always cool in this room, like the most perfect spring day. Tall bookshelves are across from the bed, and I have labored over putting books and pictures and random objects in just the right place.

This is the dream I have dreaded. You have a gun. It's not a shotgun this time. It's a pistol. You sit on my bed, and next to you is a stranger. I can't see his face. He is nothing but shadows, and he whispers in your ear.

"I'm going to do it," you say. "I'm going to shoot myself."

I know what will happen next. Your blood will be everywhere. It will ruin the white linen hanging at the windows.

"What about all my beautiful things?" I say.

I have said the wrong thing, and so you pull the trigger.

16

Spring—beautiful, amazing, wonderful spring—when it arrived at last, after the longest winter of my life, was a Godsend. Daylight saving time was like my personal crystal meth, an addictive mix of sunshine and mild temperatures, without the rotten teeth. I had the urge to buy yellow bedding and drive a yellow convertible. I did neither, but I did purchase a yellow purse for my birthday. Like a drug, spring wasn't easy to come by. It came and went, mild on a Sunday, snowing two days later on a Tuesday, returning for a brief visit on a Friday.

I felt like I was slowly coming out of hibernation. The kids and I were looking forward to spring break in mid-March. The Emorys were taking us to Disney World. On the last day of February, a Sunday, when there was finally a hint of spring in the air and clear skies, Kate and I went to the park at her school. We walked on the nature trail that goes down the hill past the park and twists around.

"How come when parents get divorced, the dad has to pay money?" Kate asked as we walked back up the hill to the park. I can't remember what prompted this query.

I explained how it costs money to raise children, to pay for a home for them and the bills that go with that, and that the parent who doesn't live there still has to contribute to that.

"Oh. Why did you and Dad get divorced?" Before I could answer, she went on. "Oh, I know. Because he was a liar."

I had said that aloud one night not long before, when I was angry about one of the kids lying to me. I shouldn't have said it. Kate had said, "I didn't eat that piece of cookie dough, Mom. I wasn't lying." Had I really yelled at her about cookie dough? Sadly, yes.

But it's never really about the cookie dough.

"Daddy lied because he was addicted to drugs," I said. We stopped at the top of the hill. "That is what addicts do. They don't even know it's wrong sometimes because they're so focused on getting whatever it is they're addicted to.

"He wasn't a bad person. He was just sick. You understand that, right?"

She said that she did and she wanted to play on the swings for a little bit. She was ready to move on.

I watched her run ahead of me into the fenced-in playground. I hoped it was better if I explained that drugs make people do bad things.

He was not a bad person, I would tell them. I would tell myself.

Sometimes I was so angry when Kate misbehaved that I would go in my room and shut the door and curse. "She's just like you, you asshole," I'd say. Onto a dead man, I could lay the blame for that moment of lying or destruction or disrespect. But, hell, for all I knew, she could have been acting like me when she snuck the last cut-and-bake pieces of cookie dough, sat in her room eating the gooey, sugary squares and licking the dough off her fingers, and refused to admit it.

I sat at one of the tables and watched Kate run around with a couple of younger children. They decided to play hide-and-seek, and Kate stood at a corner of the fence and hid her face behind her hands and counted to 20. I put my hand up to my left cheek and held it there while I watched her.

That morning, I'd baked biscuits and scrambled eggs and fried bacon. I put a plate with paper towels on top of a burner I wasn't using and turned on the burner next to it to heat up the skillet for the bacon. After a couple of minutes, as I stood over the stove scrambling the eggs, I heard a loud pop, and the plate cracked in two and the paper towels burst into flames.

I started blowing on the paper towels to put the fire out. I turned off the burner and used an oven mitt to move the shattered pieces of the plate. The left side of my face felt weird, sort of tingly, and the sensation traveled from my ear to my jaw. From the loud noise? I probably busted a blood vessel from the stress.

It was a continual battle to get my head on straight. What was I thinking? I finished scrambling the eggs. I pulled another plate from the cabinet and set it on the counter next to the sink rather than on the stove. Then I put paper towels on it for the bacon. Once I'd fixed the kids' plates and carried them to the table, I stood in the kitchen and breathed in and out and tried to calm myself.

This is how it always went. You have to finish what you are doing before you can take a second to breathe, to slow your pounding heart.

Hours later, my cheek still felt odd, as if I were feeling the last tingling sensation of blood rushing back into a limb that had fallen asleep. My chest still felt tight. Loud, unexpected noises unsettled me. One day in counseling, Joan said, "What will happen when you hear the sound of a gunshot again?"

I didn't know. I was going to do my best to avoid that situation. In my memories of that night when Charles died, the sound of the shotgun was the thing I could not recall. I would have been unable to describe it if someone had asked me. I could say it was loud, but this felt like a fact I had read somewhere and not experienced. I could only see the effects of the explosive sound. Maybe what I saw overwhelmed my senses and whatever I heard got lost in the sight of something unreal and incomprehensible.

One day I might hear it again and recognize it. I did know that the sound I heard was nothing like the fake gunfire you hear on television.

"Mom! Come play with us!"

I focused my gaze and saw Kate waving me over to the play equipment. The two little Indian boys she was playing with were watching me, waiting for my answer. The boys' mom was Jacob's algebra teacher, Mrs. Uswatte. Their dad stood nearby watching. Another boy and girl had arrived at the playground with their dad.

"Come on! You can be *It!*" Kate called from her perch atop the slide.

"OK," I said. I covered my eyes and bent my head toward the tabletop and started counting.

Friday night, Erin, Stacey and I went to a Yoga Nidra class at a yoga and Pilates studio in downtown Homewood. Yoga Nidra is a form of meditation or yogic sleep in which you lie in savasana (corpse pose) for 45 minutes. You relax into a subconscious state, but you never fall asleep (if you can help it).

Savasana was my favorite yoga pose. At the end of a long yoga session, this pose was the reward. Five minutes of lying on your back, sinking into the floor, breathing in and out. I still hadn't done yoga since the day Charles died, but I was eager to try anything that might calm my mind or soothe my battered spirit.

I had written a list in my journal.

I'm so afraid of a million things:

That I will never be good at my job again.

That I will be alone forever.

That when Kate and Jacob have both gone to college that my life will close in on me, becoming so small that I won't be able to move.

That I will be at Southern Living, *struggling every day until the day I get laid off, and then I will be unable to find a job. Talent doesn't matter. I have no skills. I can't think. I can't focus. I am broken.*

That the wall I've put up around me will crush me.

That August 3 will come again, and that winter must follow it, bringing with it cold and darkness once more. I am afraid of this, and it's months and months away.

That I will cry a million tears, and that some of them are for Charles, but most of them are for me.

In the dimly lit studio, we sat down on yoga mats lined up in rows. There were about a dozen people in the class. We began by moving through several yoga poses before lying down in savasana and closing our eyes. The instructor provided bolster pillows to put beneath our knees as we lay on our backs. We also had blankets. Some people even brought pillows.

"You will repeat to yourself your statement of purpose," the instructor told us. We were to come up with a positive goal of some kind, something to plant in the rich soil of our subconscious so that this thought could become reality.

What did I want to plant? What goal did I have for myself? I wanted answers. I wanted peace. I wanted to find a way out. But how to do that? I didn't want to say to myself something vague and slippery and too big to wrap my head around.

"I want to write this down," I thought. "I will write my story."

The instructor told us to repeat this statement of purpose to ourselves three times. Then she led us through a full body scan, like taking a tour of our own bodies. As she named each body part, we were to focus on it. She went up the body, from the foot to the head and then back down again.

The room was chilly. I should have worn socks. The instructor told us to focus on our breathing. In and out. As it passed through the nostrils. A man in the corner was already lightly snoring. That man had paid $20 for a nap.

In the next segment, she asked us to call up certain sensations and emotions.

"Imagine you are cold." My feet were already cold.

"Imagine you are hot." I thought of hot sand at the beach, the yellow sun blazing down.

"Recall a moment of intense joy."

Kate, right after she was born. After she'd been cleaned off and swaddled in a blanket, she was carried over to me. Everyone left the room, and I held her. For at least five minutes, it was only the two of us, me and my girl.

"Recall a moment of intense sorrow." Just one?

The instructor began taking us through rapid visualization. In her soothing monotone, she read from a list of items that we were to picture before quickly moving onto the next.

"White rose, waterfall, the symbol for Om, river, cross, white rose..."

For a flash, I landed on an image I did not want—the image of Charles in the garage that would always be with me. I used all my mental strength to shove it away, to return to the list. White rose, waterfall, the symbol for Om.

Eventually, the instructor asked us to repeat our statement of purpose.

It felt like 15 minutes had passed, but, as the instructor led us through light stretching, I discovered that 45 minutes had passed. Somewhere in there, amidst the white roses and the sound of the waterfall, I'd managed to lose myself for a little while.

"What did you think?" Erin asked as we rolled up the yoga mats and folded the blankets.

"It was amazing. I can't believe how the time went by so quickly. I feel so relaxed. I had a hard time with the visualization at first," I said. A flash of an image that would not disappear.

I said, "It was more like white rose, cross, ocean, George Clooney."

"White rose, ocean, white wine," Erin chimed in.

"Yes, wine," Stacey said. "Let's have some."

Four days later, I turned 37. I was still in my existential waiting room, waiting for my "real life" to begin. I had to get through all this mess to get to it. What this real life would entail, I wasn't quite sure. Did it include love from a man who wouldn't hurt me? Did it include liking my job again? Would it include feeling settled again, not having to constantly fight off depression and horrible memories? Would it include sunlight, something warm and yellow?

When you're going through a bad patch, it feels as if it's never going to end. Knowing that it will—that the truest thing is the phrase "This too shall pass"—only helps a little.

On Sunday, Rose Darby had thrown a party for me at her house, and we watched the Academy Awards. Rose Darby and her husband, Drew, had high-definition, and it made me feel better to see the flyaways in the glamorous up-dos, and the wrinkles that couldn't be hidden by makeup. It helped to watch George Clooney and his silly facial expressions as he reacted to jokes made at his expense. It helped to see that his girlfriend of the moment wasn't flawless and could have used better, smoother undergarments under her shiny red dress. Everyone contributed money to a small, tin bank that had a retro-style photo of two women on it and the phrase: "I'm saving up for a rich man."

When I opened it, someone said, "That's babysitting money. So you can get out again."

When I woke up the morning after my birthday, I saw that I had two missed calls from the night before. Lollie had called to say, "Happy Birthday." The other call came after 10 p.m. and was from my dad. He'd left a message on my voice mail. When I got to work, I had a message from him there, too.

I waited until that evening to call him back. We hadn't spoken since August 6. When he answered, he said he was at dinner with colleagues (he was at a conference somewhere) and asked if he could call me back in a bit. Sure, I said. That's fine.

By 9:15, I was already in bed, Kate asleep beside me, but I sat up and opened my laptop to go online and stay awake. The actor Corey Haim had died that day, and people were saying it was a drug overdose. He was 38 and had spent his life sobering up and relapsing, like Charles. The comments under the story on People.com were a mix of sympathetic and cruel. Some people said drug addicts get what they deserve. Those people couldn't possibly understand the death grip that drugs and alcohol could have on a person. Wouldn't Charles have quit if he could?

There was another story on Marie Osmond. Her son had committed suicide a few days earlier, and the story said that Marie had gone ahead and performed her Las Vegas show with her brother Donny the night before. The article told of her tearfulness at moments.

"Isn't she supposed to be grieving?" one of the comments read.

Why are there so many awful people in the world? I thought. And they all post anonymous comments online. Everyone thinks they know how they would react to a tragedy or a death or a shocking event. These folks on the Internet think they know everything, when they actually don't have a clue.

I worried about this a lot, the idea of reacting properly to things.

One weekend not long after that, while I was cleaning the house, I listened to NPR and heard a rerun of a Fresh Air interview with Dick Wolf, the creator of *Law & Order*, the longest-running show on television. The show's cancellation after nearly 20 years had recently been announced.

I was in my bathroom scrubbing the toilet. I didn't clean that often. I could blame it on Charles, but I never liked cleaning the bathrooms before.

Dick Wolf spoke of his research into crime, when he accompanied police officers to crime scenes. He told Terry Gross about the blood ("Yeah, it's a lot bloodier than we show you on television.... It's surprising how much blood there is in a human body. It's much worse than we've ever shown.") and how most people confronted by someone with a gun will call that person's bluff.

"Most cops will tell you that the most common thing is never ask to be shot. Because [in] a lot of drunken altercations and a lot of street confrontations, somebody pulls a gun and somebody else says, 'Oh yeah, you're so tough. Go ahead and shoot.'"

I stopped what I was doing and kneeled down on the cold tile floor next to the toilet while I listened.

Was this true, that what I had done was not so unusual?

"In a lot of crime movies and TV shows... the hero is wise enough to know that the person doesn't have the courage to do it," Terry Gross said.

Dick Wolf said, "One homicide detective told me that it is the single most common line in homicides. 'Go ahead and shoot.'"

I stayed awake to answer my dad's phone call that night. He wished me a happy birthday. He told me about the conference he was attending. He asked how I was, how the kids were doing. Neither of us mentioned the months of silence that had passed since August 6.

Spring break arrived, and the kids and I went to Disney World with Roger and Frances. We spent a week going from park to park. We started on Monday at the Magic Kingdom. We'd come with them three years earlier with Charles, too, so his memory followed us around. At Hollywood Studios, when we passed the giant sets painted to look like New York and San Francisco, I remembered standing in front of the San Francisco streetscape for a photograph. Charles, Kate, and I posed while Frances snapped the shot. It was vivid in my mind—Charles next to me, my purse heavy on my shoulder—but I wondered if the memory was so vivid because it had been captured on film.

You start to wonder what is true and what is only a mental image of a photograph placed in an album you have looked at often, searching for clues.

On our last day, Kate decided she wanted to ride Expedition Everest, the biggest coaster at Animal Kingdom. Jacob and I had ridden twice, me screaming and Jacob planning different poses for the photo taken mid-ride. His best was the photo of him blowing a huge bubble before we plunged down the 80-foot drop.

"Just think, you can do anything for two minutes," I told Kate. "So even if it's scary, it's over so fast." I squeezed her hand. "Do what I do: Scream really loudly."

With Kate along for the ride, I screamed less. I forgot to focus on my own fear and worried about her instead.

It occurred to me, not for the first time, that were it not for Kate and Jacob, I would still be in the hole. I might never have found the strength to pull myself out again and again. Without them, I never could have stayed on this ride.

Not long after spring break, Jacob came out of his room and said, "Mom, I want to sell my Xbox. And I want to take violin lessons."

For months it seemed like Jacob had been hiding in his room. Now, at last, he was ready to come out. Like me, he was ready to move again. I joked to anyone who would listen that the ghost of an orchestra member had possessed my son.

17

Somewhere in the middle of the nearly 2-mile-long Golden Gate Bridge, it came to me that today would have been my 14th wedding anniversary. It was June 20, or was it the 22nd? (Even as I write this, I am unclear on the date. Apparently, this will forever be a curb that I trip over on my journeys into the past.)

But, on this day in San Francisco—Tuesday, June 22, 2010—I knew with certainty the date. I was alone, driving north toward Marin County, where Lollie now lived, when it hit me. I'd dropped her off at work at the VA hospital, a government facility that perches on top of a piece of property with a million-dollar view. Hell, it was probably a $20-million view, what with real-estate values in the area. The fog had rolled in, so I couldn't see the bridge. After I'd dropped her off, I drove back through the Presidio and through Sea Cliff, the exclusive neighborhood perched on the edge of the Pacific. On the way to the hospital, Lollie had shown me the house Robin Williams once lived in. She told me about the time she met him while standing in the concession line at a movie theater and how he'd teased her about her Southern accent.

I'd flown out the day before for a weeklong vacation, a getaway from Birmingham and its summer memories. Here the weather was chilly and foggy. I'd packed scarves and sweaters and a jacket. In my daily jaunts around the city over the next week, I saw numerous people, tourists who thought they were on a summer vacation and found themselves in the midst of winter, shivering in shorts and fleece jackets with "SF" embroidered on them, a souvenir forced upon them by the temperature.

The night before, when Lollie had driven me across the bridge the first time, a lane of traffic had been closed off, and we saw police officers along the walkway looking over the edge.

"Oh, of course, some dumbass—" Lollie stopped.

"Jumped?" I finished for her.

Later, sitting on Lollie's bed with my computer in my lap, I'd looked up information about the bridge online. "More people die by suicide at the Golden Gate Bridge than any other site in the world," I read out loud.

"Why would you look that up?" Lollie said.

"Oh, I was looking up information about sightseeing, and it's on here," I said, embarrassed, ashamed of my curiosity about something so morbid.

I read about how some people wanted to put up a suicide barrier. I found information about the building of the bridge. I read a poem written by the bridge's chief engineer Joseph Strauss upon its completion in 1937. The fourth and fifth stanzas read:

The passing world may never know
The epic of my grim travail;
It matters no, nor friend or foe-
My place to serve and none to fail.

My being cradled in despair,
Now grown so wondrous fair and strong,
And glorified beyond compare,
Rebukes the error and the wrong.

On this morning, I made my way north toward San Rafael, where Lollie rented the ground floor in the home of her friend Gina. As I drove through the rainbow tunnel, I thought about how this would have been our 14th anniversary, if only... if only what? I was still trying to figure out what could have been done to prevent this sorry mess. As summer had approached, my sense of foreboding about another anniversary—that of Charles's suicide—had increased. During the last days of spring, I'd planned as many trips as possible to get me out of Birmingham. Maybe I thought I could pack a suitcase without also packing in the memories of last August 3 or the months that led up to it.

August 3 came along, of course, like excess baggage for which I should have been charged an extra fee.

Earlier in the month, I'd traveled to Memphis for work, where I took a running tour with a man who had ruined his marriage and career with addiction. After he'd torn his life down, he started rebuilding it. He did this by running. I had tried this, too, by signing up for a couch-to-5k program with Rose Darby. We'd slowly built up to running 4 miles and completed our first 5k in May. I'd hoped to find some answer out on the road, my feet hitting the pavement steadily, but I'd slacked off on my daily runs. This man had found the epiphany through running that I had not. He ran marathons. He told sweating tourists facts about the hotel where Martin Luther King Jr. was killed, about Sun Records, about Beale Street. He didn't tell them the story he told me, of course. I told him my story, too. He said, "My brother committed suicide." We stood, sweaty and tired, outside the hotel where I was staying, as we shared these pieces of ourselves. We people who have suffered, somehow we recognize it in each other, I think. We know when it's safe to tell our tales.

On the flight to San Francisco, I'd sat next to a man who engaged me in conversation. He was from Indiana, and I told him that's where my dad lived, that I'd spent summers there. He asked about where I lived now, what I did for a living, what was taking me to San Francisco. "Who watches your kids when you travel?" He told me he was in the restaurant business, a pastor, a youth-group leader.

I couldn't honestly re-create the path the conversation took so that we came to the place where my ex-husband was dead by his own hand. This man told me about a dear friend of his, a former neighbor, who had a son who committed suicide. He said, "But he actually saw it happen."

I sucked in my breath. On the exhale, I said, "That's what happened to me." I had yet to meet someone like me, but here was a degree of separation between me and a man who might understand me.

"I'm so sorry," this man in the window seat said to me. We talked until we began our approach into San Francisco International Airport, the reading lights dimly shining on us, the sky beyond the windows dark and starlit. "May I pray with you?" he asked me, and I said yes. I never turned down prayers. More than a year later, the man would send me a message on a social networking site, having found me via Google.

"I don't know if you remember me or not. I sat next to you on the flight to San Francisco last year. I apologize for not contacting you sooner, but I misplaced your email address and had trouble finding you with your job change. I hope this gets through to you. How are you and the kids getting along? I have thought of you often and prayed that God would make himself real to you, guide and direct your paths. Just wanted to reconnect and see how you are doing."

Life seemed to put people in my path who understood the damage of suicide and drug addiction. Then again, maybe that's not so serendipitous; there are so damn many of us out there.

Kate and Jacob were in Louisiana for eight weeks. They would spend the bulk of the time with the Emorys, with a few weekend trips to see my mom in Natchitoches. While they were in Shreveport, Jacob was taking violin lessons. He'd been serious about selling his Xbox. He said he was bored with all his games. I went online and looked up violin instructors and, after talking to Frances about the schedule and the logistics of renting an instrument, signed him up for lessons. In early May, I'd taken him to GameStop, where he got $150 for the Xbox. In the grocery store next door to GameStop, he bought $8 worth of gum and then tucked the rest of the money away.

In the news, there were daily updates on the oil spill off the coast of Louisiana. It was getting worse every day, this story of something thick and black spreading out to suffocate life and livelihoods. The news was full, too, of mine explosions and biblical-level flooding in Tennessee and Georgia, of earthquakes. Of Lindsay Lohan in court yet again, ordered to wear an alcohol-monitoring bracelet on her ankle. Would the girl never learn? I wanted to grab her pale, freckled arms and shake her as I vented my righteous anger upon her. "Can't you see what you are doing? Do you want to die?"

I could have taken from this that life was fragile and oh-so-temporary, but mostly I thought of the profound words of Fiona Apple, who once said, "This world is bullshit." She meant the world of fame and MTV; however, I liked to use the quote when discussing the planet as a whole.

But then I would picture my teenage son playing the violin, dragging a bow across the strings in an effort to put something different and new into his world, and I would think maybe the world wasn't completely doomed.

Before we all left town, I'd finally had the back door replaced. Ten months after the break-in, I'd finally gotten rid of the reminder that someone had entered our house through the use of force, cracking the door frame and breaking off the dead-bolt. Gone was the reminder that that someone could have been Charles.

Back at Lollie's house, I showered and then took my time drying my hair and getting dressed. I wasn't looking forward to wandering around on my own all day. Lollie had to work all week; she was taking the next week off when her mother would visit. I traveled so much for work that maybe I thought I would be fine on my own, but touring a beautiful city alone is a sure-fire way to feel lonelier than you've ever felt before. This trip suddenly felt like a sad reminder of how alone I was.

On the way back to the highway, I took a wrong turn and got lost. I tried not to cry, but the tears slipped out, and I was pissed at myself. I turned around and found the highway entrance pretty quickly. I don't even know how I missed it the first time because it was so obvious. I followed the winding highway back toward the tunnel and then onto the Golden

Gate Bridge to head back into the city. I made sure I was in the correct lane for the FasTrak toll payment. Lollie had an electronic tag that I needed to remember to place on the dash when I was southbound.

People were walking along the bridge taking photographs. I thought of how I was going to spend the week taking photos of sights but never appearing in the photos, unless I asked strangers if they would please snap a shot of me. Lonely Woman on the Bridge. Lonely Woman at the Wharf. Lonely Woman at the top of a crooked street. I thought for the first time that I could go home. I could call the airline and change my ticket, and no one, other than Lollie, would have to know. I wouldn't want my friends to know that my trip had been a bust, that I'd snuck home like a child who'd gone to summer camp and been struck by acute homesickness.

The trip was supposed to be reinvigorating. In a novel or a movie, here's what was supposed to happen: Lollie wanted to fix me up with a friend of hers from work, one of the neurosurgery residents. She'd told me his name, so, of course, I Googled him, and he was seriously cute. ("Last name, please," Rose Darby said when I told her about my potential date.) So, in fiction—and in Rose Darby's supportive daydreams—we would meet and fall in love immediately, and the kids and I would move to California to live happily ever after. My own fantasy involved wandering into a quirky independent bookshop where I would engage in witty and telling banter with the owner as we stood amidst shelves spilling over with hardback books, an orange kitty asleep beneath the checkout counter. The owner would say, "I'm moving to Spain, and I need someone to run this place...and live in the apartment upstairs, rent-free...and I know you are the person to do that."

At the very least, my trip to San Francisco was supposed to be a fun adventure and a much-needed respite from a year of grieving and trauma recovery. My friends wanted that for me. I would feel sad having to tell them how I flew home after two days and spent the rest of the week on my sofa watching daytime television.

But I had been at the edge of these things many times before, and I knew well how to talk myself away from it. It was always about moving. Every house and doghouse in America seemed to have that sign from WWII, the British poster that read "Keep Calm and Carry On." While bombs were going off around them, people were encouraged to keep a stiff upper lip, remain calm, and go about their business. It was the most ridiculous response, and yet, the best response. The poster image came in every color and was plastered on dishtowels and rugs and tissue holders.

I preferred the bright-yellow traffic sign posted at the entrance to Brookwood Mall down the street from *Southern Living*'s offices on Lakeshore Drive—"Keep moving." I believed in the absolute beauty and simplicity of that directive. Keep moving. I wanted to act like a teenage hooligan and steal that sign and hang it above my front door.

Instead of pulling over to the side of the road somewhere and crying and calling the airline, I made my way farther into the city and parked in a garage near Pier 37 at Fisherman's Wharf. I wandered around awhile, going in and out of shops, before I bought a big, doughy pretzel covered with salt and a Diet Coke and carried my snack over to a bench near the end of the pier. I sat down and buttoned my jacket and wound my scarf around my neck and watched people in fleece jackets take photographs of one another with Alcatraz in the distance behind them.

I thought about offering to take photos of some of the couples so they could have pictures together, but I didn't.

Eventually, I stood up and tossed my napkin and paper cup into a trash can. I went into some more shops, but I hate shopping. I was only wasting time. I stood in front of the window of a shop selling crepes and watched a man prepare the thin pancakes and fill them with cream and fruit. I went inside and bought a vanilla latte and then wandered down to the next pier where I sat on yet another bench.

I took out my cell phone and called Mom at work. I told her I was wandering around on my own.

"Where's Lollie?"

"At work. She has to work all week," I said.

"What?"

I told her I'd already cried a little bit about my never-ending aloneness, about how today was my stupid wedding anniversary.

"What are you doing this week? How about you come out here?" I said. I laughed because clearly this was an absurd question. "Wouldn't it be great if we were the kind of people who could take off on a trip on a moment's notice?"

While we talked, Mom went online and typed in travel information. Flying out of AEX in Alexandria, Louisiana. Flying into SFO in San Francisco. We played with the idea of her actually coming out here; an invisible toy to make me happy while we bounced it between us and pretended it was real.

She typed in the departure date and the return date, and waited for the results to come up on the screen.

"If you have half the ticket price, I have half," I told her.

And suddenly it was real—this idea that my mom might come out here and save the day.

As we talked, I had gotten up from the bench and started walking down the street. I'd tossed out my latte cup. I turned left and made my way up the hill.

"I'm going to call you right back," Mom said, and we hung up.

As I walked up Leavenworth Street, the fog dissipated and the sun shone. I took off my jacket and knotted the arms around my waist, the strenuous walk making it unnecessary for a bit. By the time Mom called me back, I was at the bottom of the crooked block of Lombard Street. People were crowded on each corner snapping photos.

I heard one tourist telling a story about how the parents who lived on the street in the 1920s were concerned about the speed of traffic coming down the street, too steep for some cars to drive up.

They wanted their children to be safe in front of the homes, so they had stone flowerbeds put in to create an angular path of eight hairpin turns. While they succeeded in decreasing the speed of traffic, they exponentially increased the flow and turned it into a major tourist destination.

It was amazing the things people would do to make themselves feel safe and then find that those protective measures made them more vulnerable than ever.

Later, I looked up Lombard Street online. I found out that Jimmy Stewart's character in *Vertigo* lived on the 900 block of Lombard, that Lombard was part of the video game *Grand Theft Auto: San Andreas*, that it was the setting for parts of car-chase scenes in *What's Up, Doc?* and *Magnum Force*. That it was part of a comedy album from the 1960s. That it's not the "crookedest" street in the world; it's not even the "crookedest" street in San Francisco.

I found all that, but I found no mention of worried parents protecting their children.

When Mom called back, she said she'd called her boss about taking days off and he'd said, "Of course you should go." She'd made calls to arrange for Ted to stay with his parents while she was gone.

Knowing that Mom was coming boosted my mood greatly. I forgot about being alone and sad among hundreds of tourists standing in groups. The sun was shining. The fog would roll in again the next day, but it didn't matter. By 2:00 the next afternoon, my mom would be there, stepping off the curb outside the baggage claim area at SFO. "Like a ball of fire," Todd had said of her nearly a year earlier. Here she was again.

That Friday, Mom and I took a bus tour of San Francisco followed by a tour of Alcatraz. The bus driver took us to Golden Gate Bridge and parked while everyone shuffled off the bus and walked onto the bridge. Mom and I took photos of one another. Before we climbed back on the bus, a newlywed couple took a photo of us together, with the bridge in the background, and then I returned the favor and took a photo of them.

We drove to the Haight-Ashbury District. The driver let us off, and some people ran up the block, to where Jerry Garcia had been living when he died, to snap photos of the flowers and candles set up on the sidewalk. "I'm not supposed to stop, so if I suddenly drive off, don't worry. I'll swing back around to pick you up," he said. He drove us by the "painted ladies," and, again, he stopped so everyone could get out and take photos. "I'll go around the block if the police show up," he said.

When he dropped us off at the dock where we would board the boat to cross over to Alcatraz, Mom slipped him a tip as we got off the bus. I said, "Thanks. You were badass." And he barked out a surprised laugh.

At Alcatraz, we took the audio tour and listened through individual headsets as a narrator and a few of the former inmates told the story of the island fortress. One cellblock had windows facing the city's shoreline. The narrator said this was the best cellblock because of the natural light shining in through the skylights and windows.

The narrator said the sounds of the city would travel across the water, and a former inmate said that on New Year's Eve, the faint sounds of people laughing, of music, of celebratory sounds could be heard coming from the yacht club. The sound of real life, of what they were denied while being punished for their crimes, drifted in on the wind. I imagined what it must have been like to sit in a cold, concrete cell and hear that joy and revelry. In a way, that's what this year had been like. I was moving, but I was never fully a part of whatever was going on around me. I could hear the sounds of it from the place I had imprisoned myself.

I was claustrophobic in my cell. I was ready to start living in the moment again, to be present instead of always looking for answers to the past.

That day of the trip was my favorite day. We had a driver, so I didn't have the stress of driving us up and down those insanely steep inclines. We didn't have to plan out where we were going and what we would see. We took photos of each other making peace signs at the corner of Haight and Ashbury; in cells at Alcatraz; and pretending to blow away standing outside Alcatraz (apparently, the unrelenting wind made upkeep of anything on the island untenable).

After Alcatraz, we wandered down to a bar called Buena Vista and drank an Irish coffee. We did this as part of our Tourist Clichés of San Francisco Tour. Some people might look down on us for doing all the tourist things, for not seeking out anything off the beaten path, but screw them. I had veered off the beaten path enough for one year. I wanted to be guided through the expected, the typical, the tried and true. After we finished our Irish coffees, John the bartender recommended a drink called a Chip Shot. We liked it so much we each had another.

When Lollie got off work, she wanted to take us to dinner at an upscale French restaurant—tiny tables covered in white tablecloths, a daunting wine list. We convinced her that we should go back to her house and order pizza. So we headed north and, back at the house, changed into our pajama pants and fuzzy socks. We curled up on the sofa. Lollie fixed me a delicious, fizzy cocktail, and we watched a funny movie.

It was a wonderful day.

18

No matter how many times we corrected her, when Kate wanted me to rewind a show on the DVR, she would say, "Fast-forward it back." All summer I'd been avoiding my own urge to "fast-forward it back." I had been apprehensive of the hot days that had brought terror and violence into my house. I knew that I would end up going back.

I had filled this summer with travel to Memphis, to San Francisco, and to Cincinnati to visit Tina. We sat in Great American Ball Park, wore red, and drank and danced and cheered on the Reds. We imitated Oprah, fake-introducing people ("The cast of Gleeeeee!") and giving out prizes ("Everyone gets a new caaaaaaarrrrrr!"). Since 1990, we have always been blissfully obnoxious in the presence of one another.

In July, I drove to New Orleans and met up with Tina, who flew in, and Audrey, who drove in from Shreveport. We hung out in the tiny courtyard pool of a French Quarter hotel and drank cocktails. We met up with another high-school friend, Margaret, and she took us to a Garden District restaurant where we ate and drank decadently. We grimaced and cheered as Audrey got her nipples pierced at a tattoo parlor on Magazine Street. Tina accompanied Audrey to the back, and Margaret and I sat in the waiting room, me clutching my breasts in sympathetic pain.

If I had remained as still as possible after August 3, waiting at least a year to make any major decisions, Audrey had done the opposite in this interim between marriage and divorce. She'd gotten a few tattoos. She'd indulged her wild side. Honestly, she was more herself that she had ever been in the decade and a half of her marriage, during which she joined the Junior League and bought a house in a gated community and struggled to keep up with the Joneses. Now she'd said, loudly, "Fuck the Joneses."

When our girls' weekend was over, we said good-bye to Audrey at the hotel, and I drove Tina to the airport. Not long after, as I headed out of Louisiana, I got a text from Tina: *We've been so spoiled this summer, seeing each other twice! I cried when I walked into the airport. I miss you already.*

The hardest journeys are the ones back to reality.

As the anniversary of each sign I had ignored came and went, I went over them in my mind.
The date in March 2009 when Charles's behavior had truly grown out of control. I had returned from a weekend trip to Nashville, the one when I went out to dinner with my high-school boyfriend, and Charles had screamed at me in the kitchen, had followed me down to my car and stood behind it so I couldn't leave.

AMY BICKERS

The date in May when I told Charles that his time was up. He'd been back in Birmingham six months, living rent-free.

The date in May when I was out of town on a scouting trip to New Orleans and woke up that Sunday to a voice mail from a friend of Charles's, letting me know Charles had been arrested for driving under the influence. Kate had been spending the night at a friend's house, and Jacob was home alone.

Charles's presence in Birmingham was not going to be helpful to me. It wasn't going to make things easier for me to travel for work. It wasn't going to lighten any financial burdens. He had no savings after six months, and now he had to pay an attorney and fines.

The most frightening date, the one that should have opened my eyes to what was possible, happened in early June when I returned to Birmingham from taking the kids to Shreveport. I'd driven all day, and when I came in I found Charles asleep on the sofa. I went to my room, and Charles, having woken up, followed me as I dropped my luggage and slipped off my shoes, my eyes resting on the bed and registering the rumpled sheets. Charles had been sleeping there while I was gone.

"I was going to change the sheets, but I fell asleep," he said. His eyes were cloudy and red and unfocused.

"Shocking," I said.

In an instant, he was yelling at me, his red face so close to mine that I could smell the alcohol on his breath, see the broken capillaries on his nose.

"Nothing is ever good enough for you!" He towered over me. He was only 6 inches taller than me, but he seemed 6-feet tall. Or did I just feel small? "I'm so sick of this shit."

I pushed my way past him and over to the bed.

"Can you just get out of here? I'm tired and I want to go to bed. You said you'd change the sheets. I didn't even ask you to, so let's drop it."

"Fuck this!" He grasped the side of my door with his right hand and held it steady while he slammed his fist into it, again and again, until the weak plywood gave way beneath his unrelenting punches.

"Stop, stop, stop!" I screamed, my voice cracking from the intensity with which I expelled this cry.

He finally did, his rage released. Then he tried to make a joke, to laugh this violent episode off.

"I'm sorry," he said, when I did not respond.

"I'm moving out of here in two weeks," I said, crying now. "And now I'm going to have to pay for a new door. You've done this at every house we've ever lived in. I'm so sick of it!"

He'd punched a hole in the wall of the hallway in a duplex we lived in when Jacob was four and Kate was just born. He'd slammed his fist into a kitchen cabinet, leaving a starburst in the honey-colored wood, in a rental house we lived in after the duplex. In the house we'd bought in Hoover when we first moved to Alabama, he had left undamaged the walls and doors. But one night, when he was out late drinking and had come home belligerent, I'd told him to sleep downstairs and I'd gone into my room and locked the door, only to hear him with a screwdriver removing the door handle. "This is my bedroom, too. You can't lock me out." The door handle never went back together quite right after that. It was always too loose.

When Charles punched the kitchen cabinet or a hole in the drywall or a splintered hole in my bedroom door, it seemed clear to me that he did these things as an alternative to hitting me. It felt like this was something we both understood—and also that shoving me or crushing my hand in his or standing over me while I cowered on the floor were all substitutes as well.

And with this understanding, we both accepted the lie that Charles told throughout our lives together. "I would never hurt you."

We both accepted the lie that *I* told throughout our lives together. "It's no big deal."

But, looking back, I wonder if all that violence wasn't directed at me. There had been a day a year earlier when he had cornered me in my bathroom. This was during a time when he briefly lived in Shreveport and he was visiting the kids for the weekend. I was going to Atlanta with Stacey for the day. I don't even remember why he was upset with me. Because I was leaving? Because when he came to visit the kids, he expected me to be there, too? He stood in the doorway of my bathroom and wouldn't let me out. Then he started slamming his head into the door frame repeatedly until an angry red welt appeared on his forehead.

Was he always trying to destroy himself? Was hurting himself a substitute for hurting me? Or was he trying to reveal his pain, make what he carried inside manifest so I could see it? I often thought that he wanted to destroy me when he died, but maybe he was only trying to show me.

Did he know he would die after he showed me all his pain, after he ripped himself open and spilled his blood and sent his tortured soul into the night?

Even now, I shrink back from the drama of this, the hyperbole. Oh wounded soul, oh spilled blood, oh bullshit, bullshit.

Asshole addict with a gun blows his brains out. It ain't poetry. It's just a fact.

After he stopped hitting the door and became remorseful, I ran to the kitchen, grabbing my purse off the counter, before running to the stairs to go down to the garage. He followed me. He shoved himself past me on the stairs and blocked my path at the bottom. In my haste, I hadn't put shoes on. I had on socks, and I lost my footing and fell into a seated position on the second to last step. He towered over me, and I thought, "This is what it's like to be afraid, to be trapped."

He refused to let me up, to let me go to my car. He veered back and forth between yelling at me and begging for forgiveness, for a chance to talk to me, to explain himself.

I was so tired. I'd been driving for eight hours. Before that, the kids and I had flown in from a trip we'd taken to Kentucky for the magazine. This day had been so long. I wanted to go to bed. That's all I wanted. I wanted this night to end.

I finally relented. I was defeated.

"OK, I'll come upstairs."

Back in my room, I cried. "I want to go to bed. I'm so tired. Please leave me alone."

He wouldn't, of course. He promised to replace the door.

"I'll take it down now. I can put it in the basement," he said. He ignored my protestations that the door could stay up until the next day. He went to the kitchen and got a screwdriver and used the end to loosen the door from the hinges. He leaned the door against the wall in the hallway.

I crawled into my bed, still wearing the clothes I'd traveled in. "Please, go to bed. I'm tired. We can talk about this tomorrow," I said.

"No, I want to sit here next to you. I'm so sorry. You know that, right? I'm going to wait until you go to sleep," he said. He sat down on a yellow stool that was next to the bed.

I don't know how long it took me to fall asleep. I thought about morning. I thought about how I could get up when my alarm went off and I could go to work. I'd be able to leave my house then. I could figure out what to do after that. I could take a bag of clothes and leave this house. I was moving into the new house within two weeks. He could stay here until it was empty and the landlord came and kicked him out.

Somehow, I fell asleep. In the morning, I went to work. I waited for Stacey to come in, and I went to her cube. I told her what had happened. "If I hadn't been sarcastic, this wouldn't have happened. I keep thinking that. If I hadn't said, 'Shocking', and been a smart-ass, he wouldn't have freaked out," I said, and she assured me of the thing that I knew and did not know at the same time—that this was not my fault. I asked if I could stay with her, and she said of course. Todd went with me at lunch and came inside with me so I could pack a bag.

Charles was there sitting on the sofa. He seemed sober now. He looked tired but clear-eyed.

"Please, let me talk to you," he said.

"I'm going to wait outside, OK?" Todd said. He stepped out onto the front porch. Charles followed me into the bedroom, watched while I threw clothes into a canvas bag.

"You don't have to go. I just want to talk to you."

"I don't want to talk to you. This is it. You need to fix my bedroom door before I have to turn in my keys to this place. I'm going to stay somewhere else, and you can stay here until this weekend. My mom and Audrey are coming to help me move some stuff. You cannot be here. You need to find a place to go."

My heart was pounding. Was I so pathetic that I wanted to comfort him at that moment? I wanted to hug him and tell him it was going to be OK. I wanted to help him. I zipped up the bag and went back down the hall, through the living room, and out the front door.

Charles left the house by that weekend. His downward spiral continued. He moved into a weekly rate hotel. He failed a drug test at work and was fired. He awaited a court date for his DUI hearing.

I swore to my worried friends and to myself that I would not let him into my new house. Later, when I did let him in, I didn't tell my friends, because I was embarrassed. How did it happen? Like this: Charles called about his upcoming trip to visit Shreveport to see the kids. His brother was going to drive through town and pick him up.

"Can I please park my car at your place? I don't want to pay for the hotel if I'm not going to be there. I need a place to keep my car. It has all my stuff in it."

I said yes. He came by, and I let him in the house. I told him about a problem with a circuit breaker, and he said he'd fix it for me. "While I'm here, I can help you hang your pictures."

This was something we did. He would follow me around the house, and I'd tell him where I wanted things to go. He'd pull out his measuring tape and make sure everything was right.

This is how it happened. We acted just like we'd always acted. We played the roles we had always played.

A week or so after the trip to New Orleans, I went to Shreveport to pick up Kate and Jacob. While I was there, I returned to Charles's grave. I knew it wouldn't be satisfying even before I drove out there. I would not find peace or understanding or whatever else I was seeking.

I stood at his grave and thought about how people in movies and on television always talk aloud to their dead relatives. If you want to know my thoughts, I would prefer they were shared in voiceover and read by Morgan Freeman. I did not say one word out loud.

I read the headstone dates. These dates were the bookends to his life, but what about all the dates in between?

Dates when I didn't love him enough.

Dates when I forgave him too easily.

Dates when he pushed me to the floor and stood over me screaming.

Or the other dates?

The dates when our children were born.

The dates when we loved each other and held each other tightly and believed in our future together.

The headstone reads "Beloved son, father and husband."

Did we rewrite history since Charles and I were no longer married when he died? Yes, perhaps.

"Where are you?" I thought. When I looked at those words and numbers carved into stone, I felt a bubble of disbelief rise up inside me. He is not dead. This is not how it is supposed to be. It felt like this was the lie, and, if I could find him, he would show me the truth.

I imagined him up in a tree somewhere near this grave, perched on a limb and looking down on me. I imagined him in trees all the time, and I had no idea why.

Carved into his headstone was a tree. A deer standing beneath it. My sick inner comedian said to me, "Funny, if Charles were alive, if he were sitting quietly in that tree, he'd shoot that deer."

Shortly after I left the cemetery, Frances, Roger, and Kate arrived. They'd gone to the craft store and purchased new flowers to place at the grave. I'd asked Kate if she wanted to come with me, but she'd said no. Frances later told me that Kate changed her mind almost as soon as I was out of the driveway, but since I had no cell service, they couldn't call to tell me to turn around.

When they got back to the house, Roger and I talked about what it was like to visit Charles's grave.

"I knew I wouldn't find what I was looking for there, because I'm looking for him," I said. For months I had imagined him watching us from a distance, held at bay by the emotional restraining order I had put against his spirit a year earlier when I said out loud in the car, "You stay away from me no matter where I go on this planet."

But secretly and irrationally, I had believed that if I asked God or Oprah or whoever runs this universe to let it happen, that Charles would come back. That if I stood still and *really* wanted it, he would appear, not alive but also not dead. I would open the door to him and hold my breath.

And what was it I would ask of him? Why did you do this? Do you think of your children? Do you know what you did to them? To all of us? Are you sorry?

Are you still mad at me?

19

As the anniversary approached, in the weeks between my trip to New Orleans and Shreveport, I had started losing sleep. My heart hurt. I lay in bed and stared at the spot on the wall next to the dresser. I left the lamp on so I wouldn't have to stare into the darkness. The thing I thought I'd left behind months ago, the fear, was back again, having its way with me.

July 13: I dreamed that Charles was going to kill me. Stacey helped me hide. I woke up with a pounding heart.

July 14: I turned off the lamp and cried. I sobbed uncontrollably until there was nothing left in me. Then I reached out and turned the lamp back on.

That day I had read a few stories about Mel Gibson online. I listened to the recordings of his phone calls to his girlfriend, the mother of his youngest child. He was a man out of control, screaming vile things. When I was in high school, I stuck a sticker of Mel Gibson to the dashboard of my gold Chevy Citation. It was a picture of him from one of the *Lethal Weapon* movies. Now, Mel was a joke, one of those sad stories that spreads across the Internet like a virus.

I recognized something in those phone calls that worried me now, as I lay in my bed far away from California. I felt a little like one of those people in a movie who everyone else thinks is crazy. I thought about the demon in the garage, the one who could turn men into monsters. A man can't fight that alone. Once the demon has you, he can make you do something awful.

I shouldn't have listened to those calls, the recordings of a man ranting and raving, straining so that his voice becomes something more like the growl of a beast.

Mel, I believe you have re-traumatized me, sir, I thought. But perhaps the truth was closer to this: I had never gotten un-traumatized.

July 16: Erin, Stacey and I went to Yoga Nidra again. It wasn't as impressive as the last time. A new restaurant had opened up next door to the studio, and I could hear the comings and goings of customers. I could hear chair legs scraping back and forth, back and forth. I pictured a table of people scooting in and scooting out, scooting in and scooting out, and I pictured myself punching each one of them in the head. Why is it that when you hear people moving in a space next to you or upstairs it always sounds as if those people are throwing furniture across the room or bowling or playing the drums nonstop?

I tried to push the distractions away (unsuccessfully) and sink into the deep yogic sleep, but I never got there.

My statement of purpose had been this: "I will make peace with Charles's death."

This seemed almost as foolish as stating: "I will win the lottery this year."

I remembered Mom telling me to type "and is now at peace" in Charles's obituary after the phrase "died suddenly on August 3." I wanted that to be true. I really did. Eventually.

It did not seem fair for him to be at peace, not when I was so far from it. No, he should not be at peace until I was. I wanted him somewhere crying himself to sleep, huge wracking sobs ripping his chest apart night after night.

Peace? Not even close.

July 18: Sunday night, I went to church with Stacey. She attended one of those enormous places I liked to call "Six Flags Over Jesus" or "Chuck E. Jesus." It was situated on the other side of town off the interstate; they served free Starbucks coffee and had an indoor playground for little kids and a huge stage on which a band played praise music. Two enormous screens projected the words to the songs, and people raised their arms in the air.

Having grown up going (off and on) to an Episcopal cathedral, I felt a little squirmy surrounded by such earnestness. Midway into the service, the electricity went out and the band stopped playing. I leaned over to Stacey.

"God knew I couldn't handle all the flashing lights."

She laughed.

The pastor gave the sermon, and it was pretty good. At least, that's what I wrote in my journal entry that evening. I couldn't tell you what it was about. I was looking for a message from beyond, but I couldn't even hold a sermon message in my head for long.

All I wanted was peace for my constantly fluttering heart.

Are you listening? Are you there, God? It's me, Amy.

I didn't go back to the church the next weekend. Or ever again.

But I continued my prayer-like vigils.

I asked, "Why?" every night while I lay in bed. I did something akin to praying as I asked some unknown force for the gift of dreamless sleep.

It came to me on one of these sad, immobile missions impossible that I was not trying to figure out why this happened to Charles. What I wanted to know was why this happened to me. The thought made me feel selfish and self-pitying.

Why me? Why *not* me?

"It's nothing personal. Your name just came up," read the caption on a *Peanuts* cartoon.

Why me?

Another *Peanuts* cartoon, Charlie Brown looking for answers in the night: "Sometimes I like awake at night, and I ask, 'Where have I gone wrong?' Then a voice says to me, 'This is going to take more than one night.'"

Charles was dead, and I was alive, and all of the questions came back to my children and me. What are we supposed to learn? Who are we supposed to be now? Is there a purpose to all of this?

If I were the world's creator, I'd have been clearer about my thoughts on these matters. I'd answer questions instead of leaving people to spin in circles.

I mentally clipped out the *Peanuts* cartoons and tacked them to my mental bulletin board, where I kept all my clues and images and reminders that even bitter laughter is laughter. I saved a Shel Silverstein poem, too. In it, God hands over the steering wheel to a human, who inquires about the pay and quitting time and asks about taking a lunch break. God basically sighs and takes back the wheel.

Was I ready to steer? Was I ready to do something other than go round and round? I was tired of this year, but I was afraid of what came next. I'd been in a holding pattern, and I had zero confidence I would feel any better come September or October or another dreadful holiday season.

What next? I asked. What next, what next, what next? My heart pounded too fast, and it pounded out the rhythm of this question that I sent into the universe. I was merely marking off days.

What next?

July 19: I got into bed and I cried so much and so hard I thought my heart couldn't take anymore. To be in emotional pain is to be in physical pain. My body was exhausted, and each morning I dragged myself from bed like a soldier dragging himself from the field of battle.

I felt as if I were right where I had begun nearly 12 months earlier. If this was a hole, as I often thought of it, then all of my progress in climbing out of it had been for naught. I had slid down to the bottom again. Here I would stay until August 3 came and went.

And then what?

When I'd first taken the kids to counseling last fall, I'd said something to Jacob's counselor about how I wanted to get through the year. Do the work and serve my time. He said, "You know the anniversary will not be a magic date. You won't automatically feel better once it's past."

I nodded. Of course I knew that. But I felt a spark of anger, too. I remembered a time after a car had struck and killed our cat, Jewel, two years earlier. That day I had cried and cried. When I emailed my friend Carl about it, he answered back, "You know you're not really crying over the cat, right?"

It was true that I had driven Charles to the Greyhound station the night before the cat died. I had sent him on his way back to Shreveport to begin our separation, on his way to accept the end of us.

"Yes, I *am* crying over the cat," I typed back.

It had pissed me off a little. Just like Jacob's counselor had pissed me off.

I think people should be allowed to fool themselves if they choose, at least for a little while.

I gave in and took an over-the-counter sleeping pill. I stopped imagining a dark cloud traveling out of my garage and making its way across the country, burrowing its way into the hole in another man's soul.

I dreamed of Charles again. I could see him standing outside a window. He was smiling at me. He had on a striped shirt with a collar. He didn't beckon me closer or move. He only grinned, his eyes crinkled at the corner. Happiness. I walked closer to the window. As I put my fingers to the cold glass, I realized that he looked like a photo we have of him. Then I knew that this view of him through the window wasn't real. It was only a picture. I knew that he would only ever be who he was in my memories.

He would never again be anything more than that.

I woke up and turned on the lamp and waited for the alarm to go off.

July 22: I lay in bed and thought about why Charles could not move on, and I came to this conclusion: because I could not let him hate me. I could not do what had to be done so he could hate me.

Even now I could not bear to think of how angry he was with me. I was looking for him because I needed to know if I was forgiven.

I told my mom this. I said, "I'm afraid that he is still angry with me."

Her jaw dropped open in shock.

"*He* is the one who deserves the anger of everyone. I am still angry with him about what could have happened," she said.

Me dead first, she meant.

But he was never going to do that. He wasn't trying to hurt me. He was trying to *show* me. He needed me to see his pain.

I felt embarrassed by my worry.

This didn't stop me from repeating the same thing to my mother-in-law.

"I worry that he is still angry with me."

"Amy," she said. "When did he ever stay angry with you? Was he ever angry with you for a whole day? A whole hour?"

No. Never.

Now, Charles's pain was my pain, and I lay in bed and worried about whether or not he hated me when he did what he did.

I knew he was unhappy about Michael emailing me and asking for my phone number. I knew he was unhappy when Michael called me on that Saturday night, two days before August 3, the night when I did not answer.

I said to him, "I wouldn't answer while you're here."

But I did. When the phone rang on that Monday night, I thought it would be rude not to answer when I'd given him my number and he'd tried twice now to call.

So, see? I said to myself as the waves tossed me back and forth on that bed adrift on a fathomless sea. You are to blame. You said you wouldn't answer the phone, but you did. And the darkness said to me, "How could it not be the reason when it is clearly the reason?"

July 23: I had a counseling appointment. As soon as I sat down on the overstuffed sofa, I said to Joan, "We need to talk about something we've talked about before—about the fault and where it lies. About that stupid phone call and what happened when I hung up."

"OK," she said. This did not surprise her. "All you did was answer the phone. That's all you did. The phone rang. You answered it. Would anyone in their right mind respond the way he did?"

"No."

"Let me ask you this. What if the situation were reversed? What if he was on the phone with another woman? Would you do what he did?"

"Of course not. It's ridiculous. I know that. I do. I know it's not my fault."

One time I had imagined myself doing what Charles did. I had pictured myself walking into a room full of people and standing in front of them while I shot myself. I could see their horrified, blood-splattered faces. I wondered if I was trying to see myself—the horrified, blood-splattered person I'd been on that awful night.

"Sometimes I get caught in my ridiculous thoughts," I told Joan. "I need to say them out loud so I can hear them, so I can recognize how foolish they are."

They were thoughts born in darkness, like vampires. Exposing them to the light was the only way to kill them.

"I keep trying to find a way that I would be in control of what happened, but then I have to be responsible for it. So then it would be in my control, then I'm not powerless. Otherwise, it means that at any time anyone can do anything to you or in front of you, and you have no control," I said.

"That's right. That is the truth. If you could make him do anything, if you had any power, you would have made him sober? Isn't that right?"

Yes, I would have made him sober.

This is what I liked to call the George Clooney Conundrum. If I could make things happen with the power of my wishes, George Clooney would be my boyfriend. He would be insanely devoted to me, despite my lack of supermodel-long legs and my small breasts. If I had any power, Charles would be sober and happy and married to someone else. The kids would see him on weekends and Wednesday nights. When Charles and his new wife came by my house, there'd be a laugh track.

All our problems would be wrapped up in 30 minutes, not counting interruptions for commercials.

July 26: Rose Darby and I took a walk in her neighborhood, up and down the hills around a curving route I could not have navigated again on my own. Birmingham had always left me a bit turned around. I would drive into a neighborhood and follow the roads, certain I would come out on the other side, and somehow I would end up right back where I had begun.

We talked about writing. Rose Darby had started over on her novel. She felt the first few chapters were too confusing, so she scrapped them entirely in favor of beginning again.

We talked about my book. I'd spent as much time as possible putting down everything that came into my head. I'd turned off my filter. I could edit later. Keep moving, I told myself.

At some point on our twisted route, Rose Darby told me that the first time she came to stay with the kids, during my trip to Nashville for the photo shoot with my high-school boyfriend, she'd thought she might be afraid. She was afraid of being afraid.

Stacey told me, too, that she had been afraid of being afraid. She'd come to feed the cats for me one weekend, and she asked her boyfriend at the time to come with her so she wouldn't be alone in my house. She had seen the kitchen ceiling the night of August 3. She had seen some of what was left behind before the cleaning crew came, before I spent an afternoon painting the smooth kitchen ceiling Meander Blue.

It made me sad to think of my friends being creeped out by my house. Sad and mad. I understood it, and I hated it. Kate, Jacob, and I lived here every day, and the house was fine. I wanted my house to be a happy place. The children and I did our best to fill it with laughter and love.

I was tired of being home without the kids, that was true. But it wasn't because the house was creepy to me. I had learned long before that the garage was just a garage. Memories are what will doom you because they go with you wherever you go.

No, the house was not haunted.

I was.

July 29: Kate and Jacob were home, and life felt full again, in ways good and stressful. They yelled at each other. They took off their shoes and dropped them in the middle of the living room. They left toothpaste smeared on the sink. They didn't rinse their dishes. Kate came to the office with me each day and wandered the halls, seeking candy and entertainment. I told her to stay away from the executive end of the floor. Visit people in cubicles only.

The office culture had changed over the past year, and little girls popping in to say hello and ask, "Do you have any candy?" weren't as welcome as they might once have been. One day Kate said to an editor in the homes department, "Are you an intern?" and the editor said, "No, why do you ask?" "Because you haven't been laid off yet," Kate said.

I did not care about the comings and goings and office politics. I didn't want to be there anymore. I hid in my office. I avoided meetings. On this day, the announcement was made that the current editor would move to a newly created position, which was widely accepted as some way station on the path to retirement. The new editor-in-chief would be a man who had come down months earlier, whose opinion had suddenly been more valued than the editor. No one was surprised. If the staff were a stadium crowd, rather than doing the wave they'd have performed a collective shrug.

In six days, it would be August 3.

July 31: We drove to Tennessee to meet my dad and step-mom for vacation. My half-sister and her children were there, too. We had gone on vacation with them every year for the past seven years or so. Normally we went to the North Carolina shore, but money was tight. This year, we met up at a condo near Gatlinburg.

"Do not expect anything of him," Joan had said of Dad at my last appointment. That was how I would protect myself from disappointment.

What is it I would have wanted from him? A long, meaningful hug? An apology? An acknowledgment that we had not seen each other in more than a year?

I got none of these things. The prick of disappointment made me see that I was still expecting things.

I set it aside. More than anything, I was relieved to have left Birmingham behind for a week. I did not want to be home when the day finally arrived. Here we could sit by the pool. Here we could wander around tourist traps, eat ice cream, visit an aquarium, and hike through the forest. Here we could pull to the side of a winding, mountaintop road and snap photos of one another with a wide-open sky behind us.

August 2: *What if I wrote Charles a letter? What is it I want to say to him? Depending on the day or the hour or the minute, it might be "I hate you." Or it might be "I hope you are OK. We are OK. I forgive you." Or, "Look at what you left me with, this thing in my mind, in my memory, that will never* not *be. Do you see?"*

20

When I was in college in the '90s, I constantly clipped out *Calvin & Hobbes* cartoons. I tucked them into journals. I taped them to the bathroom mirror. I have saved them through the years, and they have grown feather-soft and yellow. I clipped out one about what is necessary for creativity ("last-minute panic"), another showing Calvin invent a "writer's block" ("You put it on top of your desk and then you can't write there anymore!"). But this is no ordinary writer's block.

Writer's block is rarely a state of paralysis. It feels closer to the act of driving in circles, avoiding the place you're supposed to be while you stop at random places nearby.

You can see the place, this destination you are avoiding, this thing you want to say, but you attempt to ignore it while you freely spill words other places, like into the "What's on your mind?" box on your Facebook page, or on that long, ranting email to a friend, or in a comment thread under a story on a decorating blog.

You just keep circling the block, trying to convince yourself to pull into the driveway of the event you promised yourself you'd attend today.

I have resisted pulling into the driveway, but I must.

I have avoided opening the garage.

But I will.

The door is never really closed.

21

On August 3, 2009, I came home for lunch and sat on the sofa with Charles. It was the last week he was staying in the house—sleeping in Kate's bedroom on her twin bed—because I was driving to Louisiana that weekend to pick up the children and bring them home from their grandparents' house. We sat together on the sofa and ate turkey sandwiches and watched a rerun of *Entourage* on HBO.

He told me he'd applied for unemployment. He wanted to know if he could use my bank account for direct deposit of any benefits he would get. That way I'd have the child support. (Also, as I found out later, his checking account was overdrawn by nearly $900. Why does a bank allow someone to withdraw that much money that they do not have? Oh, wait, I know. So they can charge overdraft fees, that's why.)

I told Charles that my dresser project was going to be on *Today* the next morning. The woman in charge of getting *Southern Living* segments on various talk shows and morning shows across the country had asked me to ship a dresser that had been featured in one of our makeover editions. I'd actually done the project years before, when Charles and I lived in the house we'd bought when we first moved to Birmingham. I'd painted an unfinished dresser a glossy rich red, something with the word "maple" in the name, and then nailed upholstery tacks into the front in a swirling design.

Rather than re-create it, the PR woman had me ship the dresser to New York. Overnight. Charles had helped me unpack the contents of the drawers and carry the dresser out to the garage. The previous Thursday, I paid (with my corporate Am Ex, of course) a company to come pack it up, crate it, and ship it. It had arrived in New York City without incident and would make its national debut the next morning.

We set the DVR to record the August 4 episode of *Today*. (When I came home more than a week later, I sped through interviews and news segments and stopped to watch Al Roker talk to the magazine's decorating editor—a woman who, in fact, never once stepped foot in the offices of *Southern Living* during her brief stint as an editor there.) She mentioned that an editor had shipped the dresser up there from her home, and Al opened the drawers to see if anything had been left in them.

For several weeks, I would crack jokes about Al Roker putting his hands in my drawers. Who am I kidding? I still crack that joke given the opportunity.

Lunch was uneventful. Charles seemed fine. "See you later," I said when I left to return to the office.

When I came home from work that evening, I changed into my workout clothes and did an hour of yoga. Charles came in and out of my bedroom while I tried to maintain standing tree pose and Warrior II, and while I lay quietly in savasana.

We sat on the sofa and ate ten-bean soup for dinner. It was leftover from Sunday night. Soup always tastes better a day later.

What else can I tell you?

I don't know what we watched on television. I don't know what we talked about. I don't know that anything was out of the ordinary. Charles's eyes were not glassy and unfocused. His speech was not slurred.

Charles stepped outside to smoke a cigarette. I thought he was making a phone call. He made numerous phone calls a day, but he was never on the phone long, usually the length of a cigarette. At his funeral, each person who spoke said that he talked to Charles at least three or four times a week, and I had wanted to say, "Yes, every time he smoked. He couldn't simply smoke a cigarette and *be* with himself."

Charles would complain that when I was on the phone with someone, the conversation went on for more than an hour. I would say yes, that's true, but I talk on the phone once every two weeks, not twenty times a day like you do.

At 7:38 p.m., while Charles stood on the front porch smoking, my cell phone rang, and I ran into the kitchen and picked it up off the counter to see who was calling. I saw Michael's name and number light up on the screen. After exchanging a few emails the previous week about his high-school reunion, his recent date with a younger woman, and some joking about our advancing age, he'd asked for my phone number, and I'd given it to him.

I think about it now, how Charles was always over my shoulder. He would step out to smoke a cigarette, and when he came back inside, he would walk over to stand behind me, to see what website I was on, who I was emailing. He made comments about Michael's emails to me in a tone that was perhaps

274

supposed to be teasing but was closer to menacing. Yes, now that I can look back on it, his tone was harsh and on edge, and I foolishly allowed myself to believe it was harmless.

Charles had made a comment that Michael probably liked me, and I'd blushed. I was out of practice and unaccustomed to flirting or being liked, and my stupid face betrayed that. Charles went off on me, yelling at me words that I can no longer remember. I think that maybe I always tried to forget his harsh words to me as quickly as possible so that I could fool myself some more.

On the phone to this man with whom I'd gone to high school, I talked about things trivial and ultimately forgettable— mutual friends who'd gotten married and divorced, other classmates who'd gone to jail or found success.

Charles came in from smoking, the smell of tobacco clinging to his clothes, and walked into the kitchen.

"Who is that?" he mouthed.

I shook my head and shooed him away.

He asked again.

"Michael," I mouthed.

"Ohhhhh," he said, as if he were a young boy teasing me. Only now do I see how a smile is sometimes a person baring their teeth at you, that this manner of teasing is so akin to being knocked down on the ground by a boy who likes you and wants your attention and, at the same time, hates you and wishes you didn't exist.

He left the kitchen.

But he came back. He bothered me as a small child would with periodic interruptions. Only weeks later, Kate would do the same thing to me and say, "You're supposed to be paying attention to *me*." And I would flash on an image of a grown man who wanted me to look at him.

I put my hand over the phone's mouthpiece and said, "Go watch TV."

"I can't. I can hear you in here talking."

He left the room. Maybe he went down to the basement garage where his car was parked.

I brought my vodka-and-cranberry juice cocktail in from the living room. I drank it and leaned on the kitchen counter and looked at the window while I talked. Michael brought up Audrey and her divorce. She'd been posting cryptic updates about the ongoing saga on Facebook. Michael wanted to know the scoop.

"Divorce sucks," I said. "People do a lot of things they shouldn't and they don't think about the consequences."

(Audrey's consequences were that a judge eventually ordered her to stop posting status updates about her douchebag ex-husband.)

Charles stomped into the kitchen.

"Don't you dare talk about me," he said.

I covered the mouthpiece again.

"I am not talking about you," I whispered. "I'm talking about Audrey."

This didn't really soothe his agitation, but he said nothing more and left the kitchen again. I tried to remain upbeat and not reveal the drama on my end of the phone. I was embarrassed by Charles's increasing belligerence.

He came into the kitchen again and stood behind me, gyrating against me, and he said in a low tone, "I don't want to listen to you on the phone with some guy who wants to fuck you. I'm about to yell 'I'm fucking here, and I'm fucking Amy.'"

I turned around and shoved him away. You wish you were fucking me, you asshole. That's what I wanted to say. I wanted to drop the phone and start screaming at him. But how could I respond? I wanted my life to seem normal. I wanted to have a normal conversation without any hint of this domestic dispute, this sad, banal bullshit.

It was all so ugly and pathetic.

I should have gotten off the phone then. I should have gotten off long before that. I should have calmed Charles down immediately. I should not have dismissed him and shoved him away and ignored him.

A year later, I didn't care what anyone said to dispute that. I couldn't stop believing it.

Charles stomped out of the kitchen again, and, still on the phone, I walked out of the kitchen through the door into the garage. I punched the button to open the garage door and stepped outside into the warm, clear evening. I have no memory of the conversation. Michael had moved out of Shreveport for a while during college. Maybe we talked about that. Maybe he told me about his job. Maybe he asked about mine. Maybe I wasn't listening and I was waiting for an opportunity to end the call. Maybe I didn't end the call right away because I knew what was waiting for me inside. (But I did not know. I did not have any idea what was waiting for me inside.)

Charles came out onto the front porch and yelled something. I strained against the restrictions of my memory for months afterward, but I still could not hear what he said. I could only see him, watching me from the porch. He stormed back into the house and attempted to slam the glass door behind him, but the arm mechanism caught it and closed it slowly and silently.

I ended the phone call. I interrupted something Michael was saying and said, "I'm really embarrassed, but my ex-husband is here, and he's throwing a fit."

"Oh, I'm sorry. Sure. I'll talk to you later," Michael said.

And the call ended.

It was 9:21 p.m.

I walked back through the open garage door and, at the stairs into the kitchen, I ran into Charles coming out of the kitchen door, his shotgun clutched in both hands. I stumbled backward down the stairs and backed toward the far wall.

"This is so hard," he cried out. "You have no idea how much this hurts."

He let go of the gun with his left hand and slammed his open palm against his chest. "Do you have any idea how much this hurts?"

I opened my phone to call someone, anyone. Who could I call? I thought I would call 911. The police could come get him, come take his gun away. I punched in the 9. A 1. Another 1.

"If you hit send, I'm going to do it! I'm going to kill myself," he yelled.

I closed the phone.

"OK, OK, just stop. Just stop a minute."

It was all happening so fast. My mind leaped ahead to tomorrow when someone could come get Charles and take him...where? To rehab? To the hospital? Who could come? If I started to dial any number, what would he do?

It is amazing how little time your mind needs to leap over the varied possibilities and search for answers. My heart was racing, my hands shaking, my eyes wide and disbelieving, but all the while my brain was tossing out names and places and words, trying to give me something to grasp onto in an attempt to fix this. Despite all this work my brain was doing, not once did it give me the image of what was really possible, what a gun could really do. It did not show me the image of death.

It showed me hospitalization. It showed me jail. It showed me Charles driving away from here. It showed me a phone call to Charles's dad. It showed me the image of the guest bedroom at Stacey's house, the walls pale blue, the furniture antique green, the air cool, the door closed, the lights off, the sound of silence, this night over and done with.

Charles lowered the gun, and I moved back toward him. If I could get in the house, I could stop this. If I got inside, he would put the gun down. He would follow me into the living room, we would sit on the sofa, and he would calm down. He wanted me to listen. I could do that. If I went inside, he would see that I would sit down and listen. I had calmed him down in the past. I could do it again.

When I stepped onto the bottom step, he gripped the shotgun with both hands again and shoved it under his chin.

"I'm going to do it!" he yelled.

I jumped back from him, and the cell phone fell from my hand to the ground; I heard it bounce against the pavement. I ran back to the far wall, to the front of my car, and I crouched down on my hands and knees. Was the phone under the car? I couldn't see it. Where was the phone? Who could I call?

I would have to call his dad. Yes, once Charles calmed down, I would call his dad and tell him that someone had to come get Charles out of my house right away. I could wait for him to go to sleep, and then I could pack a small bag and sneak out and go to Stacey's house until he was gone.

He was only trying to control me again. He wanted to punish me for moving on with my life.

"This is so hard. I'll do it. I'm going to kill myself," he said.

How long would this go on, this scene meant to frighten and control me, before he would calm down enough for me to pretend it was OK, for me to tell him he was forgiven? I was so tired of the manipulation and the emotional blackmail, so tired of the lies and the guilt, so tired of hoping for better when it always got worse. I had put him first a million times. I had let him stay in my house when he had nowhere else to go. I had let him be with his children. I had cowered on the floor while he pounded a hole in my bedroom door and screamed that I was a whore and a bitch.

"I'm going to do it," he screamed now.

I was so sick of this scene. I wanted it to end.

I said, "Then do it already."

I looked down, still searching for the phone. Nowhere. It wasn't under the car. Where the hell was it?

It was less than a second, this glance down, this moment when I was looking under the car and not at him, between what I said to him and what he said to me.

I looked up again and saw him shove the shotgun tightly under his chin, his face above it red and contorted with rage—or was it pain?

"You can remember that's the last thing you said to me before I did it."

The world exploded around me. The sound of the shotgun blast slammed against me and filled my ears. Pieces of Charles's fragmented skull hit the ceiling, and blood and flesh rained down around him. I heard the sound of it, this unholy splattering, right before his body collapsed onto the landing, and the sound of that was thick and wet and lifeless.

The garage was filled with smoke and a smell so foul and evil that I was convinced for a moment that this room was Hell and there was no longer anything outside of it. No pine trees or grass in the front yard, no stars or moon in the summer sky. No minutes. No seconds. Infinite time. There was only me, trapped forever on the bloodstained floor of my garage, where Charles had left me alone at last.

Dream: Forgetting

I receive a letter from a woman who writes that she is having an affair with you. You have been lying to me for quite some time. This woman is watching me while I read the letter, waiting for my reaction.

I decide to divorce you. I won't wait for you to come home and explain yourself. I won't forgive you. I'm going to end this right away, and I go to an attorney. He asks questions and writes down my answers. I look around his office and realize it is in a treehouse. I am sitting in a leather chair, but outstretched limbs surround me. Light shines through only the tiniest pinholes between tight clusters of glossy green leaves.

You will need to sign the papers, but you are not here. I wonder where you are, and then it dawns on me that we are already divorced. How could I have forgotten?

I watch the attorney and try to decide how to tell him that this is unnecessary. I am embarrassed. Then I remember more. I remember that you shot yourself in front of me. You fell to the floor. You are dead.

"Wait," I put out my hand to stop the attorney. I try to think of a way to explain this without looking like a fool, or worse, someone who is insane. "We don't have to do this. I forgot that my husband is dead."

The attorney acts like this is not out of the ordinary. "Good. Then you're all set."

He puts the papers in a file. His secretary appears from nowhere to carry the file away.

"You can remember." That is what you said to me before you died.

It is only in a dream that I can possibly forget.

22

It felt as if the anniversary of Charles's death was layered directly on top of August 3, 2009. Underneath the surface of this day was that other day. The clock ticked down the minutes of both days simultaneously. I imagined if I were at home in Birmingham, I would be able to hear the sound of me coming in on my lunch hour, of us watching *Entourage*, the sound of a cellphone ringtone, the deafening blast of a shotgun.

We spent the day at the swimming pool of the resort. The pool was perched on a hill overlooking Sevierville. In the distance was the helicopter tour place. From our lounge chairs, I could see a red barn in a field, a red helicopter parked next to the barn. It occasionally took off, flying tourists over the Smoky Mountains. The Titanic museum stood tall in the distance and looked like a ship floating across a sea of green treetops, its maiden voyage destined to be ruined by a roadside hotel or a go-cart track rather than an iceberg.

I was in a place I'd never been, surrounded by people I didn't know who were splashing in the pool, spreading towels across their chairs, popping open cans of soda, and underneath this day that other day was ticking by. I looked up now and then to watch Kate leap into the water or calmly tell a squabbling Kate and Jacob to give it a rest. I got in the pool and watched my nephew Cameron paddle around in his life jacket.

That evening we all gathered around the table for dinner and board games. We played a game called Cranium, which has challenges in four areas, including words. Near the end of the game, as the minutes ticked past 9 p.m., my half-sister, Katie, and her stepson, Chase, got a challenge to fill in the letters of a football strategy. They weren't able to guess it, and time ran out. The answer, I shit you not, was SHOTGUN FOR-MATION.

Sometimes I was a person who believed in coincidence.

Sometimes I was a person who believed in a higher power who had a really sick sense of humor.

I watched the clock and thought about what was happening at my house at this minute, right below the surface of this day.

I waited.

At 9:25 p.m., Charles would be dead again.

When I finally climbed into bed that night, I turned the bedside lamp on, opened my journal, and wrote this:

What do I know now, 365 days later? I know that anger and sorrow are not mutually exclusive. That I can miss you and curse you in the same breath. That I can forgive you and not myself, and then forgive myself and not you, all in the span of one exhalation. That I can look for you everywhere I go. That I never find you. That I can see Kate and Jacob walking toward me and catch a glimpse of you. That you are gone and yet not.

And then I slept.

The next morning, I logged onto Facebook and read the messages people had written on my page and Charles's memorial page to mark the anniversary. Note after note of sympathy and support. A hint of anger here and there. My mom wrote that she still felt angry but also sad. My cousin wrote: "You're a douche. WTF were you thinking?"

A valid message, no doubt, but I emailed Randy, since I no longer had access to the password, and asked him to go on Charles's page and delete it. From that very first August 4, I'd tried to project the right tone, and that couldn't include anger. Imagine the power I had in those first few days, how I could have spewed bile and venom and drawn people onto my "team"; how I could have lashed out at people who were alive; or how I could have encouraged everyone to think the worst of Charles and what he had done. But, honestly, it never even crossed my mind. Maybe there is a higher power, and that force really was with me during that time, and it said, "Love him. Remember him with kindness and understanding. Love is the answer."

And I heard that message.

Randy wrote me back and said it wasn't the "douche" comment but one my cousin had written on my page that he found so offensive. "August 3 is all about Charles," he wrote, "and she made it negative and about her."

I didn't know what Randy was talking about. I clicked over to my page and found what the cousin had written: *You're better off without that speed bump in your life. He's not here to cause you stress and strife. You can do it on your own like you always have.*

Again, it's not like it wasn't true, but I deleted it anyway.

But something stuck in my mind, and I kept coming back to it. August 3 is all about Charles. All about Charles?

Every day up to August 3 was about Charles. About his needs and wants and obsessiveness. I could feel these thoughts under my skin, biting their way out.

"For many people who love me, it is also about what happened to me and what happened to my children," I wrote back. "Isn't it understandable if those people express their grief over that, too? I know you don't want to know what he did to me, and that's fine. We'll leave it."

Randy responded: "How would you feel if someone wrote that about Jacob? How do you think my mom felt reading that about her son?"

I thought the thing that probably every mother would think because to imagine otherwise is horrifying: *But my son would not do what Charles did.*

I felt disloyal even thinking this, but I need to say something here that will scare every mother who reads it: Your son could absolutely do what Charles did.

I'd sat in the study area of the public library and read a book called *Death Becomes Them* by Alix Strauss. It was about famous people who committed suicide. I read stories about Hemingway and Hunter S. Thompson. Both alcoholics, by the way. I found out that Thompson mailed a suicide note to his wife four days before he shot himself. When he did it, he was on the phone with her. It gave all sorts of statistics like how every 34 seconds someone attempts suicide, how divorced men commit suicide 400 percent more often than women, how men use guns most often.

I scribbled these things in my journal. I copied this information from Dr. Edwin S. Shneidman, suicidologist (what an unfortunate job title). He explained that suicide would happen when three factors collide:

- The person reaches his psychological threshold for pain (cannot envision an escape other than death).
- He has easy access to life-ending tools such as a gun, knife, or pills.
- The person enters into "perturbation," an agitated state where discomfort and anxiety feel intolerable.

Knowing these things, are you like me? Are you amazed that more mothers' sons don't end up here?

Knowing these things, can you see Charles on the night he died and the way he was destroyed by three factors colliding?

"I have tried to make this as easy as I can for everyone," I wrote back, "while I am the one with the nightmares and the sleep problems and the posttraumatic stress. Please do not suggest that I am insensitive to the feelings of your parents. I have been as sensitive as I can be."

My heart was beating too fast. My hands were shaking as I typed. Randy's disregard for my feelings had been clear from the beginning. When I gave him the password to Charles's Facebook page, he immediately changed it so I would not have access. When I asked him to please remove a photo from Charles's page of Charles holding the shotgun with which he had killed himself—an unfortunate image that had sent me reeling the day I found it—he ignored me. The photo remained.

Of course it was about poor, sad, dead Charles. I was just the one left alive to deal with the fallout. I was the one who was no longer any good at her job, filled with panic by each new email about this meeting or that policy change. I was the one who got to carry around the fear that Charles's family and friends were all hiding a little seed of anger and blame that had my name on it. I remembered how his mother once said, "I wanted it to be your fault." I knew what she meant. I knew she did not believe this, and yet it's a seed, isn't it? A little seed that could be sown into anger and hatred if someone planted it and watered it a bit every day.

Of all the emotions I had felt that year, anger had gotten the least stage time. When it did threaten to emerge, I hid it behind the others—the sadness, the fear, the love, and the dark humor.

It was not for shame of it. I didn't think that was why. It was because anger was the one most likely to throw me off my steady path. It was the one most likely to put a wall between me and some of the people in our lives, people who might have been listed on a roster under the title "Charles's People."

The night of his funeral, my friend Gabi, the one who had helped Kate and I pick out dresses for the funeral and visitation, had picked me up and taken me over to Dan and Julie's house for a small get-together of Charles's closest friends in Shreveport. There were snacks and drinks and good-hearted reminiscing. At one point, someone brought up the birthday dinner we'd had when Charles was messed up on pills and wrote the message to me that read, "To the most forgiving wife ever."

Now, at this post-funeral gathering, Julie said, "Talk about denial."

The room fell silent, and I looked at her. This was the closest anyone came to saying it was my fault, to pointing out my culpability in Charles's long addiction and tragic death.

After a moment, I said, "I wasn't in denial. I drove him to rehab twice. I divorced him. I don't know what else I could have done."

The moment passed, acknowledged only by Stuart coming up to me and saying, with laughter in his voice, "Well, that was awkward."

When we drove away from the house that night, Gabi said, "You need to get back to your people. These are Charles's people. They're going to put him up on some pedestal. But I'm pissed. Your friends are pissed. You need to get back to your people."

No matter what tone I set, there was going to be this unacknowledged division. My people. Charles's people. For Charles's people, I might be a good target for blame.

I certainly wanted to blame someone. I felt it all day on August 4, 2010—this ball of blackness in my stomach that I wanted to vomit out like fire from a dragon's belly.

I went through the motions of that day, hiking along trails in the Tennessee national forest, stopping to pose for photos with the family. I smiled and I laughed and I kept my little seed of anger in my pocket. That night, everyone went to bed, and I stayed up, watching the television without seeing it, thinking all the mean thoughts I wanted to think.

"Look at me. I'm angry. I didn't deserve this, and if you think I did, fuck off!" I wrote in my journal.

Pressing the pen into the pages with unnecessary force, I wrote down all the ways it was my fault. My handwriting was messy. Perhaps someone could analyze it and diagnose a mental disorder.

I didn't kick Charles out of our lives.

I didn't suspect he robbed my home.

I didn't protect myself.

I let him stay in my house when he was homeless.

I did not take him to court when he didn't pay child support.

I dared answer the damn telephone and have a conversation.

I didn't assume he would trap me in a garage using a gun.
I didn't assume he would make me watch him die.
I'm such a fucking failure. Clearly, it's all my fault for:

1. *Always having a job.*
2. *Not being an addict.*
3. *Worrying more about my children's relationship with their father than my own peace of mind.*
4. *Never ever dating or having boyfriends or letting my guard down for a minute with any man other than Charles.*
5. *Letting him cuss me and push me down and manipulate me.*

Maybe now was the time to let anger have the stage. Poor, forgotten, ignored, neglected anger. Yes, come out from the wings and let's open the curtains. Anger wanted to know this: Is Charles at peace? Anger had the mic right now, the lights were shining on her, and Anger said, "He doesn't deserve it. As long as we're not at peace, why should he be? Someone answer that. How about one of you assholes who wants to judge my family for being even a little bit angry that someone with a gun held me captive?"

Everyone who wanted to remember how great he was, how funny and kind—and I was one of them—all those people should answer that. Everyone who wanted to imagine Charles as a sad soul who took his life in a state of misery and hopelessness, a crying mess in a hotel room listening to Sarah McLachlan songs, should come watch the images of what really went down. Here, step inside my head, where there's a nightly showing of that horror film. What if they knew that he did it out of anger and spite and pure malevolence? What if they saw it for the violent act it was? What if they were in my place, crouched on the concrete, helpless, never able to get up again?

What if they tried to imagine what they could do that would be bad enough to deserve the punishment I got?

Anger said "Fuck Charles. Fuck Charles's people. I hope he is suffering. I hope he feels what I feel. Asshole."

I was fuming, sitting in that bed in a Tennessee condo, with all the lights off save the bedside lamp and the flashing of the scenes on TV. I stayed up all night like that, rage coursing through me, leaving me itchy and restless and tense. If you have a fight with someone, it can leave you sort of shaky and make your heart beat too fast. Charles left me with this times a million. It was like the horrible thing Charles was carrying around, the demon on his back, had directed all the evil, awful, you-should-die, you're-a-bad-person energy into me.

"How was August 4?" Stacey texted me.

"It was OK but still weird. I kept thinking about where I was last year and how this year I had a bra on."

Stacey texted back: "I can see your sense of humor is still intact."

Humor was like a stage manager with one of those crazy, long hooks like you'd see in a Bugs Bunny cartoon or some old Vaudeville act. Humor had worked on the other phases of grieving. I could use it now to pull Anger off the stage, to push it back into the dressing room where Anger got outfitted in a costume, the costume of someone who was serene and cool and wasn't enraged by the absolute stupidity of people who didn't know what the hell it was like to watch a monster die and yet had the audacity to judge people who were sad *and* angry.

That costume looked like me.

Unfortunately, anger was like an illness that I couldn't shake. It stayed with me on the next day during the drive home from Tennessee back to Birmingham. The problem is that sometimes I am at my funniest when I am pissed off and railing against the bullshit of life. Anger and humor go hand in hand; ask any comedian who spends night after night on a stage straining his vocal cords trying to laugh instead of cry.

The adrenaline kept me wide awake despite the sleepless night.

It kept me up for several nights that week after the anniversary, during which I'm sure I must have slept but I never stopped grinding my teeth. I felt frightened and disturbed by the awful things I said in my head. I acted out arguments with people in my imagination and I wrote cruel lines for them so that I could, at last, scream out my defenses.

I listened to Ludacris in the car every morning on the twelve-minute drive to work. I thought this was a vast improvement over my Sorry for Myself playlist full of sad-sack alternative rock. I sang out the curse words that had filled my head for a year and I relished lyrics with words like "motherfucker" and "bitch." This made me feel better.

"I'm worried about you," Erin said.

We were in my office with the door closed, and I was ranting. When you go through the stages of grief, you should know this: Anger is the phase that will scare your friends. Anger is frightening. Anger is a pot boiling over with adrenaline, and someone will get burned.

That afternoon, I drove down a street in my neighborhood and passed a woman standing on the side of the road with her child and a large golden retriever. Mindful of the unpredictability of children and dogs, I watched them as I drove past and that's why, as I passed, I saw the woman narrow her beady eyes and mouth the words "slow down."

Anger said, "Let me out right now." I hit the brakes, backed up, and rolled the passenger-side window down.

"Do you have something to say to me?" yelled this woman, who had wrongly accused me of speeding, in a snotty tone of voice.

At last, here was someone blaming me for being a bad person. At last, here was someone I could tell off.

"I was going 27 miles an hour," I said.

"The speed limit is 25," she said.

"Come on," I said.

My face must have clearly expressed my opinion of her as histrionic, because her voice became high-pitched and righteous as she said, "I have a child here!"

Will no one think of the children?

I rolled my eyes at her and, dismissively, like she was the most ridiculous person I'd ever seen, I calmly said, "Then get out of the road, bitch."

She gasped, and her eyes grew wide with shock.

I drove away and my hands started to shake. I thought what an asshole she looked like standing there talking on her cell phone about something vitally important, like how her husband works too late, or how it's time to trade in her latest SUV, or that she doesn't know what color to paint her kitchen, or that she needs to buy a new Auburn flag because the current one is so faded. Screw her.

I couldn't get to sleep that night either. I started feeling guilty. I imagined walking down Chester Street and finding that woman and apologizing. I hated being mean. I hated knowing that someone thought I was a horrible person. See, the thing is,

I would say, "I'm having a really difficult time. I'm not a bad person."

I knew that I was the only one saying cruel things. I was really only arguing with myself. I knew this because I heard a voice in my head say, "Sorry, wrong, you *are* a bad person."

Like a fever, anger broke, and I stopped thrashing about like some street fighter who is being restrained by the bigger guy standing behind him. I was exhausted. I didn't need to lash out at the world anymore. I knew who was to blame. I'd concentrate on punishing her for a bit.

On Monday, we had a staff meeting at work. We all trekked through the main building over to the auditorium in what everyone called "the new building." The new building used to house a couple of magazines, and everyone who'd worked in it had had nice, new, adjustable office chairs and shiny, clean cubicles. The building was empty now. We'd heard the maintenance staff had to put out mousetraps. Earlier in the year, there'd been memos about snakes on the property, and everyone had joked about all the snakes being in offices at the publishing headquarters in New York.

The meeting was so that our latest editor-in-chief (EIC) could share his vision for the magazine. Less than two years before, we'd shuffled into the rows of upholstered seats for a similar meeting with the last new editor-in-chief. The crowd reaction was the silent equivalent of "Ho-hum," like we'd heard this all before, which, face it, we had. I felt bad for the EIC. I was sure he would create a lovely magazine (though he had a reputation for also creating an atmosphere of chaos and perfectionism and last-minute changes, all while the staff continued to feel burned out and unappreciated). It was the new world order 2.0.

He talked about improving feature stories, giving *Garden & Gun* a run for its money (though I'd heard *G&G* couldn't even make money and was targeted at a completely different audience, but don't let reason or reality be a part of the NWO 2.0). I wondered how I was going to do this anymore. With the last new EIC, I'd been ready to buy in. I'd enthusiastically accepted my move into a new department. I'd believed in change. This time, I felt nothing, not one ounce of enthusiasm. I knew that things around here would not change for the better.

I was more than burned out. I was no longer invested emotionally and no longer present mentally. When I thought about work, my chest hurt. Sunday night, I'd read a reader comment on the magazine's website about an essay I'd written about how I'd never learned to cook traditional Southern dishes. "Let's blame my mother," I'd written. My mother loved it. We thought it was funny.

"Wow. Just wow. I just finished reading the 'Southern Journal' article on the last page of the May issue, and I am so disappointed. I have always wondered why *SL* doesn't offer a 'letter to the editor' and I think it's because of pitiful articles like this one," wrote someone who called herself Scarlettdouble. "Amy Bickers, the author, brags about not having a cast-iron skillet, not being able to make pimento cheese, not being able to cook..."

Brags? I wasn't bragging. I was making fun of myself. Hell, I was mostly making fun of my mom. I couldn't believe I'd been so misunderstood. I sat on the sofa and cried.

My anger tried to rear up and tell a joke, something about how she must have chosen her screen name because she's two times the bitch Scarlett O'Hara was (and everyone knows Scarlett O'Hara was an enormous bitch).

But it didn't work. I cried more. I was unable to shake the feeling that I was the bitch.

I didn't belong here anymore. I knew it. Scarlettdouble knew it. Everyone knew it.

The meeting wrapped up with some lackluster applause, and we all shuffled back out of the new building and into the old one.

At my counseling appointment, we talked about work a little. We discussed my personal writing, the only thing that felt good and right lately.

My counselor said, "I'm not sure you have to include what you said to him. It doesn't matter. It was going to happen anyway, no matter what you said."

She had spent months assuring me of this truth, but it ate away at me. It woke me up at night.

Charles's death in my garage had to be my fault. If it was my fault, that meant there was some way to have stopped it. It meant control.

"If I can't figure out what *I* did so that I can make sure I never do it again, then that means at any moment someone can trap you in a room and make you watch them die."

"Yes," my counselor said. "That's right."

All I could see was this truth that I had wanted Charles to go away. I had wanted my life back. I was exhausted by his need for me that was trumped only by his need for pills. The two had become entwined, and I was like a drug for him. He would do anything to get me, and once he had me, he would use me up until I was as empty as one of his pill bottles.

I could live with his death. I really could. I just couldn't live with being the person who told him to do it already.

Writing it all out in book form was really only a longer way of saying, "I'm so sorry. This is very hard."

23

On a Tuesday, two weeks after the anniversary of Charles's suicide, Stacey called and said, "Do you guys want to go to a movie? It's Tuesday. One-dollar popcorn night at Carmike."

Yes, definitely, I said, a rare answer for a school night. I typically only enjoy a school-night movie outing if it's to see the latest George Clooney movie. I told the kids to finish up their homework early and we could go see *Ramona & Beezus*. Jacob wasn't thrilled about this, so I told him he could see something else showing at the same time.

We were the only people in the theater. The movie was sweet but sad for all of us. Kate said, "I cried when her cat died and when Ramona ran away."

I cried at the scenes between the father and daughter. Stacey cried at the love story and happily-ever-after backyard-wedding scene. OK, I cried at that, too.

When the credits started and the lights came on, I said, "Maybe we should have seen a movie about ugly people with horrible lives."

We went out into the lobby and waited for Jacob. I checked my phone and saw that I had several missed calls and a text message from my sister: Call Dad or me ASAP.

I dialed Dad's number, already knowing that something bad had happened.

"It's your granddad."

I don't know how much of the story my dad told me right then and how much he told me later. My granddad had fallen and hit his head on the built-in desk in the kitchen. They thought maybe he tripped where the kitchen's linoleum floor gave way to the carpeted eating area, that he didn't immediately understand the seriousness of the harm it had caused. He was home alone and he made his way over to the sofa to lie down. Hours later, my aunt Vickie came in from work and found him lying unconscious on the sofa. An ambulance was called, and he was rushed to the hospital, but there was too much brain damage. Later that night, the doctors would take him off the ventilator and move him to a hospice room where he would die.

Granddad hadn't been the same since my grandma's death nearly three years earlier. He didn't say much. He didn't leave the house. If you'd known the man from my childhood, you'd know this was not the man he truly was. Wes and Carlene (my grandparents) had "happiness" parties. They drank. They smoked. They laughed and loved. And loved and loved. They had a love story that we had mythologized over the years, illustrated by black-and-white photos of my gorgeous grandma.

My granddad, at 15, saw a photo of her, a girl of 14 looking back over her shoulder with a wink and a smile, and I imagined he knew then that she was the loveliest thing he would ever find. Why would he look for anyone else? He snatched her up and married her when she was 16 and he was 17. My dad was born the next year.

After my parents' divorce, during our summers with my dad, my brother and I spent a good bit of our time with our grandparents. They owned a pontoon with seats covered in bright orange fabric, and we spent the summer days floating on Geist Lake in Indiana. We ate O'Malia's fried chicken and Mike-Sell's Old Fashioned Potato Chips.

At the end of the day, when the sun was setting and the temperature dipped, I always wanted to sit next to Grandma, wrapped in a beach towel and in her arms. She had dark hair and green eyes, olive skin that made her a tiny bit exotic.

My younger brother, Tim, would "drive" the boat with my granddad, and I would sit close to Grandma. She was soft and always warm. I've never forgotten the silkiness of her skin when I would snuggle up against her.

We would listen to Abba and Neil Diamond cassettes as we crossed the lake to the boat dock. During the school year, when I was back in Louisiana, I would cry when I heard Neil Diamond songs. Who am I kidding? I still cry if I catch the opening notes of "Love on the Rocks" or "Hello Again."

My brother and I spent hours playing "pretend" at my grandparents' house. Our favorite game was "detective." I wore my grandma's sundress and played the part of the femme fatale. I don't think we knew what a femme fatale was then, but I was glamorous and I needed a crime solved. The dress I wore was white with black polka dots and red trim. It wasn't the kind of dress grandmas wore. But then, my grandma wasn't your typical grandma. She was the stuff of movies. She was a film-noir star. She let me wear her jewelry. All of her necklaces hung from a hook in the bathroom. I remember a red bead necklace. I remember a gold necklace with a butterfly hanging from it.

We would run around that tri-level house and make up mysteries and then solve them. When we weren't playing "detective," we played soda shop. My grandparents' family room had a bar, and we would serve up vanilla ice cream in glasses and pour root beer, foaming and fizzing with abandon, on top of it. When it was time for lunch, my grandma would indulge my preference for cheese and mayonnaise sandwiches. Afterward, we would eat marshmallow cookies.

I remember one night, sitting on the porch swing, when my grandma talked to me about what it felt like to have parents who were divorced. No one had ever really talked to me about how it *felt* before. I remember the dark night, the porch lit softly from the glow of the living-room lamps beyond the windows. There was something about sitting in the half-light, the mix of inside and out, that made it easier to say exactly how something felt.

When I was in college, my mother, Ted, and I decided to drive to Indiana to visit Tim, who had moved there the year before, wanting to be near our dad and figure out the kind of man he wanted to be after years of living with me and my mom.

Even after the divorce, my mom had still called my grandma and granddad "Mom and Dad." That's the kind of people they were. When they loved you, they loved you forever. When we showed up, years and years after my parents' divorce, with my stepdad in tow, they welcomed him with open arms. They hugged him and led my parents and me out to the screened-in porch and put out snacks and poured us drinks.

My mom and stepdad had brought my grandma a Creedence Clearwater Revival CD, knowing she loved their music. When my grandparents said they didn't own a CD player, my mom and stepdad went out that day and bought them one.

If you had had the chance to be with these people, to be loved by them, you would have bought them a CD player, too. You would have bought them a CD player, and you would have played them a hundred songs they loved.

I grew up seeing my granddad look at my grandma with an expression I'd never seen outside movies. On their 50th wedding anniversary, she wore a pale-yellow suit, and he looked at her with adoration, like he was in love with her.

A few years ago, my granddad had been in a hospital across town for something relatively minor. My grandma was at home, unable to make the trip to visit him. As her grown children left the house to see their father, my grandma said, "Tell him I adore him." It was her last message to him. Within days, my grandma would be in another hospital, and my granddad would leave his own hospital bed to go to his one true love and hold her hand as she slipped out of this world.

Now, on the day after the 62nd anniversary of the day he married my grandma, my granddad was dead, too. I wanted to imagine she was waiting for him when he left this world and entered the next, her arms wide open to welcome him back to her. "Hello again," she might have said.

I honestly don't understand people who don't cry when they hear Neil Diamond songs.

Stacey hugged me, and it occurred to me that I was exactly where I needed to be on this school night, with a friend who could hug me when I hung up the phone. I told the kids that my granddad was going to pass away this evening and we would probably leave Birmingham the next afternoon.

Kate hugged me and said, "I'm sorry about your granddad."

We tossed our $1 popcorn containers and drink cups in the trash can on the way out.

The next day, I waited to hear from my dad about the arrangements while I packed the kids' suitcases and took my gray sleeveless dress out of the closet. We were going to another funeral.

My dad cried on the phone. Even as an adult, you can feel like an orphan when you are left in this world to fend for yourself. It doesn't matter if you are 6 or 16 or 60.

I still felt a huge gulf between us, and I worried that it might never be repaired. Underneath my sadness for his loss, I could feel my anger that he had not hung up after the call from my mother and driven to Birmingham on August 4 of the previous year. I could not imagine not being there for my granddad's funeral, to hug my loved ones, to share memories. It reminded me that my dad was not here for me when I had needed him. Two weeks earlier, on the vacation in Tennessee, he had not said one word about Charles. He had not hugged me extra hard after not seeing me for an entire year. To my face, he had not said the words, "I'm sorry. I was wrong."

My mom had suggested I ask him to take a walk with me on one of the evenings during our vacation.

"Maybe," I'd said.

And she'd said, "You won't do that, will you? You'll wait for him."

I felt bad for carrying this anger, but I didn't really know what to do about it.

The funeral was on Saturday. There was a service at the funeral home, and then we drove to the cemetery for graveside services. After they lowered the casket into the ground, the children, grandchildren, and great-grandchildren tossed roses onto the coffin. At Grandma's service, we had tossed in daisies, my grandma's favorite. There are people who look down on flowers like carnations and daisies, and there are people who appreciate them for their sweet simplicity. I can only speak from my experience, but a person who loves daisies will love you so much and so well that, even years after they die, you will still feel them loving you.

Afterward, everyone made their way back to their cars. Kate and I walked together with Tim and Jacob behind us, probably saying funny things to make each other laugh. On the drive into the cemetery, Tim had said, "I can see Granddad getting to heaven, and there's Grandma and all his friends and family to welcome him. And there's Charles, and Granddad sees him and says, 'Who's that guy?'"

I could see it—my granddad turning his head to the side slightly, rubbing his chin, while he grinned and his kind eyes lit up. If he teased you, he only ever did it lovingly with a sweet smile. Despite my lack of religious faith, I liked the idea of our loved ones carrying on in another world greater than this one. I wanted to think of my grandparents hugging Charles and *loving* him and making sure that he knew we were OK, that we still loved him, too.

Kate tucked herself under my arm as we walked and said, "I've tried really hard not to cry all day."

Her eyes filled with tears. There is nothing more certain to cause tears than to say aloud how much you are trying to hold them in.

"I wish I could have put one more thing in Daddy's casket."

She'd been thinking about him all day, of course. While all around her, 50- and 60-year-old people mourned the loss of their father, she was remembering her own father and his funeral. Here she was, 10 years old and already a year into life without her daddy.

I stopped walking and leaned down slightly, my arm still around her, and said, "What would it have been?" but she did not know.

What she wanted was another minute with her dad, not an open grave to toss daisies into.

"Even if you could put something in, it would never be enough," I told her, my throat thick with tears unshed and things unsaid. "I think I want to give him one more hug, but it wouldn't be enough. You know?"

And she said, "Yes, I know."

I hated that she already knew that nothing would ever be enough to make right the loss of her father.

Mourners gathered at Dad and Carolyn's house afterward. The kids and I changed out of our funeral clothes. I fixed a bourbon and Diet Coke and sat in the family room. On the television, a video played that Sue had put together for my grandparents' 50th wedding anniversary 12 years earlier. Family photos went by on the screen, slowly and set to music. The occasional Neil Diamond song would come on.

A photo of Charles and Jacob came up on the screen. Jacob was only a year old or so in the photo. I put my hand up to my eyes and cried for a moment, but I wasn't caught off guard like I had been the night before during the visitation.

This same tape had been playing on a TV in the corner of the room at the visitation. I'd avoided watching it, for the most part. Carolyn had asked me to come over and say hello to the Walters, their neighbors from Columbus. Tim came over, too, and we were all chatting, Tim beginning to explain what had taken him from Arizona back to Louisiana.

It was at that moment that someone in the crowd moved; I glanced to my left and saw, on the screen, a photograph of me and Charles sitting on the porch swing at my mom's former house in Natchitoches. Charles, with a big grin on his face, had his arm around me.

"Oh!" I said, like it was a moment of recognition. Not unpleasant, just unexpected, like running into someone you know at the grocery store. But then, right on the other side of this "Oh" moment (not to be confused with one of Oprah's Aha! moments), was something else—a realization. It was the feeling of being punched in the gut, a sharp intake of air. A sharp intake of *facts*. He is dead. You know this because you saw it. You can remember that.

"I have to leave for a minute," I said and—what's that phrase?—I turned heel and fled. Whatever the phrase, I started to go and heard Tim say, "I'm sorry," and, as I kept walking, I said brightly, "No, I'm fine." I tossed this lie over my shoulder as I hurried from the room.

Brightly is how I imagine I said it, so that the words and the tone might downplay the act of fleeing.

I walked to the restroom off the parlor area and stood in the stall. What had just happened? My heart was racing. I knew I could choose now to bawl or to hold it in. I breathed deeply in and out and put my hand against the cold metal door, leaning into it slightly. Breathe.

I'd been caught off guard, that was all.

Breathe.

After a few minutes, I stepped out and washed my hands and looked at my totally normal-looking face in the mirror. When I stepped back into the parlor, I saw Sue, and she motioned for me to follow her. We walked out to the parking lot, and she handed me a Xanax.

"Here, take this," she said, and, for once, I did not decline.

It hadn't been too strong at all, just enough to slow my heart rate to normal.

This time, I was not caught off guard. I'd been sitting there on purpose, watching the photos flash by, and I'd been waiting. I had chosen to see the full pink cheeks of my sweet baby boy, wearing his denim overalls and his Winnie the Pooh turtleneck, grinning up at his dad. I had chosen to remember this.

Sunday, I decided we would stay one more day. I could have powered through the eight-hour drive home, but I knew it would be a *long* eight hours. Was it so bad if the kids missed one more day of school and I missed another day of work? A quote from *Office Space* popped into my head:

"Looks like you've been missing a lot of work lately."

"I wouldn't say I've been *missing* it, Bob."

We were all moving slowly. Tim had woken up late and, even though Dad had sped him to the airport, he still missed his flight. He was at the airport waiting for another flight out, closer to noon.

I took my journal and a Diet Coke out to the screened-in porch and sat at the round iron table. I wrote about the funeral and the burial. I wrote about Kate and what she'd said to me. The next entry in my journal is from two days later, but I didn't write about how my dad came out onto the screened-in porch to talk to me. I never wrote down how he apologized, how he finally came to me and said the things I needed to hear.

Now I don't remember exactly the words he said. I know that we talked for quite awhile, stopping sometimes when my nephew Cameron came out and ran around. I know my dad told me that he was sorry, that he had made the wrong decision a year ago. He admitted that, decades ago, when he and my mom divorced and we moved away, he had turned our lives over to our mother. He had relinquished his claim on our "real lives."

The day before, when a group of us had been sitting on the screened-in porch, my sister Katie had spoken about the words Aunt Vickie said at the service, about how Granddad had always been there for his children when they needed him.

"I realized that's what you've done for us," Katie said to Dad. "You're always there for us."

I'd remained silent. What could I say? Obviously, this was not true for Tim or me. The truth was that Katie and I had grown up with the same man as our father, and yet we'd had different dads. As sad as it made me for Tim and me, it made me sadder for my father.

I don't know if it was during this conversation or sometime later, but somehow I figured out what to do about my anger. I let it go. It was a decision I made, like setting down a piece of luggage I was tired of carrying. The epiphany was realizing that I could actually choose to set it down.

"I thought as long as you guys had your mom you were OK," my dad said now. "I've always underestimated my importance in your lives."

I thought of Kate and Jacob, of how Charles had removed himself from their "real lives," how he had underestimated his importance in their lives. I hoped they would be OK as long as they had me.

OK or not, my children will always have questions about their father's death. Will Kate, a sassy and impatient force of nature, always be the one to voice them? Will Jacob, laid-back

THE GEOGRAPHY OF YOU AND ME

and peace-keeping like his mom, always wait for the answers to reveal themselves to him over time?

On Monday, during the drive back to Birmingham, somewhere on I-65 next to an Indiana cornfield, Kate said, at last, after a year, "Mommy, where were you when Daddy was in the garage?"

We'd been listening to a news report on NPR, something to do with drug addiction or alcoholism. I'd said, grasping this "teachable moment" as I always did, "See? That is why drugs are so bad. They make you do things you would never do otherwise."

Again and again, I needed them to remember that drugs were what fueled their father's violent destruction. I needed them to never do drugs. My greatest fear was that they would inherit the monkey that rode on Charles's back.

It was somehow a relief to have her ask me this. This information—the geography of Charles and me on the day he died—was one more thing I did not have to wait for her to ask me about, one more thing she did not have to wonder about. I have never wanted his suicide to be a mystery with which my children could become obsessed with solving.

"I was in the garage, too," I said.

"Oh," she said.

I glanced at her in the rearview mirror.

"You know how Daddy always needed me to be with him? Well, I think he needed me to be there that day."

This was enough for now.

"OK," she said.

After a few minutes, she said, "Hey, can we listen to 'Mr. Blue Sky'?"

"Yeah!" Jacob chimed in.

"Of course," I said.

I picked up my iPod and scrolled through the songs until I found the one by Electric Light Orchestra. If I'd had an official Cheer the Hell Up playlist, something to counteract the Sorry for Myself playlist, this would have been the first song on it. It was the number-one song the three of us agreed on that year. The kids always asked me to turn it up, and we sang along loudly.

"Mr. Blue Sky please tell us why
You had to hide away for so long
Where did we go wrong"?

This is the way it was. For every moment of difficulty, there was another moment of laughter or singing. For every time one of us acknowledged the damage the world could inflict, there was a moment of survival. For every question about the past, there was a determination to live in the present.

"Hey you with the pretty face
Welcome to the human race
A celebration, Mr. Blue Sky's up there waitin'
And today is the day we've waited for"

People say it's darkest before the dawn, but the truth is closer to this: Darkness and light exist simultaneously. Sometimes when all you see is black, it is only because you have closed your eyes to the light.

"Hey there Mr. Blue
We're so pleased to be with you
Look around see what you do
Ev'rybody smiles at you"

I cannot recommend highly enough the power of singing this song at the top of your lungs. If you have two of your favorite people in the world to accompany you, all the better.

24

I thought about Botox. The middle of my forehead was constantly creased. By the end of each day, it felt like a little weight was sitting between my eyebrows. Could I do with a little paralysis up in here?

I felt like I'd stayed still, stuck in one place all year. This place was Grief. It's like some tourist town where it always rains. Every day you wake up and see that the skies are overcast. And sure, you can check out for a bit, but you can never leave. OK, maybe it wasn't so much like a town as it was like The Eagles' "Hotel California."

Like a gift or a penance, I had offered up this year to Charles. I had made no major decisions. I'd let life carry me along on its tides while I waited it out. I had surrendered the months to sorrow and guilt and the hard work of grieving. I'd

picked up books seeking answers. Sometimes I'd almost immediately put the books down again.

Kate and I had taken our weekly trip to the library, and,
while Kate wandered through the children's section, I'd looked
up a book Joan had mentioned in one of our sessions. *The Ver-
bally Abusive Relationship* was shelved in nonfiction,
262.8292EVA. I pulled it off the shelf and flipped through it,
but I decided not to get it. The idea of reading it made me
tired.

On the shelves above the books about abuse—and there are
so many books about abuse—were the books on suicide. I spotted one titled *The Myths of Suicide.* I pulled it off the shelf and
flipped to the back inside jacket. I always looked at the author
information first. Who is he? Why did he write this book?
What I really wanted to know was *how* he wrote this book. The
son of a man who committed suicide had written this one.
There are a lot of books written by the children of suicides. Not
so many by the wives or husbands.

I checked the index. I always did this next. I looked for a
listing that said, "witness to suicide." There wasn't one. There
were several pages listed after "murder suicide."

I flipped to the table of contents. I flipped to a page about
anger. One of the myths of suicide, the author wrote, is the
pervasive idea that people commit suicide to get revenge on
others or that it is an act of aggression against someone. The
author briefly—the part I needed was always brief, it seemed—
touched on the case of a man who shot himself in an ex-
girlfriend's front yard.

I wanted to know if she was there. I wanted to know if he
spoke to her before he did it. What did he say to her? What did
she say to him? Wasn't he angry? Wasn't he trying to exact
punishment somehow? Where was she now? Was she OK?

I'd read another book on suicide that had briefly told the story of a woman whose husband, a police officer, shot himself while they were in bed together. They had made love only moments before. After he did it, she ran from her house screaming, naked and devastated. The book said that her mother-in-law blamed her, so she moved away and met someone else. She married him and had his children. And she never told him about her first marriage, about the day a man died in front of her.

I stood in the narrow aisle and read the entire chapter. The author stated that, despite some suicides who do it in front of someone, the fact that people do it because they are angry is a myth. People commit suicide because they feel isolated. They believe they are alone. They believe they have no other choice.

It is a fact that you can hold an open book in your hands while you stand in the nonfiction section of a library, while you hear the low murmur of conversation between a tutor and a student at a round table nearby, and yet be somewhere else. You can be in a garage watching the last few moments of someone's life, while you search his face for the truth.

"You have no idea how much this hurts," he had said. He'd clutched his heart with one hand and the barrel of the gun with the other. He was miserable. He was desperate. He was hopeless. Was he angry? Was he vengeful?

He made me watch him do this horrible thing. He said something cruel.

The author wrote that the survivors, family members and friends, were often angry after the suicide, so they projected their anger onto the victim. Psychologists had done studies that showed that angry people tended to perceive aggression in others' facial expressions.

So was it me who was angry?

I shut the book and slid it back onto the shelf. I walked out of the nonfiction department and went back to the children's section to find Kate.

What I was ready to consider is that who was angry, who was being punished, or who deserved to be punished were questions I was tired of asking. I no longer wanted Charles to be stuck in what I had wished upon him so many times, a purgatory that was some twisted mirror image of the pain I was feeling. I hoped he had learned whatever he was supposed to learn, that he was free of guilt and pain and that the hole he couldn't fill was, at last, no longer empty. I hoped that he was somewhere with love and laughter.

If he was free, maybe I could be free, too. Both of us could leave the garage behind.

I'd had enough paralysis. I'd had enough of being stuck in the mud of a wet and gloomy tourist trap.

I'd had enough of this damn weight between my eyes.

Sitting at my desk at *Southern Living*, I was reading articles on a blog, my right hand on the mouse, clicking from smart-ass comment to smart-ass comment, my left elbow leaning on the desk, the fingers of my left hand stretching out the skin of my brow. I was engaging in this compulsion of middle age, while wasting the remaining hours of the morning, when Spencer knocked lightly on my open office door.

"Hey, can I come in?"

"Of course," I said.

As he stepped in, he closed the office door behind him and quickly said, "It's nothing bad."

Closed office doors weren't considered good omens in those post-downsizing days.

Spencer said that, after the staff meeting in which he spoke about his vision for the magazine, the new editor-in-chief had told the executive editors that he wanted to make an offer to anyone who no longer felt enthusiastic about the job. The EIC had asked the powers that be to free up money to pay for severance packages for anyone who wanted to volunteer to leave.

As Spencer spoke, I could feel the muscles of my face wanting to pull into a smile. It was like having someone break up with you and you know you should probably look serious about this turn of events, but all you can think is, "Yes, yes! I don't have to date you anymore, and I don't have to be the one to say it!"

"Anyone who wants to be on the list to be considered for a package has to submit their name by Labor Day," Spencer said. "Now, there's no guarantee about who will get one, of course."

"OK," I said. "That's interesting."

Be cool, I thought.

I was not cool. I was excited.

This was it, right? This was the universe talking to me. I remembered the day I'd come home from Charles's funeral and walked through the front door of my new life and promised myself not to make any major decisions for a year. The year was up. Was I hearing a message now? Was this the universe or God or Oprah, knocking down a door and throwing open a window?

Spencer reminded me again about the deadline and said, "If you have any questions, call Catherine in HR. She can explain it all."

He smiled, and I smiled, and he left my office.

Then I left my office, too, and hurried down the stairs and out of the building to my car. I dialed my mom's number at work and waited for an answer.

"I haven't heard you this excited in a long time," Mom said.

As soon as she'd answered, I'd told her what Spencer said. I said, "So, listen, I need you to pray to Jesus and let me know what he says."

This is a joke between my brother and my mom and me that we always ask her to ask Jesus. "You can talk to Jesus, too," she'd always say, laughing. "I know," I'd say, "but you're better at listening to him!"

Let's be real. She was simply better at believing in something I just could not buy into. But I did buy into the wisdom of my mother.

"I don't want to be foolish, but I'm so sure I'm supposed to leave. I really am," I told her.

I'd been wishing for the universe to move me on, out of this job and onto the next thing. I had felt led, utterly compelled to write my story and to share it with others. It felt like what I was supposed to be doing right now rather than dragging myself into an office and wasting away under the harsh glare of fluorescent lighting.

"I think you're right," Mom said.

"Yes! I do know that I'm the mother of two children, and I am the only person responsible for all of us. I have to be able to pay our bills. I don't want to put the kids at risk in any way."

While Mom was calling Jesus, I could make a list of things that had to be in place for me to leave my job. An accurate household budget, a list of what debts could be paid off while I was still receiving severance, a list of places I could freelance for, etc. This list flashed through my head, but mostly I felt like smiling.

I felt like I was on the verge of leaping into the blue skies of the "What next?"

That afternoon I went upstairs and met with Catherine in Human Resources. She said the decision would be made pretty quickly and people would probably be notified by the week after Labor Day. (This would turn out to be wildly untrue. The decision was dragged out for months.)

Catherine said to give it some thought and let her know by Labor Day. "It's not going to be decided by whose names are on the list first," she reassured me.

"That's good," I said. "Because I was picturing a bunch of us shoving each other as we raced up the stairs to HR."

My image was not so far off. The decision took so much longer because, rather than two or three people requesting a package, more than 15 people on staff, including three executive editors, asked for one.

I assured her I would think about it carefully, told her that I'd asked my mom to please consult the Son of God, and then I walked back down to my office on the third floor.

There was little point waiting. I knew the answer. The next morning I emailed Catherine: "Jesus told my mom I should go for it."

When I told her I was leaving *Southern Living*, Kate cried. She liked the trips we had taken, the photo shoots we'd been on, and she liked visiting the office and collecting candy and other treats from my coworkers. I told her we would still take trips. We would still see our friends. But it was time for me to move on. To move *forward*.

I drove Jacob to school one morning, and he said, "How much longer do we need to live in the house?"

"You mean until I won't have to pay back the tax credit? About a year and a half. Why?"

"So, I'd be a junior in high school?"

Something in the way he said this let me know that he was asking if he'd have to move, leave his school and his friends, now that I was leaving my job.

"And you don't want to move in the middle of high school."

"No. Wait until I'm done, and then you can move."

"Don't worry about that," I said. "We're not planning to move. We'll see what happens."

It wasn't a promise, but I hoped it was enough.

Our house was the place where Charles died and where I watched him die. Despite this, it was our home. It was not haunted. It was filled with the sound of our laughter, sibling fights, and me yelling for Jacob to take out the trash. Charles dying here was not the most important thing about this house. I refused to believe that. I could see so clearly that my children didn't believe it either.

My father, stepmother, and half-sister came down to visit one weekend in September, and my father spent all of that Saturday afternoon replacing the locks and doorknobs on my front door and on the door in the kitchen that leads to the place where Charles died. It was also simply the place where I parked my car.

My dad fixed the door so that it remained closed without having to turn the deadbolt.

As he worked on the front door, my dad asked where my tools were. He followed me into the kitchen, and I pulled out a plastic storage bin from a lower cabinet. It was filled with tools and nails and random parts.

I handed him the screwdriver.

"Are any of your friends in town handy?" he asked.

"No, I don't think so," I said.

He looked up from the tool in his hand and said, "I'll have to come down more often then."

Whether this would prove to be true or not did not matter to me then, and it doesn't matter to me now. I love my dad. I enjoy loving him. I think he is a good and kind person. I like his brown eyes and his policeman-style mustache. I like remembering how he would flex his arm and I would hang from his bicep. Certainly, he had made decisions that hurt me, but he had also, on every single day of my life, loved me.

There is freedom in choosing love over anger.

There is freedom in choosing the side of light.

Not long after my dad fixed the latch and replaced the locks, I painted the door to the garage a sunny shade called Raincoat Yellow, an appropriate name for something to ward off the storms. With two coats of paint, the door became different than it was on August 3, 2009.

I knew that my memories would come with me wherever I went. The job of keeping the door to them closed was mine alone. Sometimes I would open it and look around and see something I didn't want to see, and that might never change. But the glossy yellow paint made me smile.

One night in early November, not long after I signed my termination papers at *Southern Living*, I lay in bed with Kate beside me. She still slept with me, and I rarely spoke to her about changing that. When the time came for her to go back to her room alone, she would know.

Kate was on her back, her hands squeezed together over her chest, and she said, "Mom, I can feel my heartbeat. Try it."

I laid the book I'd been reading across my legs and put my hands together.

"Like this?" I asked.

"Now squeeze them together, tight."

I couldn't feel anything at first.

"I close my eyes," Kate said helpfully.

So I closed my eyes. Suddenly, I could feel the pulse in my hands.

"I feel it!" I told her.

"Isn't that cool?" she said. Then she unclasped her hands and reached her left hand out to me. "Hold my hand," she said.

I held her hand while she went to sleep.

When Charles read a book, he liked for it to have a lot of what he called "stopping places." He loved James Patterson novels in which a chapter might be only a page or two. Every time a new one came out—which, by my estimation, was about every six weeks—I pictured Charles sitting on the sofa reading and only taking breaks to step outside and smoke.

The chapters zip along. When you look ahead, you aren't intimidated by long running text. You see a place where you can stop in case life comes calling and you need to set the book aside for a bit. The trick, though, is that when you see another stopping place, you decide to keep going. Just a few minutes more, only one more chapter. It's so doable. And suddenly you are at the end.

Life goes by like that, I think, a collection of short chapters that fly by, and suddenly you are looking back on an entire story.

I needed a stopping place. I needed a place to pause and catch my breath.

I was next to my daughter under a down comforter, but I was also at the end of something, about to leap into the unknown. I pictured a life without the job that had brought me to Birmingham and to this point in my life.

I had one goal in mind, and it was to write what I needed to write. I knew that I had to do it soon. I could not imagine a life spent writing this book in my head. I needed to release these words into the world and maybe release some of the weight on my chest, the weight between my brows. Or, as Kate said to me one day, "Stop carrying around that emotional luggage."

It was time to fast-forward it back and tell my story. I didn't know what would happen after that, but, miraculously, I wasn't worried about it.

I held Kate's hand in mine and closed my eyes.

And I could feel my heart beat.

epilogue

In the fall of 2011, Kate, Jacob, and I signed up for a walk to benefit suicide prevention. We formed a team with some of our close friends (Laurey, Stacey, and Rose Darby), Kate's friends Molly and Norah, and Norah's mom, Rebekah—people who had been there for us in the days after August 3 and hundreds of days since. Friends and family who couldn't be there donated money, wrote kind words of support.

On the day of the walk, we drove south on the interstate to Cahaba Valley Road. The sky was bright blue, the temperature mild, the surrounding hillsides painted in broad strokes of orange, red, yellow, and green. When we arrived at Heardmont Park, there were hundreds of people milling about. Laurey had ridden with the kids and me, and, as we slowly circled the parking lot looking for a spot, we all expressed surprise at the size of the crowd. You can feel like you're alone in this thing, the loss of a loved one to suicide, when the truth is you are one of millions.

In the weeks leading up to the walk, our team raised more than $1,400. It felt good to do something concrete, something that could be tracked. It felt like a way to fight against something, even if that something might feel like a battle we had already lost, a battle we didn't even know we were fighting in the first place.

We signed in and collected our free T-shirts. We went to another table and picked up plastic bracelets to represent our purpose there. Red for those who'd lost a spouse. Purple for those who'd lost a friend. Blue for those who support the cause. Kate and Jacob picked up gold bracelets to represent the loss of a parent.

I hesitated for a moment. Since Charles and I had been married, should I have red? Since we were then divorced, should I have purple to represent the loss of a friend? I didn't linger long. I chose red. I tried not to think too much about my feelings, which were complicated and colored by guilt and regret and love, by indignation and resignation.

Over the past year, I'd moved forward in so many ways. I finally said yes to a date. Then another one. One evening in the spring, after powerful storms knocked out the electricity in our neighborhood, the kids and I had gone to the bookstore to waste some time. A man approached me and said, "Can I introduce myself to you?"

I thought perhaps he was going to try to sell me something, but he said, "I mean, where are you supposed to meet people?" He blushed. He was tall and broad and slightly balding, but his blush made him seem like a vulnerable teenager. It was charming. "I was hoping I could get your number and invite you to lunch sometime? In a public place, of course."

I laughed and said, "Sure. OK. Why not?"

He was a kind man, also divorced with children. The day we went to lunch was a pleasant day in April. We had a good conversation. But we did not go out again.

As I drove away, I was overwhelmed by the feeling of missing Charles, of wishing I'd had lunch with him, of wanting to talk to him and hear his laugh. I didn't want to cry. I turned off the interstate and drove to the bookstore. When I needed comfort, I went to the bookstore or the library. I wandered among the shelves. Before I went inside, I decided to call my mom.

"I miss Charles," I told her. "And I realized that I feel ashamed of that, like I'm some battered wife who misses her abuser."

"First of all," she said, "I'm glad you're still in counseling."

We both laughed.

"I don't miss the bad side of him," I said. "I don't miss the person I had to push away from me all those years. I miss my friend."

She said, "Maybe you should think of it this way: You are allowed to love him now. You can love him if you want to. You can love him without being afraid."

The walk was largely ceremonial. There was no one keeping time. This was not a race to the finish. If you have ever grieved a loss, then you know that it is a walk that never really ends.

In the crowd, there were groups of people wearing matching T-shirts honoring the person for whom they were walking. Some of the T-shirts had photos on them. Others had quotes. "A life well lived" read one. I thought that I would like to have one for Charles that read, "A life well loved."

"Next time we should have matching T-shirts with a picture of your dad on them," I said to the kids. Kate was walking next to me, holding my hand, Jacob on the other side of her.

"Yes! Can we use the photo of dad swinging his shirt over his head? The best photo ever," Jacob said, laughing.

The photo was from New Year's Eve 1998. Audrey and I had hosted a party at her house. The invitations read "Party like it's 1999." Remember when 1999 seemed like a long way in the future? Now it felt so long ago. The party was full of Prince songs and drinking and laughing and dancing. At some point, Charles untucked his plaid, button-down shirt from his blue jeans and pulled it off, swinging it over his head.

Jacob had discovered the photo on the computer a few months earlier while he was helping me transfer my music collection from the desktop to my laptop. I used to have a print of the photo that I kept underneath the tray of my jewelry box. It always made me laugh when I saw it.

If we had kept track of the laughter Charles gave us in his life, if we could add it up like the generous donations people gave us, I believe the laughter would add up to more than the tears. I believe this will always be true.

On the morning of the walk, I was listening to the songs on my iPod while I cleaned the kitchen. A George Strait song came up on shuffle. It's called "The Chair." At the end of the song, George Strait sings, "Baby, do you think there's a chance that later on I could drive you home? No, I don't mind at all."

When it got to this part, I momentarily stopped mopping the floor and burst into laughter. Charles would sing this song, but he'd wiggle his eyebrows up and down, suggestively, and sing, loud and off-key: *"Baby, do you think there's a chance that, later on, I could drive IT home? No, I don't mind at all."*

Jacob had the right idea. If we were going to have T-shirts with his dad's picture on them, the photo would have to be something that made us laugh. Laughter was what saved us when we were suffering. Laughter was what kept his dad's memory alive.

After our team made its way around the walking path, we headed to a grassy area in front of a stage (which was really a flat-bed truck parked in the lot). The kids ate free ice cream out of serving-size containers and free popcorn out of paper bags.

A woman went to the microphone and, from a piece of paper, read the words of a Native American legend about butterflies: "If anyone desires a wish to come true, they must first capture a butterfly and whisper that wish to it. Since a butterfly can make no sound, the butterfly cannot reveal the wish to anyone but the Great Spirit who hears and sees all. In gratitude for giving the beautiful butterfly its freedom, the Great Spirit always grants the wish. So, according to legend, by making a wish and giving the butterfly its freedom, the wish will be taken to the heavens and be granted."

If you could whisper your wish to a butterfly, what would it be? The answer is never as simple as it seems.

Another woman stepped forward with a large white box and opened the lid. This was when I discovered something fascinating about butterflies: They do not immediately flee their captors. They stay still in the box. They emerge slowly. Their wings lift them into the air softly and with no hint of impatience. The promise of freedom is all around them, and yet, they linger.

A Josh Groban song, the sort of song that will wreck you even on a good day, played over the loudspeakers. I sat between Kate and Jacob on the grass, and we watched as the butterflies slowly made their way above the crowd and over the treetops.

Yes, I could love Charles. I could send that love out into the world. I could set it free from me.

If I did this, maybe some day I could love again.

My love is yellow like the sunshine, and it floats away on the breeze.

Dream: You and Me

Maybe a day will come when I will dream of you and I won't know anything that has come before. There will be no fear or regret. I will dream of you and me and nothing more.

Maybe we will be on a beach. You are the person I was with the first time I saw the ocean. I was 21, and you were 23. We were happy and young standing on the Florida shore along the Gulf of Mexico.

We will walk barefoot on white sand. You will smell like coconut, sunscreen slathered across your freckled arms and back. You always were responsible about that. I won't use sunscreen. It's the one way I've always been irresponsible.

The sea will spread out around us—calm and glassy the way it is before the tide rolls in—and the truth will stay beyond the horizon, too far for either of us to see it.

You always asked if we could stay friends, and now I will tell you that we can. I am your best friend, and you are mine, and this will be enough. You won't ask for more.

Not once in this dream will I remember that I am here and you are not. We will be in this place without memory. For a minute or an hour or the forever that lasts until morning, this will be the geography of you and me.

Acknowledgements

This page has caused me the most angst of any page in this book. It is impossible to list every person who, at some point in this process, provided the support and love and friendship I needed to complete this project. There are too many moments of well-timed grace, love, and humor to share here. Forgive me for my imperfect efforts at acknowledging all those who deserve my gratitude.

To my family: How many words can I put down in this lifetime to express how much I love you all? A million is not enough.

For the kind of friendship that deserves medals of honor, I am endlessly grateful to Tina Rollman, Todd Childs, Emily Goodin, Gretchen Auer, Laurey Glenn, Lollie Rockefeller, Katie Crawford, and Jennifer Camilletti. I could fill another book with all you have done to keep me going during the worst times and all the fun we've had during the best times. Chris Davis, thank you for allowing me to use your gorgeous painting for the cover of the book, for hugs, laughs, tiny clay sculptures of platypuses, dollar movies and sitting through the credits with me while I cried. Thank you, Stephanie Gibson Lepore and Tracey Beck Clark, for all you did for me after Charles's death. Thank you, Erin Shaw Street, for encouraging me to start a blog, for encouraging me to write this book, and for inviting me into the gold dining room for celebration, support, and the smooth sounds of Michael McDonald. Thank you, Scott Thigpen, for answering all my questions along the way and designing a beautiful book cover. If this book reads well and has commas in the right places, it is only because of the editing talents of Carla Jean Whitley and Lisa Bailey. If there are mistakes, I am solely to blame. Thanks to author Lars Anderson for his guidance and support during the early stages of the writing of this memoir and its proposal.

To the readers of Vodka Cranberry Clooney, who listened when I first needed to tell this story, in bits and pieces and random thoughts. Some of you sent messages that touched my heart when I desperately needed to hear someone say they understood. This act of kindness is no small thing.

I'd like to include a special acknowledgement of the following Kickstarter backers and friends: Patrick Axford, Dawn Cassidy, Janay Commons, Lane Crockett, Carl Dubois, Emily Goodin, Alicia Holland, Jill Hurley, Katherine Embree Kalmbach, Michelle Maloney, Sandy Nadeau, Kiki Redhead, Sheena Tait, and Sharon and Ira Turner. This book would not have been published without your generous support.

Love and gratitude today and always for Sara Askew Jones and Tim Greening, writers and dear friends who were taken from us too soon.

And, finally, Adam Abeyta, thank you for remembering me all those years after we met at the Flying Saucer in Little Rock, for sending me a "friend request", for making me laugh, and for joining our little family even though we had cats. I love you.

Geography of a Memoir:
An Interview with Amy Bickers
By Javacia Harris Bowser

I met Amy Bickers on March 24, 2011, the night of the very first See Jane Write Birmingham event. That night Amy told me about a book she wanted to publish — a memoir. "What's it about?" I asked jovially. "Well," she said, "my husband killed himself in front of me."

I was speechless. I wanted to know how she could survive something like that. I wanted to know how she could ever be whole again. But I didn't ask her because I knew these were questions only a memoir could answer.

In this candid interview Amy talks about how she found the courage to finally share her story.

When did you decide to write this memoir and how long did it take you to do it?

I kept a journal in the year following my ex-husband's suicide and writing in it was incredibly therapeutic. Writing everything down as I felt it was a huge part of my healing process.

The idea of a book was always there, though. I've been writing since childhood, when I first wrote short stories that were very obvious rip-offs of *Sweet Valley High*. For me, the best way to give myself peace from something is to write it down. I told myself that maybe if I told the story now I wouldn't have to spend my entire life rewriting it in my head. It was, in part, an exercise in acceptance.

It took me about a year and a half to complete the memoir. I began it one evening in the summer of 2010 at the Hoover Library in one of the study carrels. Now I can't remember how many words I wrote that first time, but I remember feeling a great sense of accomplishment. I wrote most of the book in that library or at coffee shops. Cliché, I know! But I cannot write at home unless everyone is gone and all the laundry is done. Otherwise, I'll just procrastinate, fold clothes, and watch *Sex and the City* reruns.

What doubts did you face about writing this memoir and how did you overcome them?

I never really had any doubts about writing this book. I felt driven to do it. Since childhood, I've wanted to write a book, although I always thought it would be fictional, and, as an adult, I always worried a bit about revealing too much (even in fiction). Something about the traumatic experience loosened whatever chains I'd put on expressing myself.

Whenever I did worry about what others would think, I would remind myself that I wanted to share the truth of this experience so that others could know they weren't alone. I wanted to give people, who otherwise might not understand, a glimpse inside depression and grief and the complexities of grappling with suicide. And I was focused on sharing that truth from a place of love and understanding for the humanity of everyone concerned.

You've described the book as "a memoir of suicide, grief, healing, dark humor, too much cursing, some vodka, and a perfectly healthy fixation on George Clooney." How did you approach writing about a topic like suicide with the care and compassion one

might assume it would call for while still maintaining a bit of an irreverent tone?

I've always been a fan of dark humor. I love Kurt Vonnegut, who had an excellent way of expressing serious things with humor. I love comics who can take something rooted in sadness and make you laugh your ass off about it. I adore Tig Notaro. She did a set about her cancer diagnosis that became sort of legendary in stand-up circles, and it is one of the most raw, funny, real examples of how we can use humor to find a way through the hardest times.

Humor has been my coping mechanism for as long as I can remember. It's my go-to for alleviating the weight of a difficult experience. Plus, it's a good reminder that things aren't always going to be so terrible. You can find a way to laugh again. I often call my mom crying and I always, always get off the phone laughing. She's like a magician. That laughter is a sign that I've regained some perspective.

Humor also can be a way to share an experience with someone else while making it easier for them. It can put the other person at ease. I would rather make someone laugh than cry, but if I can make them laugh AND cry, all the better. Feel the emotions, people!

All that said, I write early on in the book about how my go-to coping mechanism was no longer the appropriate one and it left me lost. I had relied on that so heavily all my life. Eventually, I found it again, that balance between grappling with trauma and putting it into perspective with humor. One of the ways I did this, for my children, and myself, was to tell them funny things their dad said or did. I wanted them to remember those things, how he danced to "Ice Ice

Baby" or made up silly words to country songs, and I wanted them to know they were free to laugh. Sometimes people feel like the rules of mourning are that you must wear black, you must cry, you must never laugh heartily. I say laugh heartily as often as possible, because it is going to give you the strength to make it through the crying you do alone.

Any advice or words of wisdom for other women who want to write a memoir, especially those struggling to do so because the topic is so difficult?

I think my first piece of advice would be to keep a journal. Write about the experience for your eyes only. And then, when you're ready, you can refer back to those emotions and experiences you wrote about freely. Remind yourself of the things you said when no one was looking.

Too often we write as if there is an audience already there judging every sentence we put down. There is no better way to stymie your writing voice than to turn every sentence into an imagined public performance. People say of public speaking to imagine the audience naked; writing a memoir is to actually force yourself to be naked in front of a mirror. You cannot write a memoir without acknowledging painful truths about yourself.

No matter what "secret shame" you share about yourself, so many people will say, "Oh, me too!" This is a gift we can give to one another.

So write it the way you want it. No boundaries. For me, nothing was more important than putting the truth into words. Too many people try to make things a little glossier, a little flashier, a little more socially acceptable. I wanted it to be real.

My other piece of advice is, if you have experienced something traumatic, to go to therapy. Therapy was incredibly helpful to me and it helped me to say aloud the things that kept me up at night, to have someone else say those things back to me and make me see how hard I was being on myself.

Take plenty of breaks! Unless you already have a book deal – and if you do, shut up, don't talk to me, I'm kidding, I'm so happy for you – there is no deadline. Don't tell yourself you have to get it all down in a month or a year or even two years. If you need to take a two-month break to do nothing more than drink cocktails on the back patio with a cute guy all summer, do it. OK, yes, I did that. I needed a break from all the thinking and feeling. And I gave myself that break. When I was ready, I came back to the story I needed to tell.

Over the course of this, I've given myself several breaks along the way. Somehow, during those breaks, I was finding my way back to being the person I want to be.

Your Kickstarter campaign has been a huge success. What do you think you did right to promote it and why do you think so many people were willing to back this project?

I've joked a few times that the key is to "Write a blog and, in that blog, be sure to whine for three years about how no agent will take you on as a client." And that's really just a way of saying the most annoying phrase writers will hear today, and that is "Build a platform." My blog readers are loyal and ready to support this book. And that only happened over time by sharing my story, my love for George

Clooney, my taste for vodka and cranberry cocktails, in bits and pieces on the blog.

Once I knew I was going to do a Kickstarter, I did a lot of research. I looked at successful Kickstarter campaigns. I looked at unsuccessful Kickstarter campaigns. I watched videos. I read article after article about what to do and how to do it. And only after I'd done all that for months did I begin my own campaign. This sounds like I'm very organized, but this process was probably two-parts preparation, one-part procrastination. *Sex and the City* airs daily on E!

I mentioned before that I love to paint rooms (crazy, I know) and I always say that prep work is the secret to a good paint job. It's no different for Kickstarter. Prepare your product, prepare your pitch, prepare your emotions. It's a roller coaster, to say the least. I have been overwhelmed and humbled by the success of this. The first day, I burst into tears every time a pledge came through.

Build a team of people who believe in you and believe in what you're trying to accomplish. Have people in your corner who are ready to celebrate with you or comfort you.

What other advice would you offer to aspiring authors?

If you're thinking of writing about something, do it. Just begin with one sentence, even if that sentence is only "Once upon a time this really crappy thing happened." The rest will come. Eventually, you'll find yourself looking at a word count that seems incredible. It's really kind of thrilling. It's like adding steps to your pedometer! (I just got a Fitbit and I'm obsessed with my step count.)

If you need a break from writing, take it. Be kind to yourself. Self-care is vital in a world so full of expectations and rushing about. Write your book for you first. Forget everyone else.

If you become discouraged, wallow in it a bit. You're allowed. The world is full of dumb celebrities writing dumb books and getting huge, dumb book deals! Rant and rave and curse. (I love cursing.) But then try again. If one road is blocked to you, stomp your feet a bit and then find another path.

I like to listen to a certain Ludacris song when I'm angry as hell and I can't take it anymore. I highly recommend this. I believe the best way to tackle any challenge is to enter it the way Ludacris enters a song – with boldness and by telling the world your name. Luda!

When you ask yourself "Why bother?" remember how Kurt Vonnegut responded to that question: "Many people need desperately to receive this message: 'I feel and think much as you do, care about many of the things you care about, although most people do not care about them. You are not alone.'"

Originally published April 2015 at seejanewritemagazine.com.

Amy Bickers was born and raised in Louisiana, where the first question visitors get asked is, "Would you like a drink?" (The second question is "Would you like another?")

In 2003, Amy moved to Birmingham, Alabama, where the first question newcomers are asked is, "Who do you root for? Auburn or Alabama?" (The second question: "Do you have a church home?")

Amy has worked as a professional writer for nearly two decades, including seven years as an award-winning newspaper journalist and seven years as a staff writer at *Southern Living*. Her work has appeared in a number of national publications. Several of her essays are featured in *Southern Living Heirloom Recipe Cookbook* and *Southern Living Comfort Food*.

Amy lives in Birmingham with a very tall man, a cantankerous teenage girl, and an enormous white cat. Her son moved out and Amy texts and calls him a reasonable number of times each week to ask him questions about his life.

Author photograph by Kate Mercer
Front cover design: Scott Thigpen
Back cover design: Dana Brown

Made in the USA
Las Vegas, NV
25 January 2023

66259368R10204